THE SECOND TWENTY YEARS AT HULL-HOUSE

By
JANE ADDAMS

THE SECOND TWENTY YEARS AT HULL-HOUSE

September 1909 to September 1929

WITH A RECORD OF A GROWING WORLD CONSCIOUSNESS

By

JANE ADDAMS

New York

THE MACMILLAN COMPANY

1930

SET UP BY BROWN BROTHERS LINOTYPERS
PRINTED IN THE UNITED STATES OF AMERICA
BY THE FERRIS PRINTING COMPANY

To all those who have contributed to Hull-
House of service, of money, of devotion throughout forty years, this book is affectionately
dedicated.

CONTENTS

CHAPTER I

CHAPTER II

SOCIAL SERVICE AND THE PROGRESSIVE PARTY
SOCIAL TRENDS BETWEEN 1909 AND 1912 SUGGESTING A NEW POLITICAL ALIGNMENT

CHAPTER III

THE DEVIL BABY AT HULL-HOUSE

CHAPTER VI

POST-WAR INHIBITIONS
1919-1929

CHAPTER VII

CONTRASTS IN A POST-WAR GENERATION
1919-1929

CHAPTER VIII

A DECADE OF PROHIBITION
1919-1929

CHAPTER IX

IMMIGRANTS UNDER THE QUOTA
1921-1929

CHAPTER X

EFFORTS TO HUMANIZE JUSTICE
1909-1929

CHAPTER XI

PLAY INSTINCT AND THE ARTS
1909-1929

CHAPTER XII

EDUCATION BY THE CURRENT EVENT
1909-1929

ILLUSTRATIONS

THE SECOND TWENTY YEARS AT HULL-HOUSE

CHAPTER I

INTRODUCTION

THE following statement was made concerning a young Frenchman, who, in the spring of 1914, recorded his last reflection upon life:

When we are young we do not immediately know where we shall hear those voices of our own time to which our virginal hearts will deeply and instinctively respond. They must come from figures of our own time, older than we are or they would not have found expression, but not old enough to have "arrived," so that we do not at once learn of their existence. Our teachers, as well as popular fame, thrust upon us the figures of the last generation, by whom they had themselves been inspired in youth, and these are, in general, precisely the figures to whom our instincts are most rebellious.

1

It is always difficult for a given individual to know just when he has become "a figure of the past generation" against whom youth's instincts rebel, and I confess now to a sense of risk in writing of another twenty years—especially with autobiographical notes—the end of which brings me so very close to threescore years and ten.

But, after all, the young compose a smaller proportion of the world, year after year, as the prolongation of life increases and we are authoritatively told that never before, in the history of mankind, were there so many people—both actually and proportionately—living upon the face of the earth who are more than sixty-five years old, as are living here at present. Not that we have done very much with that increased span of life to feed our pride! In fact, the young people themselves in moments of exasperation have been known to say that many of the follies of which they are accused in cabarets and other frivolous places are really affected by older people who, equipped with the foolish clothing and the brilliant complexions of the young, are dancing and drinking to an extent that fills the actual young with dismay, and that most unfairly discredits the coming generation. Although these excessive imitators of youth may be few in number, they are symptomatic of a widespread tendency to prolong unduly the springtime of life.

Is it not possible for this newly enlarged elderly

group, or at least for some of the individuals who compose it, to refrain from imitating another group simply because the latter possesses the natural glamour of youth; isn't it possible for each group to make its own contribution, if only because we know that the present moment—which after all must concern us more than the disappointing past or the iridescent future—is in the hands of the mixed lot of us; that we are of all ages and of all degrees of social usefulness; that happily the generations are never clean-cut, but are always inextricably mixed from the new-born babe to the admitted octogenarian. If these intermingling groups must push the world along as best they may, it is hardly fair for one of them, the older at that, to lazily pull out by pretending that it isn't there!

I am confident, therefore, that it is dangerous to insist upon simulating the ardors of youth, as if to be young were a virtue in itself, and that we may thus easily upset the balance; that if we carefully suppress all differences with youth even those inescapable differences of old age, we run the risk of destroying a form of variety which has a tried social value.

Our hope of achievement apparently lies in a complete mobilization of the human spirit, using all our unrealized and unevoked capacity. The situation requires limitless patience and comprehension, which ought to be supplied more readily by those who have been subjected to life's training.

One happy result has issued from the current situation. The freshly accumulated group of the elderly at least avoid giving advice, and sedulously refrain from making critical comments upon the passing show. Perhaps this multitude of "sixty-fivers and past sixty-fivers" merely shirk formulating their empirical knowledge, or have never learned to reflect, or their vision has never become sufficiently keen and purged to attract the favorable notice of the young. More likely, they have failed to demand the truth from life and are therefore disconcerted when they find that youth will brook no insincerity and is also most impatient of secondhand opinions and platitudes.

Even as I write these words I reflect that there is always a chance that the garnered wisdom of the old may turn out to be no wisdom at all, and there is an awful possibility that the aged in their strategic position of domestic tyranny and general dogmatism will retard all attempts at progress simply because such attempts necessarily imply a change in the customs with which they have been long familiar. I uneasily recall what happens in certain Oriental countries, where old age claims all its prerogatives. During a journey I once made around the world, I became much discouraged, suffragist as I was, concerning the influence of old women; those in China insisting that little girls' feet must be firmly bound, although the practice had been forbidden by law and hotly repudiated by all of Young China; the old women in India insisting upon purdah at home and veils in the street, although some of the Indian women were voting and sitting as members of the City Council of Bombay; the old women in Turkey and eastern Europe—but why continue this doleful recital, when it is quite obvious that if, or rather when, old women actually do exert themselves they become a social menace? Probably there is nothing more dangerous in the world than the leadership of prestige based solely upon the authority of age.

In contrast to this eastern attitude, I recall an eightieth birthday party, given in Chicago long ago, at a table garlanded with eighty roses and seating eighty guests. Some one asked the birthday child how she had always kept so young and she promptly replied, that it was because she had always adopted an unpopular cause; first, the abolition of slavery, when, as a young woman, she had lived in the pre-war South, and then votes for women which she thought would last her to the end. She explained that no one put you on a pedestal and treated you with respect just because you were old, if you were the advocate of an unpopular cause—you had to defend it and discuss it and take your chances with the wits of the young.

One thing is clear out of all the contradictions; that the task of youth is not only its own salvation but the salvation of those against whom it rebels, but in that case there must be something vital to rebel against and if the elderly stiffly refuse to put up a vigorous front of their own, it leaves the entire situation in a mist. Even if we, the elderly, have nothing to report but sordid compromises, nothing to offer but a disconcerting acknowledgment that life has marked us with its slow stain, it is still better to define our position. With all our errors thick upon us, we may at least be entitled to the comfort of Plato's intimation that truth itself may be discovered by honest reminiscence.

I shall attempt therefore in this record of the Second Twenty Years at Hull-House, to avoid the pretensions both of old age and of youth, in the only way possible, by setting down as carefully as I may what I deem significant in the way of experience or reflection from September, 1909, to September, 1929.

The period easily divides into two decades, the first of which subdivides into five years of peace and five years of war. The second decade is continuously filled with the effect of the gregarious panic, which inevitably follows war and the rumors of its attendant revolutions.

So closely is the life of the individual or that of a public-spirited group in the modern world

What is arising or to arise in the States? I think of it as some mood of planetary consciousness. I cannot get a more precise word. . . . The biological ancestors of the people in the States are European, Asiatic, African, with some survival of the aboriginal American. Nature will find in this multitude the materials to blend to make a more complex mentality than any known before, with wide-reaching affinities in the subconscious. I notice, too, that the writers who form the spiritual germ-cell of American culture— Emerson, Whitman, Thoreau, and their school—think and write of themselves almost as naturally being children of earth, as being American citizens. That group manifest in their writings something like a cosmic consciousness. American statesmen, too, are beginning to formulate world policies, leagues of nations, world peace, a sense of duty to the world struggling up through the intense self-interest and pre-occupation with their own affairs. The American benevolence is world-wide. The Rockefeller Foundation thinks of the health of humanity, not merely of the American people. . . . A planetary consciousness I surmise will grow up through centuries in this astonishing people, warring with its contrary idea which also has its own meaning and just basis. Our human faculties are burnished by their struggle with opposites in ourselves. And it is no less true of the ideas which become dominant in great civilizations. I imagine centuries in which in the higher minds in the States a noble sense of world duty, a world consciousness, will struggle with mass mentality and gradually pervade it.

It lies with us who are here now to make this consciousness—as yet so fleeting and uncertain— the unique contribution of our time to that small handful of incentives which really motivate human conduct. Such a motive has certainly been a definite factor in the last twenty years at Hull-House, and an effort to define it as well as to illustrate it, must be my apology for much of the succeeding pages which may seem unduly autobiographical and also far afield from the corner of Halsted and Polk streets, Chicago.

CHAPTER II

SOCIAL SERVICE AND THE PROGRESSIVE PARTY

BY 1909 the beginning of the third decade at Hull-House, we had already discovered that our intellectual interests, our convictions and activities were all becoming parts of larger movements and that research into social conditions was gradually being developed in the universities and by the great foundations. Based therefore on a more careful knowledge of the situation to be remedied, the five years to 1914 were filled with a veritable zeal for social reform throughout the United States. The efforts both in volume and type were differentiated from those of the preceding two decades. The immediate influence was the Pittsburgh Survey which, financed by the new Russell Sage Foundation and begun as early as 1907, was the first of the community surveys. It was described as

An appraisal of how far human engineering has kept pace with the mechanical developments in the American steel districts.

The results were published in the then new *Survey Magazine,* itself a combination of two publications, one which had been fostered by the Charity Organization Society of New York and the other by a settlement, the Chicago Commons.

The Pittsburgh Survey aroused the entire country to conditions of work in the great American industries. The report challenged the belief that it was primarily an employer's business to produce goods and that he was not expected to discover and prevent social waste and injury. The American settlements claimed a share in the Pittsburgh Survey, both Kingsley House and the Columbian Settlement in the city itself had collaborated throughout the undertaking; Paul Kellogg, the director of the survey, was a resident of Greenwich House in New York; the advisory group, all of whom wrote sections of the report, consisted of Florence Kelley, living in the Henry Street Settlement in New York, Robert A. Woods of South End House, Boston, with Professor John Commons of the University of Wisconsin who had the habit of spending his vacation in one settlement after another.

The public reception of the report revealed a
compunction which had long been felt by a
minority within the church who had sought for
new forms in which to express their enlarged sense
of justice and compassion. It was similar to the
compunction responsible for a movement in England in the days of Charles Kingsley and Maurice
or to the adventures in altruism made later by
ardent high churchmen of the Oxford Movement.

Certain denominations, of which the Methodist
church was the pioneer, began to make their own
researches into the stupid atrocities of contemporary life, its arid waste, its meaningless labor,
its needless suffering, and its political corruption.
This church effort proceeded slowly at first, for
there was inevitably both honest doubt as to its
wisdom and downright opposition on the part of
those who sincerely believed that the church was
going outside its proper field. But at least one
organization, the Men and Religion Forward
Movement, obtained active adherents in many
parts of the world and the Commission on Social
Service of the Federated Council of Churches of
Christ in America, representing altogether hundreds of thousands of members, added an unequivo-
cal declaration against the twelve hour day and
the seven day week to their protests concerning child labor and other recognized social
wrongs.

In such an insurgent mood men reëxamine from

time to time the social institutions upon which they have been relying and renew their faith in human volition as a power which may really direct and shape social conditions. In the five years before the outbreak of the world war, therefore, our general efforts were more and more interrelated with many other movements. I recall, although it may seem far afield, the enormous interest we all felt in 1909 in the brilliant minority report issued by the Royal Poor-Law Commission to the English Parliament with its challenging statement concerning the unemployed, the underemployed, and the unemployable.

The year of 1909 was at the end of the decade in which the so-called "muck-raking" articles dealing with political corruption in American cities had been carried forward by *McClure's Magazine* and other publications of nation-wide circulation. It seemed at the moment as if the subject of political corruption could be approached only through such journals, because the local newspapers were too timid and found their personal affairs were too involved with the *status quo* of their own cities to deal with it.

When Chicago therefore in 1909 witnessed a personal demonstration against political corruption, which should have banished it from our city forevermore, the experience was all the more startling and proved to be almost unbearably poignant. This tragic protest was made by Dr.

Theodore Sachs, whom we had known for many
years at Hull-House through his skillful and unremitting efforts to reduce tuberculosis in our section of the city. One of the Hull-House residents,
under his direction, had once made a careful study
of one block—lung blocks, we used to call them
—in the Russian Jewish quarter in which the
tuberculosis rate had been phenomenally high.
Day by day we had been impressed anew with the
universal testimony of gratitude and affection
showered upon him by the poorest of his com-
patriots. We rejoiced with many people throughout the city when Dr. Sachs was made head of
the Municipal Sanitorium for Tuberculosis.
Although we knew that he encountered unending
difficulties with the officials of a corrupt city
administration in his efforts to care for his patients
properly, we were all aghast one morning to learn
that this brilliant, sensitive man had committed
suicide as a protest against the entire situation.
He himself had explicitly stated his desperate
hope that some reforms might thus be induced
which would result in better conditions for those
poor people in Chicago who were suffering from
tuberculosis.

One was inevitably reminded of John Ball, who
five hundred years earlier had looked out over the
wretched conditions in England, and with his
heart burning within him, had cried aloud, "The
saints in heaven are forebearing, and yet bidding

me not to forebear." Certainly that city is fortunate, as was mediæval England, who finds even one such among its sons, irrespective of the form of expression which his protest may take. This tragic ending of a beneficent life made a profound impression upon thousands of people, especially among those who had known Dr. Sachs and his wellspring of tenderness for the hardships of the poor. The residents of settlements, perhaps more than other people, are brought close to the mysterious shortcoming on the part of life itself; they become oppressed by that "grief of things as they are" over and above the griefs of circumstance or wrongdoing; they have been forced to realize that what we need in the world over against it, is a certain power of compassion, that humanity requires a standing force of self-pity as an elementary ingredient in our social atmosphere if we are to live in it at all. As was predicted at the huge memorial meeting held in Dr. Sach's honor, his spirit has carried on in the splendid fight against tuberculosis, which has resulted in Chicago's exceptionally low death rate from that dread disease. But, unhappily, political indifference and corruption are still with us and at the moment strongly intrenched.

Curiously enough, while the situation in which Dr. Sachs found himself clearly indicated the need for civil service administration of city affairs, and above all for the removal of the callous politician from the possibility of interfering in the care of the sick poor, it was not long after his tragic death that we had in Chicago a demonstration of the most ruthless disregard of both. The president of the County Board of Commissioners, to which body is committed the care of the sick, the insane, the aged poor and the dependent children, in a spirit of Rabelaisian gayety, scattered to the winds all the safeguards which a decade of the merit system had built up. This new president, in evidence of his devotion to the poor, dismissed the medical head of the County Hospital for the Insane as well as the trained nurses, and "fired" the corps of Civil Service employees; he also turned his attention to the Juvenile Court, which had been too long under the influences of reformers. After many pathetic tales of dependent children—and what in the history of the world has ever been more touching than a little child, deprived of parental care—he managed to make the chief probation officer responsible in the eyes of the public for all their ills, and this officer was dismissed after the farce of a civil service trial lasting for three months. It was hard to prove to the community that efficiency is also tenderness; that untrained service results in cruelty, and that the last things to depend upon are the vagaries of a self-seeking politician.

At the next election, a very different type of man was made president of the County Board.

Since Alexander A. McCormick as a young man had resided for several years at Hull-House, we had had opportunity to learn how fine his basic attitude was toward the humanitarian aspects of his office. One of his first undertakings was to reorganize the Civil Service Board and to appoint as a member of it an able woman, long identified with the Chicago settlements. Anna Nichols did much to dissociate civil service from the conception of a cold and correct public official versus the kind-hearted and open-handed politician. Perhaps the protagonists of the merit system had over-emphasized its usefulness in keeping the rascals out and had thus allowed it to become stranded in the shallow water of negative virtue, failing to launch it upon the deep seas of popular affection. I recall a party Miss Nichols gave in the Civil Service rooms of the County Building and overflowing into the other departments, to all the employees of the public charitable institutions as well as to those who served as volunteers. It was attended by both distinguished physicians and the women who scrubbed the floors of the hospitals. One of the latter, after the speeches were over, said to me, "I have felt something like that ever since I have been scrubbing in the Public Dispensary Division. I take lots of the poor things home who can't go on the cars by themselves, sometimes because they are too weak and sometimes because they haven't the price of the fare."

It was at this time that Dr. Cabot in Boston was working out his system of hospital social service, since extended throughout the country. Who can tell in how many work-hardened hands it had been lodged before?

In this same year of 1909, President Roosevelt called together in Washington people from all parts of the country to consider the best type of care to be given to dependent children. It brought the entire subject before the country as a whole and gave to social work a dignity and a place in the national life which it had never had before. We did not realize this at the moment, however, for during the conference itself we were all absorbed in the hope that the gathering might solidify the movement for home-placing versus institutional care for dependent children which at that moment was being discussed throughout the country. President Roosevelt was much amused by a small incident. As the evening speakers were waiting to file upon the platform, the young man in charge, a little overcome by his responsibilities, said, "Are we all here? Yes, here is my Catholic speaker, my Jewish speaker, the Protestant, the colored man, and the woman. Let's all go on." I remarked to Booker T. Washington, "You see, I am last; that is because I have no vote." He replied: "I am glad to know the reason. I have always before been the end of such a procession myself."

II

Events moved rapidly in the five pre-war years. In 1911 a Commission on Occupational Diseases, which had been appointed by the governor of Illinois the year before, reported its findings, and as a result an act was passed by the state legislature for the protection of workers in poisonous trades. One of the Hull-House residents, Dr. Alice Hamilton, in the course of her investigations for the commission, had found conditions in the town of Pullman which seemed to expose the men unnecessarily to the dangers of lead poisoning. She reported the situation to one of the Hull-House trustees, Mrs. Joseph T. Bowen, who was a large stockholder in the Pullman Company. Although there is nothing more difficult to act upon than that evanescent tie which binds the men of a large corporation to the stockholders of that corporation, Mrs. Bowen made such an intelligent protest that the manager, after acknowledging the accuracy of her statements, agreed to carry out the reforms which she recommended. This, of course, was not accomplished without some difficulty. When she appeared before the executive board of the Pullman Company, she was asked why she did not sell her stock if she so disapproved of their methods, and she spiritedly replied that she preferred to stay in and change those methods.

It was during this time that Josephine Gold-
mark published her noteworthy study on *Fatigue
and Efficiency,* which material was used as the
basis for briefs filed in various courts including
the Supreme Court of the United States, in defense
of laws limiting hours of work for women. The
decision of the United States Supreme Court,
which reversed the adverse decision of the State
Court of Oregon, was a milestone in American
effort to secure adequate labor legislation.

In spite of the success of many of these detached
efforts, I cannot tell just when we began to have a
sense of futility and came to feel that what was
needed was a great cause which should pull
together the detached groups in the various states
that they might not only work simultaneously for
the same things, each group in its own state, but
that they might have the help and backing of the
Federal Government itself. The need for action
upon an international basis from time to time also
asserted itself. A bill passed by Congress in the
spring of 1912 gave assurance to the American
Association for Labor Legislation, of which I had
long been a vice president, that the United States
was ready to coöperate with other countries in
such regulation of industrial diseases as could only
be made effective if international. Nine other
countries had signed a treaty in the effort to eliminate phossy jaw from the world, and many other
countries were taking similar action. It had been

considered impossible for our Federal Government to consider industrial legislation, but at last a law was passed prohibiting the import and export of poisonous phosphorous matches, and placing a prohibitive revenue tax on their manufacture in the United States. The bill was significant in that it not only exhibited a readiness on the part of Congress to coöperate in an international undertaking to rid the world of a hideous industrial disease, but that it also recognized the necessity and practicability of federal action in such a matter. Years afterwards, I was taken by a young physician from the Rockefeller Institute to see a case of phossy jaw in a match factory in Peking. China had agreed to this convention for abolishing the use of the obnoxious preparation of phosphorous, but did not at the moment have a central government strong enough to enforce its factory legislation. My guide remarked that this was probably the last case of phossy jaw to be found in the entire world for its possibility had been outlawed throughout civilization.

This attempt to regulate the conditions of industry through the Interstate Commerce Acts was permitted to stand, although a similar effort to regulate child labor by prohibiting the interstate carriage of commodities in the manufacture of which the labor of children had contributed, had been declared unconstitutional by the Supreme Court of the United States. Was public opinion insufficient to uphold this difficult situation or was this first federal effort of the United States to protect its own children, too negative to arouse enthusiastic support?

The final act creating the Federal Children's Bureau passed the House of Representatives on April 2nd, 1912. The idea of a Federal Children's Bureau had emanated from a Settlement. It had been suggested and pushed by Lillian D. Wald of the Henry Street Settlement in New York; she and Florence Kelley, long a resident in settlements, had made the first outline of the matters to be investigated by such a bureau, an outline which corresponded closely to the act creating the bureau as finally passed. We all rejoiced when President Taft appointed Julia Lathrop of Hull-House as chief of the new bureau. She brought to it a fine preparation both as a volunteer social worker and as a state official, as she had twice been a member of the Illinois State Board of Charities. Miss Lathrop was also identified with the establishment of the first Juvenile Court, and was an early chairman of the voluntary committee to supply the court with probation officers and proper places of detention for the children, and at the very time of her appointment, was identified with the first attempt to give psychiatric examinations to wayward children.

It was during the campaign to obtain backing for the establishment of the Children's Bureau and also at three Congressional hearings in its behalf, that we constantly encountered the familiar argument of states rights and the insistence that states alone were concerned in such matters. It became clear that the Federal Government could interest itself in agriculture and fisheries, but not in childhood. There was evidently confusion in the minds of many of our fellow countrymen between self-government and local government. Americans have thought for a long time—perhaps the idea is inherited from the town meetings—that unless government is localized they do not exercise self-government at all. Such a conception, if persisted in, must narrow our notion of government and circumscribe our national life. We forget that politics are largely a matter of adjusted human relations through any unit of government which best serves the purpose. More and more, social workers, with thousands of other persons throughout the nation, had increasingly felt the need for a new party which should represent "the action and passion of the times," which should make social reform a political issue of national dimensions, which should inaugurate an educational campaign with leaders advocating its measures to the remotest parts of the country, which should send representatives to Congress and to the state legislatures who had been publicly committed to social reform and who were responsible to constituents for specific measures.

Only such a party could crystallize the advanced public sentiment to be found in various localities, and make of it a force for national progress. But to obtain a collective effort with a widespread attempt both to understand life and to modify it, was apparently the difficulty. There was already a vast array of specific proposals in process of realization in various states, and there was earnest agitation in others for reforms dependent upon legislation, but it all lacked unity and coherence.

III

In the very first years of the American settlements, we had been afraid to be identified with the word charity, partly because the word itself was obnoxious to many of our neighbors, and partly because we wished to be of service to self-respecting working people as well as to the very poor. As time went on, however, we found ourselves naturally identified with the activities of the National Conference of Charities and Corrections, partly because the charitable people themselves were constantly more concerned with social conditions and partly because we saw how largely our interests were mutual. At the annual conference of the national body, held in Buffalo in 1909, I was elected national president. The fact that a woman held the office shocked a goodly number of the older members, as did the fact that social workers tended more and more to discuss the eco-

nomic conditions underlying the low standards of
living, the overwork, the poverty and disease
which we were seeking to ameliorate. This movement gathered momentum at the Buffalo Conference in 1909, when a committee on Occupational
Standards was appointed which entered upon a
three years' program. The work was begun under
the chairmanship of Paul U. Kellogg and a report
made at the National Conference in St. Louis in
1910. It was carried forward to new lengths the
second year under the chairmanship of Florence
Kelley. Owen Lovejoy, at that time secretary of
the National Child Labor Committee, was chairman the third year, 1912, when the National
Council met in Cleveland. Judge Julian Mack who
was the president that year, said with all the
authority of a Federal judge: "This country will
surely lose its supremacy if the hands of the present
generation are to be so effectively tied by a dead
past that it cannot at the proper time emulate
European countries in their social legislation." It
was at this same conference that a group of social
workers after a spirited discussion agreed that if
the groups in America who were filled with
similar social compunctions and who knew that
our social legislation was falling behind the rest
of the world, really hoped to secure the help of
intelligent and conscientious people, it would be
necessary to place these questions before the entire
country as a coherent political program. The

group was convinced that it was not the social workers alone, but many others, who believed that industry should be subjected to certain tests of social efficiency and should measure up to standards necessary for public health and safety.

The final report of the committee appointed by the Conference of Social Work was written after much discussion with physicians, employers and labor leaders. It presented as components of the standard of living, first, wages; second, hours; third, safety and health; fourth, housing; fifth, term of working life; sixth, compensation or insurance and ended with the statement that "The conservation of our human resources contributes the most substantial asset to the welfare of the future." The National Conference adopts no resolutions, but the section meeting on occupational standards adjourned as such, reconvened as individuals and adopted a program of industrial minimums which was subscribed to in this fashion by representatives of twenty national organizations.

A wise man, Professor Simon Patten of the University of Pennsylvania, wrote of this period: "The great advance in the past decade has been the growth of social expression. Reform is at last able to talk the English language. We could not have had political conventions to advance the cause of social justice if social workers had not coined words that reshaped the sentiments these conventions evoke. The victory will not be won when a majority of the American people cast their ballots in favor of reform; it was won when the first group of social workers saw the real facts and found words to convey to each other what they saw." We were gradually learning that new ideas can never gain wide acceptance unless the persons who hold them confess them openly and give them an honest and effective adherence. It was only later we discovered that when the idea and measure become part of a political campaign we command an unrivaled method for their understanding.

The report of the committee of the Conference of Social Work was issued in June, 1912, only a few weeks before the program was swept into the insurgent political movement. During the month of July a group of social workers who had been identified with the committee's report held a memorable conference with Colonel Roosevelt. Of this Paul Kellogg writes to me as follows: "This report was all grist to T.R.'s, mill in launching the Progressive Party during that summer. Through the initiative of John Kingsbury we had a session with him out at Oyster Bay. I wrote some paragraphs which he more or less put into his keynote speech at the Chicago Convention; and he took over the Cleveland program of standards of life and labor practically bodily, and it was, as you know, incorporated in the Progressive platform."

IV

From various directions, therefore, people were drawing toward a new political party. It was at first as if one heard in the distance the grave and measured tread of history, but the pace increased during the first half of 1912 and became absolutely breathless by midsummer. It was in August, 1912, that the Progressive Party was organized.

Suddenly, as if by magic, the city of Chicago became filled with men and women from every state in the Union who were evidently haunted by the same social compunctions and animated by like hopes; they revealed to each other mutual sympathies and memories. They urged methods which had already been tried in other countries, for righting old wrongs and for establishing standards in industry. For three days together they defined their purposes and harmonized their wills into gigantic coöperation. Among the members of the Platform Committee for the new Progressive Party were the social workers who had approved three successive reports at the National Conference conventions, others who had been closely identified with the Men and Religion Forward Movement who thus felt the challenge to give political expression to the religious motive, and still others who embodied largely the standpoint of the scholar. One sub-committee would seem to me like a session of the National Conference of

Charities and Corrections; another, like a session of the American Sociological Society, with a liberal sprinkling of American Authors in both. The various groups were confident that unless a sufficient number of persons would act as if the increasing human liberation were there, the human mind would never find out how true it was. We were convinced that the nexus between citizens could be more scientific and durable and at the same time more understanding and heartfelt. Sometimes when we encountered members of the American Economic Association or of the Civil Service Reform League, and similar bodies, we feared that a few students of social conditions were endeavoring through the new party to secure measures which, although worthy, had after all recommended themselves to only a very small group out of all the nation. To an incorrigible democrat this was naturally very alarming, but I gradually discovered that the situation was in reality the very reverse of this. The dean of a university law school acted as chairman of the Resolution Committee, and men conversant with the later developments in social legislation supplied nomenclature and information concerning similar legislation abroad; but these men, with the so-called practical members of the committee, were not representing the opinion of any individual nor the philosophy of any group. They were trying, as conscientious American citizens, to meet that fundamental obligation of adapting the legal order to the changed conditions of national life; in the words of a Kansas member, "to formulate our own intrinsic self-vindicating laws." The members of the committee had all experienced the frustration and disappointment of detached and partial effort. They had come to this first national convention of the Progressive Party not only to urge the remedial legislation which seemed to them so essential to the nation's welfare, but to test its validity by the "inner consent" of their fellow citizens, to throw their measures into the life of the nation itself for corroboration.

They believed that the program of social legislation placed before the country by the Progressive Party was of great significance to the average voter quite irrespective of the party which might finally claim his allegiance.

The platform, in the hope that the political organization of the nation might never again get so far away from the life of the people, advocated equal suffrage, direct primaries, the initiative and referendum. We quoted to each other the saying of Walt Whitman, that as he looked abroad, it seemed to him unendurable that large bodies of men should follow those who do not believe in men and we placed at the head of our precious new party, "born of the nation's awakened sense of justice," two men of political sagacity who had shown an understanding not only of the social demands of the people but also of the people themselves. We realized that Colonel Roosevelt possessed a unique power "to put the longing of the multitude into words that they do not forget, and to banish their doubts and fears by the sheer force of his personality and the vital power of his courage." In spite of our belief in our leader, I was there, and I think the same was true of many others, because the platform expressed the social hopes so long ignored by the politicians; although we appreciated to the full our good fortune in securing on their behalf the magnetic personality of the distinguished candidate. Perhaps we felt so keenly the uplifting sense of comradeship with old friends and coworkers not only because we had all realized how inadequate we were in small groups but because the very sentiments of compassion and desire for social justice were futile unless they could at last find expression as an integral part of corporate government. At any rate, it was evident that measures of industrial amelioration and demands for social justice, so long discussed by small groups, were at last thrust into the stern arena of political action.

We were all quite well aware that the Convention was far from being a coherent demonstration, but it seemed to us at the moment as if it were much more. Certainly, for the time being, all dogmas and group egotisms were dropped, or rather, melted down by overwhelming good will and enthusiasm. During those hectic days and nights I lived with my friend Mrs. Wilmarth in the Congress Hotel, in which the headquarters of the new National Party had been established. By night and by day, through much enthusiastic discussion, the platform seemed to be coming nearer to our hearts' desire, and singing and marching days that followed were filled with that "political affection" in which the Greeks believed.

The Progressive Convention has been described many times, and perhaps never quite adequately. It was a curious moment of release from inhibitions, and it did not seem in the least strange that reticent men and women should speak aloud of their religious and social beliefs, confident that they would be understood. Because we felt so at home in that huge Coliseum, there was a quick understanding of those hidden scruples which we were mysteriously impelled to express.

During the three days of the Progressive Convention one fairly heard at times the breakdown of the well worn slogans which had furnished the old parties with their election cries for half a century; the sound was not unlike the psychic uproar which accompanies a great religious conference when the sword of the spirit bursts through its scabbard. It was more obvious, when a man got up to speak whose early political training in words visibly contended with his personal knowledge of national affairs; a man who was not ready to give up *a priori* reasoning, so often mistakenly called idealism, for the pageant of life itself. The old line politicians were as much surprised to find that politics had to do with the matters discussed at the Progressive Convention as the philanthropists were delighted to discover that their long concern for the human wreckage of industry, had come to be considered politics. Nevertheless in spite of the careful platform building, the entire noisy convention was well described as the "barn raising of a new party."

The women who identified themselves with the Progressive Convention inevitably experienced moments of heart searching and compunction. It is hard to understand it now, after we have possessed the ballot for a decade and have come to deem it a virtue "to enter politics" but at the moment we felt it necessary to give to the public our reasons for thus identifying ourselves with a political party. We said that when a great party pledges itself to the protection of children, to the care of the aged, to the relief of overworked girls, to the safeguarding of burdened men, it is inevitable that it should appeal to women and should seek to draw upon the great reservoir of their moral energy so long undesired and unutilized in practical politics—that one is the corollary of the other; a program of human welfare, the necessity for women's participation.

Later we learned to say that when a number of

women deliberately accept this responsibility, it may indicate that they are ready to give up the short modern rôle of being good to people and to go back to the long historic rôle of ministration to basic human needs. After all, we asserted, our philanthropies have cared for the orphans whose fathers have been needlessly injured in industry; have supported the families of the convict whose labor is adding to the profits of a prison contractor; have solaced men and women prematurely aged because they could find no work to do; have rescued girls driven to desperation through overwork and overstrain.

V

But these days of platform building and ratifying were not all halycon. We were, first and foremost, faced with the necessity of selecting from our many righteous principles those that might be advocated at the moment, and deciding which must still wait for a more propitious season. To illustrate from my own experience: For many years I had advocated the cause of international peace and had been a member, sometimes an official, of various international, national, and local peace societies, committed to international arbitration. But, when I sat as a delegate in the convention of the Progressive Party, I voted to adopt a platform, as a whole, which advocated the building of two battleships a year, "pending an international agreement for the limitation of naval forces"—so much we did secure. I confess that I found it very difficult to swallow those two battleships. I knew only too well the outrageous cost of building and maintaining them—that fatal seventy cents out of every dollar of federal taxes which is spent indirectly for war; and I would have liked to see the Progressive Party declare itself against this preposterous unnecessary burden and courageously commit the future to arbitration. It was a serious matter even to appear to desert the cause and the comrades with which I had been for so many years identified. In my long advocacy of peace I had consistently used one line of appeal; contending that peace is no longer an abstract dogma; that a dynamic peace is found in that new internationalism promoted by the men of all nations who are determined upon the abolition of degrading poverty, disease and ignorance, with their resulting inefficiency and tragedy. I believed that peace was not merely an absence of war but the nurture of human life, and that in time this nurture would do away with war as a natural process. It is doubtless true that we prepare ourselves for sudden deeds by an infinite series of minor decisions previously made, and that our convictions are, after all, determined by our sincerest experiences. The figures given out in 1912 were such as these: the total number of casualties suffered by our industrial army is sufficient to carry on perpetually two such wars at the same time as our Civil War and the Russo-Japanese War; that the casualties in the structural iron trade, in the erection of bridges and high buildings, bear the same percentage to the number of men engaged as did the wounded to the total number of troops in the battle of Bull Run; that fifteen thousand of our fellow citizens are killed in industry every year—as if every adult male in a city of seventy-five thousand were put to death; and that every year a half a million men are crippled—as if every adult male in a state the size of Minnesota were annually maimed. It was not sufficient for our peace of mind that a small group of public spirited citizens were constantly agitating in various state legislatures for a system of industrial insurance. Such problems belong to the nation as well as to the state. These facts should be made public to the entire country, for it was not a matter of abstract theory but of self-preservation. Legislation forced by actual conditions is like the earliest statutory laws which were reactions to felt needs. It seemed to me that I was not being presented with a choice between protesting against the human waste of industry or against the havoc of war, but that I had an opportunity to identify myself with a political party which did protest and advanced well considered legislation in regard to one of them. Was it pure rationalization when I persuaded myself that the political party most

surely on the road toward world peace was the
one which had pledged itself to work for "effective
legislation, looking to the prevention of industrial
accident, occupational diseases, overwork, involun-
tary unemployment and other injurious effects
incident to modern industry."

I came to believe that "the ancient kindliness
which sat beside the cradle of the race," cannot
assert itself in our generation against the waste of
life in warfare, so long as we remain indifferent
to the shocking destruction of life in other areas.
To protect life in industry may be a natural
beginning, a response to the brother we have
seen.

On the whole the plank upon fortifying the
Panama Canal was really harder for me to accept
than any other one. It seemed as if the wonderful
sanitary system and daily regimen which preserved the life and health of the workers who dug
the Panama Canal, ought to make it very difficult
for the same government to build upon the same
spot huge fortifications to threaten with destruction that same sort of human stuff which it had
so painstakingly kept alive. In my unavailing
arguments against this policy was I perhaps
vaguely anticipating the "point" made so short a
time later by President Wilson against the fortifi-
cation of strategic waterways, or was it evident
even then that to fortify the canal would make it
less "a life artery for the world" than an axis of

our naval power. Madariaga wrote in the *Forum* last March after the canal had long been fortified: "the canal has led the United States from intervention to intervention, and from naval base to naval base. It is evident that the Caribbean is fast becoming another Mediterranean."

VI

The real interest in the measures advocated in the party platform came however during the campaign itself when it was possible to place them before many groups throughout the country. Sometimes the planks in our platform were sharply challenged, but more often regarded with approval and occasionally with enthusiasm. I recall a meeting in Leadville, Colorado, made up altogether of miners who were much surprised to find that politics had anything to do with such affairs. They had always supposed that hours of labor were matters to be fought for and not voted upon. It was very exhilarating to talk to them, and it seemed to me that I had never before realized how slow we had been to place the definite interests of the workingmen in such shape that they could be voted upon. As a campaign speaker I was sent from town to town in both Dakotas, in Iowa, Nebraska, Oklahoma, Colorado, Kansas and Missouri. The comradeship which a like minded group always affords, combined with the heartiness of western good will, kept my spirits at high tide in spite of the fatigue of incessant speaking.

The Progressive Party campaign remains in my mind as a wonderful opportunity for education not only on the social justice planks in the platform but on the history of the idealogy back of them. Aristotle is reported to have said that politics is a school wherein questions are studied not for the sake of knowledge but for the sake of action. Out of his wisdom he might have added, that politics is most valuable as a school because the average man has an inveterate tendency not to study at all, unless he sees the prospect of action ahead of him. During the Progressive campaign, measures of social amelioration were discussed up and down the land as only party politics can be discussed, in the remotest farmhouse to which the rural free delivery brought the weekly newspaper; certain economic principles became current talk and new phrases entered permanently into popular speech. Certainly those of us identified with the campaign were convinced that people are ready to grapple with social problems whenever a well considered program is laid before them.

I was in Kansas City the very last night before the election. A relative of mine who remained faithful to the Republican Party, was quite sure that we were overestimating our strength in the West, and when I challenged him with the huge audience which his city afforded us, he insisted that every Progressive in town had come to the meeting because they were too eager and impatient to stay at home. He predicted that the Progressive vote in Kansas City would be just about the number of men in the audience, in which prediction he proved to be quite right. It was hard to believe it at the moment, however, in the midst of a torch-light procession. The Kansas City Progressives said that they had not meant to have such a procession, but somebody proposed it and the procession seemed to form itself. It was a mile long, marching bands, and all the rest of it.

The campaign renewed one's convictions that if the community as a whole were better informed as to the ethical implications of industrial wrongs whole areas of life could be saved from becoming brutalized or from sinking into hard indifference. We craved the understanding support which results from a widespread and sincere discussion of a given subject by thousands of our fellow citizens before any attempt should be made to secure legislative action. At moments we believed that we were witnessing a new pioneering of the human spirit, that we were in all humility inaugurating an exploration into the moral resources of our fellow citizens.

All this was somewhat in the minds of the National Executive Committee of the Progressive Party when, after the election, we adopted a plan, submitted by Frances Kellor of New York, for the

mending a down-and-outer sitting on a park bench, as ready to give the visitor more time than a busy citizen would and equally able to tell the story.

But why write longer of these glowing plans which have long since been abandoned? Possibly the time was not ripe for the organization of a new political party or more likely we did not recognize the nation's actual needs and desires. Certainly the time for such a movement is long overdue now, for striking changes are taking place in the parliamentary form of government all over the world, and the usefulness of the old-fashioned political party is being challenged as never before. We have recently been told by an observant Frenchman that the political parties of the United States are not political parties in the original parliamentary sense at all, that they are really political contrivances for nominating and electing officers, and that with the possible exception of the tariff, the present platforms are ordinarily made up of what the party leaders consider the most popular issues. He further contends that the advocacy of moral and economic aims associated with political parties in most parliamentary countries, is carried on in the United States by voluntary organizations; and points out that while we have no labor party, no piece of legislation affecting labor is brought into Congress before the American Federation of Labor has been directly or indirectly "sounded"—while we have no busi-

nessmen's party, the National Association of
Chambers of Commerce and similar organizations
maintain headquarters in Washington that their
interests may be safeguarded; we have no third
estate representing the professions but that the
American Bar Association would inevitably be
consulted before any change would be advocated
in legal procedure. He further points out that the
most striking piece of popular legislation of this
century was achieved not by either of our great
political parties but by a voluntary agency called
the Anti Saloon League. He might have added
that the failure of the United States to enter the
League of Nations, affords a marked example of
the results of a departure from this non-partisan
appeal and a deplorable attempt to use the strictly
party method.

It was during the committee meetings in New
York that I came to know Colonel Roosevelt well,
although I had known him slightly for many years.
I recall him first at Hull-House when he reviewed
the Boy Scouts of the entire West Side of Chicago
in our largest hall. Our boys' club band, the
fifty members of which crowded the platform,
played lustily throughout the ceremony, but never
once did their distinguished visitor wince, and
indeed he went the length of asking for one more
tune before he tore himself away. Colonel Roosevelt had come to Chicago as the guest of the
Union League Club to speak in the armory before

the immigrants who had received their second papers during the year and had thereby become entitled to their first votes. After the armory meeting at which I had also spoken, my hat could not be found. It had most likely been trampled into an undistinguishable mass by the dense crowd of men. As we came back in an open motor, Colonel Roosevelt insisted upon riding without a hat in order to make me more comfortable in my hatless state. The Union League Club, thus knowing of my loss, sent me fifty dollars with which to buy a new hat. I returned the check to the treasurer, stating the hat had cost ten dollars when it was new and was already two years old. The newspapers jocosely took up the incident as an example of admirable economy, stressing the fact that a hat which had cost so little had yet lasted so long; when the milliners in alarm also used the incident, but this time as a warning that one who had been so careless in securing a hat, had never been able to secure a husband. Any story connected with Colonel Roosevelt always had full newspaper publicity, owing, doubtless, to what had been described as his "high degree of visibility"; so the incident, enlarged and embellished, appeared in print for a long time. Colonel Roosevelt sent me a number of these newspaper clippings, with a hearty appreciation of the fact that a suffragist was obliged to submit to so feminine a judgment.

I also recall his being in Chicago at a time when

the Hull-House Players were giving Galsworthy's
Justice. He was much impressed with the play
and most generous in his praise of the young man
who took the part of the criminal at the bar.
Colonel Roosevelt had at that time never heard of
Galsworthy, but left Chicago with all the Galsworthy books obtainable in order that he might
read them between Chicago and New York. The
Hull-House Players had, a short time before, had
the privilege of entertaining Mr. Galsworthy at
breakfast, and the praise from Colonel Roosevelt
added to this fact, uplifted them indeed.

It was possible, however, to know Colonel
Roosevelt in quite a different way during those
meetings of the National Committee of the Progressive Party, for although he was not a member
of the committee and scrupulously stayed away
from its meetings unless he was specially invited,
it was always a red letter day when he came.
"Peace" was forever a bone of contention between
us, although the discussions were never acrimonious and sometimes hilarious for he loved to remind
me that it was he who had received the Nobel
Peace Prize and that he had therefore been internationally recognized as the American authority
on the subject.

VII

Perhaps the Progressive Party once more demonstrated what political history has many times

made evident, that new parties ultimately write the platforms for all parties; that a cause which a new party has the courage to espouse is later taken up by existing political organizations to whom direct appeal has previously proved fruitless.

A leading Progressive has recently written:

If from the Roosevelt camp, with somewhat jealous eyes, we watched the progressive Democracy create a tariff commission, a federal reserve system, and a federal trade commission; and write laws to promote the welfare of wage-earners, to protect seamen and to prohibit child labor, at least we were compelled to join in the applause.

Persistently the progressive Democrats urged the Roosevelt leaders to join them in advancing the Wilson two-party strategy; liberal Democrats opposing conservative Republicans—a third progressive party should be discouraged. Eventually many of our old companions in arms went Democratic.

Certainly President Wilson's first term was characterized by a series of measures which induced many of us to vote for him in 1916. Some of us whole-heartedly campaigned for his second term with profound admiration for his abilities and achievements and also because he had "kept us out of war."

When the successful issue of the 1916 campaign was celebrated at a victory dinner given by President Wilson at the White House, I inevitably found myself speculating upon the contrast between the only two presidential campaigns in which I had participated. As the diners extolled the triumph of principle over the forces of reaction and predatory greed, I vividly recalled another post-campaign banquet, at which we had congratulated each other upon our opportunity to have thrust the dry sticks of principle into the moist fruitful earth and to find them returned to our hands so fresh and blooming that we no longer wished to use them as measuring rods for the evildoer, but wondering, held them as a new-born pledge of the irresistible power of nature to quicken and to heal. In the face of such an extravagant statement—perhaps only permissible in an after-dinner speech—I should explain that in tracing the connection between social service and the platform of the Progressive Party, I am not foolish enough to claim any special perspicacity on the part of a social worker. I should say that if he at times saw the need before the politician did, it may be due to the fact that when we face a social situation in which certain values are but dimly emergent, a socially unified group may fail to tap its resources because they all see it very much alike. By the same token it may be possible for the social worker living in the midst of divers groups whose history, language and customs show the tremendous variability of human nature, to find clues to a new life pattern in such a situation because, although all the groups feel alike that something should be done about it, each group sees it differently and one may find the way out.

A time of tension when old values are at hazard may be the very moment when the groups seeking new adjustments, are driven to give attention to half formed purposes which may precipitate into experimental action. If I may be permitted to use a mixed metaphor; in the midst of the storm they scramble out of a welter of broken boats and cling together to a new safety device which the passengers in sounder boats profoundly distrust. But the device itself may be the beginning of a new method of transportation destined to replace and to transcend the comfortable boats in which the careful passengers sit tight.

CHAPTER III

The Devil Baby at Hull-House

IN the late winter and early spring following
the Progressive campaign my friend, Mary Rozet
Smith, and myself spent three months in Egypt
and Syria. The panoramic procession of Egyptian women filling their jars from the waters of
the Nile and bearing them upon their heads to the
parched fields which at the best produced barely
enough to keep their children alive; the glimpses
into the smoking huts at the end of the day when
each child received his meager portion from his
anxious mother; induced a new sense of the unending effort of women throughout the earth that
human life might be maintained upon its surface.
These somber reflections may have prepared me

49

for the visit of the Devil Baby at Hull-House which occurred soon after our return. Although I must apologize because I have already used the incident in another connection [1] I venture to repeat the story here because it gives a certain aspect of life at Hull-House which nothing else so adequately conveys.

The knowledge of his existence burst upon the residents of Hull-House one day when three Italian women, with an excited rush through the door, demanded that the Devil Baby be shown to them. No amount of denial convinced them that he was not there, for they knew exactly what he was like with his cloven hoofs, his pointed ears and diminutive tail; the Devil Baby had, moreover, been able to speak as soon as he was born and was most shockingly profane.

The three women were but the forerunners of a veritable multitude; for six weeks from every part of the city and suburbs the streams of visitors to this mythical baby poured in all day long and so far into the night that the regular activities of the settlement were almost swamped. The Italian version with a hundred variations dealt with a pious Italian girl married to an atheist. Her husband in a rage had torn a holy picture from the bedroom wall saying that he would quite as soon have a devil in the house as such a thing, whereupon the

[1] *The Long Road of Woman's Memory*—The Macmillan Company, 1917. Chapters I and II.

devil incarnated himself in her coming child. As soon as the Devil Baby was born, he ran around the table shaking his finger at his father, who finally caught him and in fear and trembling, brought him to Hull-House. When the residents there, in spite of the baby's shocking appearance, wishing to save his soul, took him to church for baptism, they found that the shawl was empty and the Devil Baby, fleeing from the holy water, was running lightly over the backs of the pews.

The Jewish version, again with variations, was to the effect that the father of six daughters had said before the birth of a seventh child that he would rather have a devil in the family than another girl, whereupon the Devil Baby promptly appeared.

Save for a red automobile which occasionally figured in the story and a stray cigar which, in some versions, the new-born child had snatched from his father's lips, the tale might have been fashioned a thousand years ago.

Although the visitors to the Devil Baby included persons of every degree of prosperity and education, the story constantly demonstrated the power of an old wives' tale among thousands of men and women in modern society who are living with their vision fixed and their intelligence held by some iron chain of silent habit. To such primitive people the metaphor apparently is still the very stuff of life, or rather, no other form of statement reaches them; the tremendous tonnage of current writing for them has no existence. It was in keeping with their simple habits that the reputed presence of the Devil Baby should not reach the newspapers until the fifth week of his sojourn at Hull-House—after thousands of people had already been informed of his whereabouts by the old method of passing news from mouth to mouth.

For six weeks as I went about the house I would hear a voice at the telephone repeating for the hundredth time that day, "No, there is no such baby"; "No, we never had it here"; "No, he couldn't have seen it for fifty cents"; "We didn't send it anywhere, because we never had it"; "I don't mean to say that your sister-in-law lied, but there must be some mistake"; "There is no use getting up an excursion from Milwaukee, for there isn't any Devil Baby at Hull-House"; "We can't give reduced rates, because we are not exhibiting anything"; and so on and on. As I came near the front door I would catch snatches of arguments that were often acrimonious: "Why do you let so many people believe it, if it isn't here?" "We have taken three lines of cars to come and we have as much right to see it as anybody else"; "This is a pretty big place, of course you could hide it easy enough"; "What are you saying that for, are you going to raise the price of admission?"

II

We had doubtless struck a case of what the psychologists call the contagion of emotion added to that æsthetic sociability which impels any one of us to drag the entire household to the window when a procession comes into the street or a rainbow appears in the sky. The Devil Baby of course was worth many processions and rainbows, but I will confess that, as the empty show went on day after day, I quite revolted against such a vapid manifestation of even an admirable human trait. There was always one exception, however; whenever I heard the high eager voices of old women, I was irresistibly interested and left anything I might be doing in order to listen to them. It was a very serious and genuine matter with these old women, this story so ancient and yet so contemporaneous, and they flocked to Hull-House from every direction; those I had known for many years, others I had never known, and some whom I had supposed to be long dead. But they were all alive and eager; something in the story or in its mysterious sequences had aroused one of those active forces in human nature which does not take orders but insists only upon giving them.

During the weeks of excitement it was the old women who really seemed to have come into their own, and perhaps the most significant result of the incident was the reaction of the story upon them.

It stirred their minds and memory as with a magic touch, it loosened their tongues and revealed the inner life and thoughts of those who are so often inarticulate. They are accustomed to sit at home and to hear the younger members of the family speak of affairs quite outside their own experiences sometimes in a language they do not understand, and at best in quick glancing phrases which they cannot follow; "More than half the time I can't tell what they are talking about," is an oft-repeated complaint.

Perhaps my many conversations with these aged visitors crystallized thoughts and impressions I had been receiving through years, or the tale itself may have ignited a fire, as it were, whose light illumined some of my darkest memories of neglected and uncomfortable old age, of old peasant women who had ruthlessly probed into the ugly depths of human nature in themselves and others. Many of them who came to see the Devil Baby had been forced to face tragic experiences, the powers of brutality and horror had had full scope in their lives and for years they had had acquaintance with disaster and death. Such old women do not shirk life's misery by feeble idealism, for they are long past the stage of make-believe. They relate without flinching the most hideous experiences: "My face has had this queer twist for now nearly sixty years; I was ten when it got that way, the night after I saw my father do my mother to death with his knife." "Yes, I had fourteen children; only two grew to be men and both of them were killed in the same explosion. I was never sure they brought home the right bodies." But even the most hideous sorrows which the old women related had apparently subsided into the paler emotion of ineffectual regret, and they seemed, in some unaccountable way, to lose all bitterness and resentment against life, or rather to be so completely without it that they must have lost it long since.

None of them had a word of blame for undutiful children or heedless grandchildren, because apparently the petty and transitory had fallen away from their austere old age, the fires were burned out. Perhaps because they had come to expect nothing more of life and had perforce ceased from grasping and striving, they had obtained, if not renunciation, at least that quiet endurance which allows the wounds of the spirit to heal. Some of these old women had struggled for weary years with poverty and much childbearing, had known what it was to be bullied and beaten by their husbands, neglected and ignored by their prosperous children, and burdened by the support of the imbecile and the shiftless ones. They had literally gone "Deep written all their days with care."

One old woman actually came from the poorhouse, having heard of the Devil Baby "through a lady from Polk Street visiting an old lady who has a bed in our ward." It was no slight achievement for the penniless and crippled old inmate to make her escape. She had asked "a young bar-keep in a saloon across the road" to lend her ten cents, offering as security the fact that she was an old acquaintance at Hull-House who could not be refused so slight a loan. She marveled at some length over the goodness of the young man, for she had not had a dime to spend for a drink for the last six months, and he and the conductor had been obliged to lift her into the street car by main strength. She was naturally much elated over the achievement of her escape. To be sure, from the men's side, they were always walking off in the summer and taking to the road, living like tramps they did, in a way no one from the woman's side would demean herself to do; but to have left in a street car like a lady, with money to pay her own fare, was quite a different matter, although she was indeed "clean wore out" by the effort. However, it was clear that she would consider herself well repaid by a sight of the Devil Baby and that not only the inmates of her own ward, but those in every other ward in the house would be made to "sit up" when she got back; it would liven them all up a bit, and she hazarded the guess that she would have to tell them about that baby at least a dozen times a day.

As she cheerfully rambled on, we weakly post-

veritable temptation to give her a full description
of the Devil Baby, which by this time I knew
so accurately (for with a hundred variations to
select from I could have made a monstrous infant
almost worthy of his name), and also to refrain
from putting too much stress on the fact that he
had never been really and truly at Hull-House.
I found my mind hastily marshalling arguments
for not disturbing her belief in the story which
had so evidently brought her a vivid interest long
denied her. She lived alone with her young grand-
son who went to work every morning at seven
o'clock and save for the short visits made by the
visiting nurse and by kind neighbors, her long day
was monotonous and undisturbed. But the story
of a Devil Baby, with his existence officially corroborated as it were, would give her a lodestone
which would attract the neighbors far and wide
and exalt her once more into the social importance
she had had twenty-four years before when I had
first known her. She was then the proprietor of the
most prosperous secondhand store on a street full
of them, her shiftless, drinking husband, and her
jolly good-natured sons doing exactly what she
told them to do. This however was long past, for
"owing to the drink," in her own graphic phrase,
"the old man, the boys, and the business, too, were
clean gone" and there was "nobody left but little
Tom and me, and nothing for us to live on."

I remember how well she used to tell a story

when I once tried to collect some folklore for Mr.
Yeats to prove that an Irish peasant does not lose
his faith in the little people nor his knowledge of
Gaelic phrases simply because he is living in a city.
She had at that time told me a wonderful tale
concerning a red cloak worn by an old woman to
a freshly dug grave. The story of the Devil Baby
would give her material worthy of her powers,
but of course she must be able to believe it with
all her heart. She could live only a few months
at the very best, I argued to myself; why not give
her this vivid interest and through it awake those
earliest recollections of that long-accumulated
folklore with its magic power to transfigure and
eclipse the sordid and unsatisfactory surroundings
in which life is actually spent? I solemnly assured
myself that the imagination of old people needs
to be fed and probably has quite as imperious a
claim as that of childhood, which levies upon us
so remorselessly with its "I want a fairy story, but
I don't like you to begin by saying that it isn't
true." Impatiently I found myself challenging
the educators who had given us no pedagogical
instructions for the treatment of old age, although
they had fairly overinformed us as to the use of
the fairy tale with children.

The little room was stuffed with a magpie collection, the usual odds and ends which compose an
old woman's treasures, augmented in this case by
various articles which a secondhand store, even of

the most flourishing sort, could not sell. In the picturesque confusion, if anywhere in Chicago, an urbanized group of the little people might dwell; they would certainly find the traditional atmosphere which they strictly require, marveling faith, and unalloyed reverence. At any rate, an eager old woman aroused to her utmost capacity of wonder and credulity was the very soil, prepared to a nicety, for planting the seed-thought of the Devil Baby. If the object of my errand had been an hour's reading to a sick woman, it would have been accounted to me for philanthropic righteousness and if the chosen reading had lifted her mind from her bodily discomforts and harassing thoughts so that she forgot them all for one fleeting moment, how pleased I should have been with the success of my effort. But here I was with a story at my tongue's end, stupidly hesitating to give it validity, although the very words were on my lips. I was still arguing the case with myself when I stood on the threshold of her room and caught the indomitable gleam of her eye, fairly daring me to deny the existence of the Devil Baby, her slack dropsical body so responding to her overpowering excitement that for the moment she looked positively menacing.

But, as in the case of many another weak soul, the decision was taken out of my hands, my very hesitation was enough, for nothing is more certain than that the bearer of a magic tale never stands

dawdling on the doorstep. Slowly the gleam died
out of the expectant old eyes, the erect shoulders
sagged and pulled forward, and I saw only too
plainly that the poor old woman had accepted one
more disappointment in a life already overflowing
with them. She was violently thrown back into all
the limitations of her personal experience and surroundings, and that larger life she had anticipated
so eagerly was as suddenly shut away from her
as if a door had been slammed in her face.

III

The vivid interest of so many old women in the
story of the Devil Baby may have been an unconscious, although powerful, testimony that tragic
experiences gradually become dressed in such
trappings in order that their spent agony may
prove of some use to a world which learns at the
hardest; and that the strivings and sufferings of
men and women long since dead, their emotions
no longer connected with flesh and blood, are thus
transmuted into legendary wisdom. The young
are forced to heed the warning in such a tale,
although for the most part it is so easy for them
to disregard the words of the aged. That the old
women who came to visit the Devil Baby believed
that the story would secure them a hearing at
home was evident, and as they prepared themselves with every detail of it, their old faces shone
with a timid satisfaction. Their features, worn

and scarred by harsh living, as effigies built into
the floor of an old church become dim and defaced
by roughshod feet,. grew poignant and solemn.

Sometimes in talking to a woman who was "but
a hair's breadth this side of darkness," I realized
that old age has its own expression for the mystic
renunciation of the world. The impatience with
all non-essentials, the craving to be free from ham-
pering bonds and soft conditions, recalled Tolstoy's last impetuous journey, and I was once more
grateful to his genius for making clear another
unintelligible impulse of bewildered humanity.
Often, in the midst of a conversation, one of these
touching old women would quietly express a longing for death, as if it were a natural fulfillment of
an inmost desire, with a sincerity and anticipation
so genuine that I would feel abashed in her presence, ashamed to "cling to this strange thing that
shines in the sunlight and to be sick with love for
it."

From our visitors to the Devil Baby it gradually
became evident that the simpler women were
moved not wholly by curiosity, but that many of
them prized the story as a valuable instrument in
the business of living. From them and from the
surprising number of others who had been sent by
the aged and the bed-ridden to secure an exact history and description of the child, the suggestion
finally became quite irresistible that such a story,
outlining a great abstraction, may once have per-

formed the high service of tradition and discipline in the beginnings of a civilized family life. The legend exhibited all the persistence of one of those tales which has doubtless been preserved through the centuries because of its taming effects upon recalcitrant husbands and fathers. Shamefaced men brought to Hull-House by their womenfolk to see the baby, but ill-concealed their triumph when there proved to be no such visible sign of retribution for domestic derelictions. On the other hand, numbers of men came by themselves, one group from a neighboring factory on their "own time" offered to pay twenty-five cents, a half dollar, two dollars apiece to see the child, insisting that it must be at Hull-House because "the women had seen it." To my query as to whether they supposed we would, for money, exhibit a poor little deformed baby, if one had been born in the neighborhood, they replied: "Sure, why not?" and "it teaches a good lesson, too," they added as an afterthought, or perhaps as a concession to the strange moral standards of a place like Hull-House. All the members in this group of hardworking men, in spite of a certain swagger toward one another and a tendency to bully the derelict showman, wore a hangdog look betraying that sense of unfair treatment which a man is so apt to feel when his womankind makes an appeal to the supernatural. In their determination to see the child, the men recklessly divulged much more concerning their motives than they had meant to do. Their talk confirmed my impression that such a story may still act as a restraining influence in the sphere of marital conduct which, next to primitive religion, has always afforded the most fertile field for irrational taboos and savage punishments.

What story could be better than this to secure sympathy for the mother of too many daughters and contumely for the irritated father; the touch of mysticism, the supernatural sphere in which it was placed, would render a man quite helpless.

The story of the Devil Baby, evolved in response to the imperative needs of anxious wives and mothers, recalls the theory that woman first fashioned the fairy story, that combination of wisdom and romance, in an effort to tame her mate and to make him a better father to her children, until such stories finally became a crude creed for domestic conduct, softening the treatment men accorded to women. Because such stories, expressing the very essence of human emotion, did not pretend to imitate the outside of life, they were careless of verisimilitude and absolutely indifferent to the real world. Possibly the multitude of life's failures, the obscure victims of unspeakable wrong and brutality, have embodied their memories in a literature of their own, of which the story of the Devil Baby is a specimen, crude and ugly in form, as would be inevitable, but still bringing relief to the surcharged heart.

During the weeks that the Devil Baby drew multitudes of visitors to Hull-House, my mind was opened to the fact that new knowledge derived from concrete experience is continually being made available for the guidance of human life; that humble women are still establishing rules of conduct as best they may, to counteract the base temptations of a man's world. I saw a new significance in the fact that thousands of women, for instance, make it a standard of domestic virtue that a man must not touch his pay envelope, but bring it home unopened to his wife. High praise is contained in the phrase, "We have been married twenty years and he never once opened his own envelope," or covert blame in the statement, "Of course he got to gambling; what can you expect from a man who always opens his own pay." The women were so fatalistically certain of this relation of punishment to domestic sin, of reward to domestic virtue, that when they talked about them, as they so constantly did in connection with the Devil Baby, it often sounded as if they were using the words of a widely known ritual. Among the visitors to the Devil Baby were many foreign-born peasant women who, when they had come to America, had been suddenly subjected to the complicated and constantly changing environment of city life, and, finding no outlet for many habits and tendencies, might easily have been thrown into that state described by psychologists as one of baulked disposition. To them this simple tale with its direct connection between cause and effect, between wrongdoing and punishment, brought soothing and relief, and restored a shaken confidence as to the righteousness of the universe. Because the Devil Baby embodied an undeserved wrong to a poor mother whose tender child had been claimed by the forces of evil, his merely reputed presence had power to attract to Hull-House hundreds of women who had been humbled and disgraced by their children; mothers of the feeble-minded, of the vicious, of the criminal, of the prostitute. In their talk it was as if their long rôle of maternal apology and protective reticence had at last broken down, as if they could speak out freely because for once a man responsible for an ill-begotten child had been "met up with" and had received his deserts. Their sinister version of the story was that the father of the Devil Baby had married without confessing a hideous crime committed years before, thus basely deceiving both his innocent young bride and the good priest who performed the solemn ceremony; that the sin had become incarnate in his child which, to the horror of the young and trusting mother, had been born with all the outward aspects of the devil himself.

IV

As if drawn by a magnet, these forlorn women issued forth from the many homes in which dwelt "the two unprofitable goddesses, Poverty and Impossibility." Occasionally it seemed to me that the women were impelled by a longing to see one good case of retribution before they died, as a bullied child hopes to deal at least one crushing blow at his tormentor when he "grows up," but I think, on the whole, such an explanation was a mistake; it is more probable that the avidity of the women demonstrated that the story itself, like all interpretative art, was one of those free, unconscious attempts to satisfy, outside of life, those cravings which life itself leaves unsatisfied. At moments, however, baffled desires, sharp cries of pain, echoes of justices unfulfilled, the original material from which such tales are fashioned, would break through the rigid restraints imposed by all Art, even that unconscious of itself.

With an understanding quickened, perhaps, through my own acquaintance with the mysterious child, I listened to many tragic reminiscences from the visiting women; of premature births, "because he kicked me in the side"; of children maimed and burnt because "I had no one to leave them with when I went to work"; women had seen the tender flesh of growing little bodies given over to death because "he wouldn't let me send for the doctor," or because "there was no money to pay for the medicine." But even these mothers, rendered childless through insensate brutality, were less pitiful than some of the others, who might

well have cried aloud of their children as did a
distracted mother of her child centuries ago:

> That God should send this one thing more
> Of hunger and of dread, a door
> Set wide to every wind of pain!

Such was the mother of a feeble-minded boy, who
said: "I didn't have a devil baby myself, but I
bore a poor 'innocent' who made me fight devils
for twenty-three years." She told of her son's
experiences from the time the other little boys had
put him up to stealing that they might hide in
safety and leave him to be found with "the goods
on him," until grown into a huge man he fell into
the hands of professional burglars; he was evidently the dupe and stool-pigeon of the vicious and
criminal until the very day he was locked into the
state penitentiary. "If people played with him a
little, he went right off and did anything they told
him to, and now he's been sent up for life. We
call such innocents 'God's Fools' in the old country, but over here the Devil himself gets them.
I've fought off bad men and boys from the poor
lamb with my very fists; nobody ever came near
the house except such-like and the police officers,
who were always arresting him."

There were a goodly number of visitors to the
Devil Baby of the type of those to be found in
every large city, who are on the verge of nervous
collapse, or who exhibit many symptoms of mental

aberration, and yet are sufficiently normal to be at large most of the time, and to support themselves by drudgery which requires little mental effort although the exhaustion resulting from the work they are able to do, is the one thing from which they should be most carefully protected. One such woman, evidently obtaining inscrutable comfort from the story of the Devil Baby even after she had become convinced that we harbored no such creature, came many times to tell of her longing for her son, who had joined the army eighteen months before and was now stationed in Alaska. She always began with the same words:

"When Spring comes and the snow melts so that I know he could get out, I can hardly stand it. You know I was once in the insane asylum for three years at a stretch, and since then I haven't had much use of my mind except to worry with. Of course I know that it is dangerous for me, but what can I do? I think something like this: 'The snow is melting, now he could get out, but his officers won't let him off and if he runs away he will be shot for a deserter—either way I'll never see him again; I'll die without seeing him'—and then I'll begin all over again with the snow." After a pause, she said: "The recruiting officer ought not to have taken him, he's my only son and I'm a widow. It's against the rules, but he was so crazy to go that I guess he lied a little—at any rate, the government has him now and I can't get him back. Without this worry about him my mind would be all right; if he were here he would be earning money and keeping me and we would be happy all day long."

Recalling the vagabondish lad, who had never earned much money and had certainly never "kept" his hardworking mother, I ventured to suggest that, even if he were at home he might not have work these hard times, that he might get into trouble and be arrested—I did not need to remind her that he had been already arrested twice—that he was now fed and sheltered and under discipline, and I added hopefully something about his seeing the world. She looked at me out of her withdrawn harried eyes, as if I were speaking a foreign tongue. "That wouldn't make any real difference to me—the work, the money, his behaving well and all that, if I could cook and wash for him. I don't need all the money I earn scrubbing that factory. I only take bread and tea for supper, and I choke over that, thinking of him."

She ceased to speak, overcome by a thousand obscure emotions which could find no outlet in words. She dimly realized that the facts in the case, to one who had known her boy from childhood, were far from creditable, and that no one could understand the eternally unappeased idealism which, for her, surrounded her son's return. She was even afraid to say much about it, lest she should be overmastered by her subject and be considered so irrational as to suggest a return to the hospital for the insane.

Those mothers who have never resisted fate nor buffeted against the black waters but have allowed the waves to close over them, worn and bent as they are by hard labor, subdued and misshapen by the brutality of men, are at least unaffrighted by the melodramatic coarseness of life, which Stevenson more gently describes as "the uncouth and outlandish strain in the web of the world." The story of the Devil Baby may have made its appeal through its frank presentation of this very demoniac quality, to those who live under the iron tyranny of that poverty which threatens starvation, and under the dread of a brutality which may any dark night bring them or their children to extinction; to those who have seen both virtue and vice go unrewarded and who have long since ceased to complain.

V

A sorrowful woman, clad in heavy black, who came one day, exhibited such a capacity for prolonged weeping that it was evidence in itself of the truth of at least half her statement, that she had cried herself to sleep every night of her life for fourteen years in fulfillment of a "curse" laid upon her by an angry man that "her pillow would be wet with tears as long as she lived." Her respectable husband had a shop in the red light

district because he found it profitable to sell to the
men and women who lived there. She had kept
house in the room over the store from the time
she was a bride newly come from Russia, and her
five daughters had been born there, but never a
son to gladden her husband's heart.

She took such a feverish interest in the Devil
Baby that, when I was obliged to disillusion her,
I found it hard to take away her comfort in the
belief that the Powers that Be are on the side of
the woman when her husband resents too many
daughters. But, after all, the birth of daughters
was but an incident in her unmitigated woe, for
the scoldings of a disappointed husband were as
nothing to the curse of a strange enemy, although
she doubtless had a confused impression that if
there were retribution for one in the general
scheme of things, there might be for the other.
When the weeping woman finally put the events
of her disordered life in some sort of sequence, it
became clear that about fifteen years ago she had
reported to the police a vicious house whose back
door opened into her own yard. Her husband had
forbidden her to do anything about it and had said
that it would only get them into trouble, but she
had been made desperate one day when she saw
her little girl, then twelve years old, come out of
the door, gleefully showing her younger sister a
present of money. Because the poor woman had
tried for ten years without success to induce her

husband to move from the vicinity of such houses, she was certain that she could save her child only by forcing out "the bad people" from her own door yard. She therefore made her one frantic effort, found her way to the city hall and there reported the house to the chief himself. Of course, "the bad people stood in with the police" and nothing happened to them save, perhaps, a fresh levy of blackmail, but the keeper of the house, beside himself with rage, made the dire threat and laid the curse upon her. In less than a year from that time he had enticed her daughter into a disreputable house in another part of the district. The poor woman, ringing one doorbell after another, had never been able to find her, but her sisters, who in time came to know where she was, had been dazzled by her mode of life. The weeping mother was quite sure that two of her daughters, while still outwardly respectable and "working downtown," earned money in the devious ways which they had learned all about when they were little children, although for the past five years the now prosperous husband had allowed the family to live in a suburb where the two younger daughters were "growing up respectable."

Certain of the visitors, although confronted by those mysterious and impersonal wrongs which are apparently inherent in the very nature of things, gave us glimpses of another sort of wisdom than that expressed in the assumptions that the decrees

of Fate are immutable. Such a glimpse came to me
through conversation with a woman whose fine
mind and indomitable spirit I had long admired;
I had known her for years, and the recital of her
sufferings added to those which the Devil Baby
had already induced other women to tell me,
pierced me afresh.

"I had eleven children, some born in Hungary
and some born here, nine of them boys; all of the
children died when they were little but my dear
Liboucha. You know all about her. She died last
winter in the insane asylum. She was only twelve
years old when her father, in a fit of delirium
tremens, killed himself after he had chased us
around the room, trying to kill us first. She saw it
all, the blood splashed on the wall stayed in her
mind the worst; she shivered and shook all that
night through, and the next morning she had lost
her voice, couldn't speak out loud for terror. After
a while she went to school again and her voice
came back, although it was never very natural.
She seemed to do as well as ever and was awful
pleased when she got into high school. All the
money we had, I earned scrubbing in a public dispensary although sometimes I got a little more by
interpreting for the patients, for I know three
languages, one as well as the other. But I was
determined that whatever happened to me,
Liboucha was to be educated. My husband's
father was a doctor in the old country, and

Liboucha was always a clever child. I wouldn't have her live the kind of life I had, with no use for my mind except to make me restless and bitter. I was pretty old and worn out for such hard work, but when I used to see Liboucha on a Sunday morning ready for church in her white dress, with her long yellow hair braided round her beautiful pale face, lying there in bed to rest my aching bones for the next week's work, I'd feel almost happy, in spite of everything. But of course no such peace could last in my life; the second year at high school Liboucha began to seem different and to do strange things. You know the time she wandered away for three days and we were all wild with fright, although a kind woman had taken her in and no harm came to her. I could never be easy after that; she was always gentle, but she was awful sly about running away and at last I had to send her to the asylum. She stayed there off and on for five years, but I saw her every week of my life and she was always company for me, what with sewing for her, washing and ironing her clothes, cooking little things to take out to her, and saving a bit of money to buy fruit for her. At any rate, I had stopped feeling so bitter, and got some comfort out of seeing the one thing that belonged to me on this side of the water, when all of a sudden she died of heart failure and they never took the trouble to send for me until the next day."

She stopped as if wondering afresh that the

Fates could have been so casual, but with a sudden illumination, as if she had been awakened out of the burden and intensity of her restricted personal interests into a consciousness of those larger relations that are, for the most part, so strangely invisible. It was as if the young mother of the grotesque Devil Baby—that victim of wrongdoing on the part of others—had revealed to this tragic woman much more clearly than soft words had ever done, that the return of a deed of violence upon the head of the innocent is inevitable; as if she had realized that, although she was destined to walk all the days of her life with the piteous multitude who bear the undeserved wrongs of the world, she would walk henceforth with a sense of companionship.

At moments it seemed possible that these simple women, representing an earlier development, eagerly seized upon this story because it was so primitive in form and substance. Certainly, one evening, a long-forgotten ballad made an unceasing effort to come to the surface of my mind as I talked to a feeble woman who, in the last stages of an incurable disease from which she soon afterwards died, had been helped off the street car in front of Hull-House. The ballad tells how the lover of a proud and jealous mistress, who demanded as a final test of devotion that he bring her the heart of his mother, had quickly cut the heart from his mother's breast and impetuously returned to his lady, bearing it upon a salver; and how, when stumbling in his gallant haste, he stooped to replace upon the silver plate his mother's heart which had rolled to the ground, the heart, still beating with tender solicitude, whispered the hope that her child was not hurt. The ballad itself was scarcely more exaggerated than the story of our visitor that evening, who was carried through the door of Hull-House in a desperate effort to see the Devil Baby. I was familiar with her vicissitudes; the shiftless, drinking husband and the large family of children, all of whom had brought her sorrow and disgrace, and I knew that her heart's desire was to see again, before she died, her youngest son, who was a life prisoner in the penitentiary. She was confident that the last piteous stage of her disease would secure him a week's parole, founding this forlorn hope upon the fact that "they sometimes let them out to attend a mother's funeral, and perhaps they'd let Joe come a few days ahead; he could pay his fare afterwards from the insurance money. It wouldn't take much to bury me." Again we went over the hideous story: Joe had violently quarreled with a woman, the proprietor of the house in which his disreputable wife was living, because she had withheld from him a part of his wife's "earnings," and in the altercation had killed her—a situation, one would say, which it would be difficult for even a mother to condone. But not at all. Her thin gray

face worked with emotion, her trembling hands
restlessly pulled at her shabby skirt as the hands of
the dying pluck at their sheets, but she put all the
vitality she could muster into his defense. She
told us he had legally married the girl, who supported him, "although Lily had been so long in
that life that few men would have done it. Of
course such a girl must have a protector or everybody would fleece her. Poor Lily said to the day
of her death that he was the kindest man she ever
knew, and treated her the whitest; that she herself
was to blame for the murder, because she told on
the old miser, and Joe was so hot-headed she might
have known that he would draw a gun for her."
The gasping mother concluded: "He was always
that handsome and had such a way. One winter
when I was scrubbing in an office building, I'd
never get home much before twelve o'clock, but
Joe would open the door for me just as pleasant
as if he hadn't been waked out of a sound sleep."
She was so triumphantly unconscious of the
incongruity of a sturdy son in bed while his mother
earned his food, that her auditors said never a
word, and in silence we saw a hero evolved before
our eyes, a defender of the oppressed, the best
beloved of his mother, who was losing his high
spirits and eating his heart out behind prison bars.
He could well defy the world even there, surrounded as he was by that invincible affection
which assures both the fortunate and unfortunate

CHAPTER IV

ASPECTS OF THE WOMAN'S MOVEMENT

THERE are certain days which remain in our memories because we then seem to have broken through into that reality which ever lies beneath the outward appearance. I spent such a day in the summer of 1913 with delegates to a convention of the International Suffrage Alliance, traveling from Vienna by way of the Danube to the beautiful old city of Buda-Pest. These women from many nations sitting upon the deck of a river steamer felt that curious stimulus which comes from the discovery of like-mindedness between people of varied nationalities. If culture is a combination of traits of purely local origin with those supplied by race diffusion, building up that totality which

as the conquests of Alexander or as the Crusades—
fit subjects for poetic recital. It was the portrayal
of a past grown tranquil because it was apart from
life. The heroes belonged to other centuries far
from our own. We could not anticipate the rough
measure and poignant reproach with which our
contemporary young poets would deal with war
nor could we then understand that it is "only the
living poets who express a feeling that is actually
being made and torn out of us at the moment. We
do not recognize it as poetry in the first place and
too often for some reason we fear it."

Curiously enough however, a long discussion on
the use of force, of military tactics versus constitu-
tionalism, was carried on during that voyage on
the Danube. Only the day before, news had been
received of Emily Davison's death, incurred in
her efforts to take a message to the King concerning Votes for Women. It was part of the campaign
carried on by a section of the English suffragists,
which was at its height in that summer of 1913.
Other women seeking to exercise the ancient right
of petition had been intercepted by the police.
Emily Davison believed that utilizing the great
day of the Derby, when all England of social and
political importance was gathered together, if a
woman should interrupt the race and, as was probable, should be trampled to death by the panic-
stricken horses that the King himself would have
to know the reason; that her petition would thus

reach him at last and that it would not fail because
death itself would lift the minds of all the specta-
tors to that "High Tribunal where justice is never
withheld." To the friends of Emily Davison her
death was a supreme illustration of their endeavor
to bring the question of votes for women before
the public in dramatic form. They believed that
the news would travel around the world that a
human life, for the sake of a great cause, had been
given freely with such heroism.

Several of the women on board the Danube boat
had not only known Emily Davison, but had also
seen her in the hospital after the accident. From
their background of personal friendship and
understanding, she seemed to them to have been a
martyr in the truest sense of the word, and they
urged that a memorial meeting be held in Buda-
Pest preceding the convention. The English
women on the boat who represented the Constitutional Society felt that any such meeting would be
a great mistake, and a discussion was naturally
precipitated in regard to the whole question of
militant tactics. It is interesting to find that the
division, *pro* and *con,* did not run along the line of
reckless youth and conservative age. Among the
Constitutionalists as among the Militants were
many young and charming women, ardent in their
advocacy of parliamentary methods. Maude Roy-
don, whom I then met for the first time, took the
position that men and women could not use force

to settle a difference between them unless women
were ready to lose, for certainly in the use of force
men were admittedly superior! That the vote
itself had been an historic effort to substitute
reason for the sword. There were also those who
advocated a passive resistance, among them Mrs.
Cobden Sanderson, representing the Tax Resistance League—a body of women refusing to pay
taxes to a government in which they were not
directly represented. Of the able talk of these
women on the Danube boat who came from many
countries I recall that of a distinguished scholar
quoting doctrines of Tolstoy, reminding us that
the early Christians had abjured the use of force
for three hundred years and that the later church
had failed to work out a technique for applying
this basic Christian teaching to political affairs.
She somewhat wistfully expressed the hope that
when Christian women received the vote they
might at least experiment in this direction.

That convention in the summer of 1913 in the
fine old capital of Hungary, gave an impressive
view of the woman's movement. For several years
I had served as vice president of the National
American Woman's Suffrage Association, when
Doctor Anna Howard Shaw was its brilliant president. I recall her vivid personality in many striking situations, but one in Buda-Pest remains most
clearly in my mind. The old city on the Danube
had long been a stronghold of Calvinism, with the

result that one of the most beautiful old churches
belonged to the Presbyterians. It had been decided
that Doctor Shaw was to give the "congress ser-
mon" there, but when the day arrived there was
great difficulty as to a woman occupying the pul-
pit. The matter was finally arranged by placing
a platform, with a reading desk upon it, in what
was the junction of the transept and the nave of the
stately old church, while the audience was seated
around the platform in four different directions.
In scholastic cap and gown, she stood on her raised
dais and with the eloquence of which she had been
past master since her early days as a pioneer
Methodist preacher, she filled the vast arches with
a valiant plea for the rights of women based on the
old historic pleas for the rights of the individual,
so dear to Calvin's heart.

The status of equal suffrage reported at the Congress by the delegates from twenty-six parliamentary nations not only gave a world-wide view of
the movement, but strikingly presented various
evolutionary stages. The very earliest stage was
doubtless represented by the women of Asia, who
were making the first struggle against traditional
barriers and customs rooted in primitive times.
The resolution, therefore, admitting the Chinese
Woman's Suffrage Society to the International
Alliance was carried with prolonged applause. It
seems incredible that the convention should have
been told that certain Chinese women had been

decapitated for the truths they had told while
fighting their battle for freedom, and that at any
day the men might find a reason to silence the
leaders of the movement when, in their enthusiasm,
they made too many converts. In spite of the
somber implications of the report, the entire Convention agreed with the thrilling words of Mrs.
Catt, the International President, that even as we
review "the slow tragic struggle upward of the
women of the West, we know there is no escape for
these Eastern women, that they must follow the
vision in their souls as we have done and as other
women have done before us."

Another stage of the women's movement was
represented by the reports from such states as
Bohemia, Silesia and Hungary, where women with
certain property qualifications were permitted to
send men as members of Parliament who would
directly represent their interests. This right of
women to a proxy vote had survived from the
days when the ownership of property was the only
basis upon which either men or women were given
the franchise. But as was pointed out in the convention, these surviving votes representing a stage
long past, were a reproach to the existing governments which made now a greater disparity between
the political status of men and women, than that
which had existed three hundred years ago. It was
upon such a basis that women a few centuries ago
sat in the English Parliament and at that moment

a small number of women were voting upon the same terms as men in the municipal government of Rangoon, in Bombay and other Indian cities.

There were also at Buda-Pest illustrations of the vote accorded to women in pioneer countries, where they had courageously endured hardships with the men who long ago gave them the franchise, in Wyoming, in Australia, and New Zealand. The fact that the latter country was able to report the lowest infant mortality rate to be found in any part of the world was accounted as a fulfillment of our hopes, and doubtless also as a confirmation of our theories. It was the northern women, however, who more than others represented the final stage of the movement. Three members of Parliament sat in the fine delegation from Finland and public servants were also found in the imposing delegation from Sweden and Norway. A most encouraging report came from Turkey, where in spite of Eastern customs, the new constitution had given women a political status, due to that tendency of each revolution to incorporate into its program the most advanced features of existing governments.

The final impression of the convention at Buda-Pest was that the movement for equal suffrage was growing, pushing and developing in all the countries upon the face of the earth, that the coming together of its representatives was no perfunctory matter, but the free exchange of genuine experiences and untrammeled hopes. The movement was everywhere surprisingly spontaneous, manifesting itself in widely separated groups within the same nation; sometimes it was sectarian and dogmatic, at others philosophic and grandiloquent; it was both amorphous and sporadic, or carefully organized and consciously directed, but it was always vital and constantly becoming more widespread. We liked to say that the entrance of women into government differed from former efforts to extend the franchise in one important aspect; that while the final entrance of the middle class was characterized by two dramatic revolutions, one in America and one in France, both of them with bloodshed, this world-wide entrance into government on the part of women was happily a bloodless one, and had been without a semblance of violence save in England, where its manifestations were not unlike those of the earlier movement among workingmen in the Chartist uprisings.

II

In those placid days before the war when we talked of suffrage we used the old abstract arguments, insisting that the adherents of representative government with its foundations laid in diversified human experiences, must concede that the value of such government bears a definite relation to the area of its base, and that the history of its development is a record of new human interests, which have become subjects of governmental action and of the incorporation into the government itself of those classes who represented the new interests.

We had certainly convinced ourselves that there was a political connection between our desire for the vote and our work for social amelioration, and we constantly declared that much of the new demand for political enfranchisement arose from a desire to remedy the unsatisfactory social conditions which are responsible for so much wrongdoing and wretchedness. We argued that because of the tendency to make the state responsible for the care of the helpless and the reform of the delinquent, to safeguard by law the food we eat, and the health of children, contemporary women who were without the franchise were as much outside the real life of the world as any set of disenfranchised free men could possibly have been in all history; never before had so large an area of life found civic expression, never had Hegel's definition of the State been so nearly accurate, that "It is the realization of the moral idea."

We believed that self-government must ever be built up anew in relation to changing experiences and that unless this adjustment constantly takes place, self-government itself is placed in jeopardy. We had also had practical demonstrations that if women had no votes with which to select the men upon whom her social reform had become dependent some cherished project might be so modified by uninformed legislatures during the process of legal enactment, that the law, as finally passed, injured the very people it was meant to protect. Women had discovered that the unrepresented are always liable to be given what they do not want by legislators who merely wish to placate them; a child-labor law exempts street trades, the most dangerous of all trades to a child's morals, a law releasing mothers from petty industry that they may worthily rear their children, provides so inadequate a pension that overburdened women continue to face the necessity of neglecting their young in order to feed them.

The need for the franchise however, was not confined to the legislative department of the government, for the administration of social reform is often quite as important as its enactment. We found that it depended upon the personnel whether the women police should be allowed to act as veritable municipal chaperons, really guarding from danger the tired young girls who seek recreation in public dance halls, or whether the women police should be reduced to such formal duty that their very presence would give a specious sense of security. The promising movement for municipal recreation so largely fostered by women might easily be irreparably injured in the very moment of its apparent success. We sometimes considered it of doubtful advantage that more and more women were appointed to positions in administra-

tive government, so long as the power of general
direction, of determining the trend and temper of
new social experiments, was lodged altogether in
the hands of men responsible only to other voting
men and politically free from the public opinion
of the women originally concerned for the
measures.

In the midst of these arguments, however, and
always in the stirring conventions whether held in
Europe or in the United States there remained in
my mind the experiences of those simple women
who could not do otherwise but make an effort for
the franchise because they needed it so bitterly for
their children's sake. This provided a sanction
quite outside of the organized movement. One
autumn during which I had spoken in five of the
state campaigns for suffrage in the West, I had
come away with a tremendous admiration for
pioneer women; I recall an outdoor meeting on the
steps of a country building in a Kansas town where
a man in the crowd ventured one of the cheap jibes
to which women suffragists had been so long subjected. An old lady who had come from Wisconsin
to help in the campaign suddenly mounted the seat
of the automobile in which she was sitting and
begged leave to reply to him. To our surprise she
evidently knew his name and the very county in
Kansas from which he came. She told of her
experiences in Kansas fifty years earlier when she
had campaigned there to secure the school vote for

women, and had then known the speaker's mother who was living in a remote part of the new state. This pioneer mother had borne six children without medical attendance or the ministrations of any woman and had buried two without the benefit of clergy. She had been eager for the school vote because she wanted a better school for her growing family, and in the midst of her cares had worked hard in the campaign. The simple tale of courageous living and high thinking was unfolded before her son and ended with the question directed to him: "Who can better vote on the needs of this state or on the needs of this great country than a woman like that?" He had, of course, no reply, and sheepishly disappeared in the crowd.

The vivid interest of pioneer women founded upon her own experience was not so unlike what I had seen among the Italian women of our neighborhood, such as their insistence that more attendants be provided for the lake bathing beaches to which their adventurous young sons repaired every hot night. There was instinctive wisdom behind their high handed demand that political action should concern itself with genuine human needs. It makes possible the age-long effort of women to bring the world nearer to their heart's desire—a better world for their children to live in. I was acting as judge of election in the Hull-House precinct one year when there was submitted to the voters a bond issue for a contagious disease hospital. The judge was permitted to go into the voting booth to assist illiterates to mark the ballot. When we were safely behind the little white curtain of the polling booth one woman after another would say: "Of course I am going to vote the way my man told me to, but I won't go out of this place until I vote for that hospital for catching diseases. The visiting nurses are forever taking a child to the hospital because the disease isn't catching but the very time it is, that is the time the nurse tells you that you must keep all the other children out of school to drive you plum crazy because there is no hospital for a disease as your child has got."

The American National Woman's Suffrage Association, as it was somewhat cumbersomely called, tried for years to secure suffrage state by state. After a vigorous campaign in 1910 in five states only two secured it, although the whole movement received an enormous impulse when New York State was won under the remarkable leadership of Mrs. Carrie Chapman Catt. A smaller group in Washington were pushing for a Constitutional amendment which should enfranchise us all at once, but they could obtain no monopoly on besieging Congress. For many years I had been one of a group of discouraged women to appear before the Judiciary committees both of the House and Senate as well as before the Platform committees of the National Party conventions. On one of these latter occasions the room had been prepared for the entry of the suffragists by carefully placing one of the committee members under the table. All would have gone well had he not been moved to groan aloud either in discomfort or in remorse for his drunken estate. On that occasion at least the time honored argument that women were not capable of using the franchise, was not advanced.

III

Much of this activity along civic lines was the result of the Woman's Clubs throughout the country. They were organized into a National Federation which met in Chicago in June, 1914, twenty-four years after it had been organized there. In its first decade it had represented a gigantic quest for culture, at the very moment society had so prided itself upon its liberality and breadth of view that an ironic Englishman had made the statement that "it would be better to be convicted of petty larceny than to be found wanting in historic mindedness." The earlier clubs continually emphasized our common spiritual inheritance as enshrined in poetry, in history, in science, in art, in drama, in music, and believed that their study might be made a great apparatus for the evocation of cultural life. It is easy to treat lightly this period of club development, but certainly the constant coördination of these fructifying specialized studies reacted intimately on the life and character of each community. When that wave of civic emotion surged into the focus of attention which had for its watchword the city beautiful it was most important that there had long been municipal art committees, that public schools had been supplied with good pictures, that trees had been planted in barren towns, that club women had been instrumental in establishing a national park. It all gave reality and background to the movement. When the new social imperative, entitled know your city, gathered momentum far and wide, so that under its impulse and sanction there was inquiry into the facts and tendencies of city life, it was again important that women everywhere had been taught the value of inspecting milk and food, the needlessness of tuberculosis, the necessity for decent factory conditions.

For many of these efforts it was found necessary to command a public opinion not only in the city or state in which the reform was needed, but throughout the country, so that any organization less widespread than the National Federation of Women's Clubs, with interest less universal, would have availed but little. In the second decade, their quest for culture yielded to their interest in child labor, home economics and public health, housing and social hygiene. The biennial meeting in Chicago in 1914 was characteristic of this attitude of club women throughout the country including the women's clubs connected with social settlements. They could all be counted upon to aid in the many efforts at social amelioration which moved forward so rapidly during the years immediately preceding the outbreak of the World War. These efforts were municipal, state, national and international in scope, illustrated often by huge exhibits; one on Child Welfare in Chicago filled the Coliseum with throngs of visitors for a fortnight.

The social settlements from the very beginning had organized groups of women in so-called clubs; first the mothers whose children attended the kindergarten, the cooking school or some similar enterprise in which the mother's coöperation was essential. One of these at Hull-House, which was true also of other settlements, had developed into a flourishing woman's club which in time came to have its affiliations with the County, State and National Federation of Woman's Clubs and to carry its full share of the joint activities. Because its members were nearer to untoward city conditions than were the women who lived in more prosperous parts of the city, it was natural perhaps that they not only gave money but their personal services to the Visiting Nurses, to the early probation officers, to the field work of the Juvenile Protective Association, to the organization extending help to newly arrived immigrants and to many another. Yet they followed on the whole the

woman's club path from culture to civic activity.
The Hull-House Club not only listened to papers
on many improving topics and to occasional con-
certs but the members themselves gave plays and
musical recitals and only later added visits to the
Juvenile Court to their formal visit to art galleries
and museums.

Concurrently with this largest woman's club
at Hull-House, whose members growing prosperous gradually moved to all parts of the city,
were clubs of immigrant women divided on the
language basis into Mexican, Greek and Italian,
although the latter also emerged into the typical
woman's club. A club of colored women obliged
to meet in the evening because they were all wage
earners by day were so absorbed in the housing
situation and so determined to find out why their
own housing conditions were so wretched that it
was impossible for the first year to interest them
in anything else. In point of fact all the woman's
clubs connected with settlements were much given
to finding out about better housing and better
house furnishings. An inter-settlement federation
of them in Chicago, as in several other cities, gave
annual exhibits with talks by experts suggesting
betterment along both lines. The Federation of
Settlement Woman's Clubs in New York City
claimed a distinct share in securing the state law
for lessening the cost of tenement house construction. I remember addressing one of their exhibit

meetings on the roof of an imposing hotel at which I received the impression that these women were taking care of their own household affairs with great intelligence and with a fine coöperative spirit which the situation required if it were to be met adequately.

During these pre-war years the settlement groups met constantly for civic discussion. I recall an incident connected with the City Club which when it was first built in Chicago was used as a meeting place for all sorts of organizations. We talked over all our causes as we ate luncheon under its hospitable roof. One day as I entered the elevator, the boy who knew me well said casually: "What are you eating with to-day—with garbage or with the social evil?" I replied: "Garbage," with as much dignity as I could command under the circumstances and he deposited me on the fourth floor where I found Mary McDowell, head of the University of Chicago Settlement, pinning on the wall blue prints of a certain garbage reduction plant. I had been a little disturbed by my conversation in the elevator, and remarked: "Isn't it amazing the way we eat and at the same time talk about these disagreeable subjects?" She went on pinning up her blue prints as she replied: "If you lived near Bubbly Creek, into which the five largest slaughterhouses in the world discharge their refuse, you would be so interested in garbage that you would talk about it at luncheon or any other time." I assured her that

I was interested in garbage, and instanced the fact that I had once been a garbage inspector myself. "Yes," she said, "you are interested, but if you lived back of the Yards you could not think that any mere talk about it was disagreeable."

And so the woman's clubs were ready at least to investigate any civic situation which seemed to call for vigorous action; and because coöperation among women was new and the companionship exhilarating they were continually "borne onward with that flood of freedom which to the open sea doth flow with pomp of waters unwithstood"—a spirit characteristic of those days which later came to seem so remote—but which is still manifesting itself in new ways, such as the third conference on the Cause and Cure of War held in Washington last January, attended by six hundred delegates from nine national women's organizations. A club woman there ventured the statement that while "the culture club is still with us, discussions of international relations are more popular than papers on the poets of the seventeenth century." She added to this the opinion that "the most interesting and unexpected turn in the tide of feminine affairs is woman's intelligent and almost impassioned interest in world affairs."

IV

The French have a proverb which has always seemed to me very charming; "Men make the roads but it is women who teach children how to walk."

It was during a meeting of women from those countries which border upon the Pacific Ocean held in Honolulu in the summer of 1928 that this saying became verified in my mind. I had been asked by the Pan Pacific Union to preside over its deliberations and from the very first moment I felt a certain vitality and a special reason why women—Oriental women at least—should throw over the mechanical method of communication in favor of personal intercourse. The entire Pacific area is nearer to a basic culture founded upon human needs than are the Occidental countries where the culture taken over from Europe has become so highly mechanized in the lives of women as well as men. One felt that these women from China, Korea, Japan, Samoa, Fiji, and the Philippines, had been less mechanized than those of us who stood nearer to Western culture. We had come to regard the advance of Western civilization as a sort of game, an effort to make one type of culture predominate, which, if too hardly pushed, may break down other cultures older and more basic. We have been accustomed to say with pride that telephone poles may be set up in a jungle, that a wireless operates as easily on sea as on land, forgetting that in our absorption in communicating culture we may easily lose the patterns and customs which give it any real value.

As the Congress at Honolulu proceeded we felt that Oriental women had unique opportunities to stand free from the tyranny of mechanization and to act upon the assumption that civilization is a method of living, an attitude of equal respect for all men. The cultural outlook on life must become as aggressive as the commercial if it hopes to be effective. There is obvious need for bolder arrangements and interactions in the distribution of education, changes which can only come about if they are carried on with that same spirit of free thinking and outspoken publication that has won in the field of natural science.

The most striking figure at the Pan-Pacific Conference was a Chinese woman who is the medical director of a large hospital for women and children; I had never heard a social worker from any country give a more sympathetic interpretation of the inner lives of her clientele than a Japanese charity visitor gave at the Honolulu conference concerning the high suicide rate of the very poor in the Japanese cities whose deep oblivion is being penetrated for the first time. Finely educated Japanese women are devoting themselves to this undertaking, bringing to it the best training the West can give them in colleges and professional schools, with an understanding of the situation all their own. One could at least claim that women who dealt with living creatures, as over against industrial machines or commercial abstractions, had the best opportunity to acquire and to retain a direct approach to life itself. As woman has always had to deal with living and growing things and as the most important food plants flourish in climates which permit a relative long growing season, woman's special contribution to agriculture has been given most lavishly in the tropics where the bulk of the world's population is found.

Was it because Oriental women still retained so much of their basic occupation that they so easily took on others in spite of their ironclad customs? Women's progress, since the beginning of the nineteenth century when it became "a movement," seems to indicate that it was based upon their increasing education followed inevitably by widening opportunities to choose a course of life for themselves. Those choices not only afforded a new scope for their faculties, but so modified public opinion concerning the activities of women that the next steps became easier for all women. This occupational development is rapidly being repeated in the East; not only do young women fill the silk mills in Japan but also the new silk factory in Bokhara, although whole villages in Turkestan have risen up in angry protest against the discarding of the veil and numerous women have lost their lives in defense of the new customs. In the good old days of suffrage speeches, we always quoted the women of Burma as perhaps the freest in the world. They have lived up to expectations and it is not strange that England allowed

them to vote at the age of eighteen although the
women of India could not vote until they were
twenty-one and the women in England itself at
that moment, were not allowed to vote until they
were thirty. The Burmese women carry on much
of the business of the country, holding responsible
positions in banking as well as commerce, and they
quite frankly use the vote to further their ends.
Perhaps the women in France are the only women
comparable to them, and although more than two
million women are engaged in business in the
United States—many of them as the heads of large
concerns and most of them carrying on successfully
—it is only in variety of occupation that the women
of these Western nations surpass Burmese women.

V

Votes for women came at last not only in the
United States but in other nations as well, so soon
after the war that it must be accounted as the direct
result of war psychology. The suffragists had predicted during the war that it might well change
woman's position, not only in industry and agriculture which it was obviously doing but that it
might also make a distinct change in woman's
political status. Many leaders of the suffrage
movement in England and Germany as well as in
the United States are convinced that votes for
women came in recognition of the fine services
women had rendered in war time when they had

accepted the orthodox conception of loyalty to the state. It has, however, always been true that a change in woman's status has been a by-product of war and that every nation after a war has used woman's strength to recover economic losses as quickly as possible and to help rebuild what war has torn down. The wars of Napoleon permanently placed the operation of small industries and petty commercial enterprises in the hands of French women although in spite of economic emancipation, the Code Napoleon put their legal status far below the place they had held under the previous code of laws transmitted from the Romans.

It is rather curious that at the present moment it is in the Oriental countries that women are making the most surprising political advance as they are also advancing in industry. Although they received the vote in India less than ten years ago, eighty women are now members of city councils, fifty are magistrates, and a Hindu woman is deputy president of the Legislative Council of Madras, a political body representing forty-five million people. A woman is vice chancellor of the Mohammedan University at Bhopal, and hundreds of them are lawyers, doctors, and teachers. And perhaps more striking is the fact that a woman living in Samarkand is vice president of the Uzbek Republic. This may be due to the fact that in the Orient woman's interest broadened into business and professional life more concurrently with the granting of the franchise, than was true in the West. The two movements flowed together more smoothly because they synchronized or it may be because men and women having received the franchise at the same time it was naturally assumed that woman would take her place in the state. In some countries as in India this may be due to the conception of the state itself.

At the Swarajist Congress held in India, June, 1924, Gandhi made the program of the Congress so preëminently social-economic that men, primarily politicians, were virtually barred from membership. The qualifications required the spinning of two thousand yards of yarn a month by each member, a staunch support of Hindu-Mohammedan unity, equal rights for Pariahs, and development of home industry—qualifications which were certainly suggestive of woman's traditional activities.

The All-India Congress of 1925 was presided over by a woman—Sarojini Naidu, a poet as well as a patriot, which was in itself a remarkable achievement for an Eastern country and could only have occurred after teachings similar to Gandhi's had penetrated the minds of many people. Mrs. Naidu had been elected a member of the City Council of Bombay in the spring of 1923. I was in Bombay at the moment and had gone from one polling place to another in an effort to see a veiled woman cast a vote. I was finally rewarded by seeing one who had come out of Purdah for this modern purpose, put it through in the most matter-of-fact manner. The next day we all rejoiced at Mrs. Naidu's election, but even then no one could have predicted that she would later be made president of the city council and thus acting mayor of the city.

At that same moment in Bombay, a group of women were protesting against certain features in the houses being built for the employees of one of the large textile mills. The traditional openings in the fretted windows were so made that the women in the house could look only downward and not straight out into the street or even up to the sky above. They could see only the feet of the passer-by who, in his turn, could see nothing but a series of small openings in the stone, at one of which it might be possible to detect a human eye. The little group of women reformers were demanding a change, if only that the Purdah women might have the normal use of their eyes. I never knew until last year when Mrs. Naidu came to Hull-House that they had failed in regard to the houses which were being erected at that moment but succeeded later when the matter had finally become one of municipal regulation. They were then coöperating of course with Mr. Joshi, whom many of us had met when he attended the Labor Congress in Washington in 1920. A member of the

Legislative Assembly in Delhi, he was asking for
the regulation of the hours of labor in factories,
and for all sorts of social legislation with which
western countries are familiar. The Social Service
League in Bombay, and in other cities, supplied
him with material, as they revealed the wretched
conditions of the people at the bottom of society.
It was analogous to the situation during the
eighties and nineties in England when the material
supplied by Charles Booth and others, concerning
East London conditions, was immediately used
upon the floor of the House of Commons. One
realized that in the West the humanitarian measures had crept into government almost surreptitiously, but in these new undertakings toward self-
government such measures were going to be recognized as basic, and as a natural field for women.

The change in the status of Oriental women
while affording a more striking contrast to their
traditions, was scarcely more sudden in point of
fact than that which occurred in southeastern
Europe. Even in cosmopolitan Vienna where in
1913 I met the venerable Madam Hainisch representing the suffrage movement in Austria. When
I attended one of her meetings, because women
in Austria were forbidden by law to belong
to any political organization, the suffrage group
always pretended that it was a literary society and
began each meeting with a paper on some well-
worn literary theme. I returned to Vienna eight

years later to find more than twenty women sitting in the Municipal Council, twelve in the lower house of the National Parliament and five in the upper house. Madam Hainisch, the mother of the president of the new republic, because she had always stood for an extension of the franchise, was eagerly honored as the leading citizen by these newly enfranchised men and women.

The Victory Convention of the National American Women's Suffrage Association and the First National Congress of the League of Women Voters were held simultaneously in Chicago, in 1920. The latter organization, with its analogous societies in all the countries in which women are voting, represents an effort to make an intelligent and effective use of the franchise which has been at last secured. The League with its combination of research, education and discipline in group thinking, with its clearly expressed objectives for its political activity demonstrates that no newly enfranchised class, from King John's barons to the workingmen, has ever prepared itself more conscientiously for the exercise of its new powers.

How long it will be necessary to keep these separate organizations for women before they unite their efforts with those of men is a question each group must decide for itself. There is no doubt that some groups remain separated too long, but that is not always the fault of the women! It is rather singular that this separation is said to be more complete in the United States than in any of the other countries.

During this first decade of suffrage women have learned that ideas change less rapidly than events, with the result that much political thought is always out of date and inappropriate to changed conditions. Perhaps their most important duty is to meet this need for constant adjustment and because they envisage the political situation afresh, they may enable the average citizen to escape from the deadening effects of worn-out conventional phrases, which so largely dominate political life. When Janet Rankin interrupted the roll call in the House of Representatives on April 5th, 1917, to say: "I want to stand by my country—but I cannot vote for war," the feminist movement was supposed to have received a knockout blow. The patriots cried aloud that women would infect politics with pacifism, an alarm, however, which the situation in Congress twelve years later unfortunately proved unfounded. There were then eight women who were members of the lower house. They were said to "disagree on the tariff, prohibition and farm relief, but were united on the issue of national defense," which they with other members interpret into more cruisers and higher appropriations for military purposes. Some of us feel that women in politics thus far have been too conventional, too afraid to differ with the men, too ill at ease to trust their own judgments, too skepti-

cal of the wisdom of the humble to incorporate
the needs of simple women into the ordering of
political life.

All these early efforts to give effective expression
to new demands, demonstrating as they do the dependence of the political machine for its driving
force upon many varieties of social fuel, not only
made clear woman's need for a larger political participation, but demonstrated that it is much easier
to dovetail into the political schemes of men than
to release the innate concerns of women, which
might be equivalent to a revolutionary force. I am
at times inclined to agree with Chesterton when he
wrote: "Many people have imagined that feminine
politics would be merely pacifist or humanitarian
or sentimental. The real danger of feminine politics is too much of a masculine policy."

VI

It is possible, however, that the present situation
does not arise from an imitative policy but that a
rather remote beginning may after all be the
natural approach to political affairs, quite as our
English ancestors in the beginning of their self-
government were absorbed in stating general principles. Perhaps it is only fair to women to remember how long it took men in the Mother of Parliaments itself to include actual contemporaneous affairs in their formal discussions. We can all dimly
recall the story of the young member of the House

of Commons who was cheered to the echo when he paused and carefully corrected a false meter he had given in a quotation from Horace. The members as a whole knew their classics and considered it of the utmost importance that the new member should be so meticulous, although John Bright and Richard Cobden at that very moment were fuming in their seats because of the postponement of the discussion on the Corn Laws which in their minds might determine the starvation or survival of thousands of their fellow countrymen. Women at least are starting far from such a point of abstraction and doubtless the nearer they can keep in their political life to their historic rôle in human affairs, the more valuable they may be.

That so many of the voting women have exhibited an intelligent and sustained interest in world affairs may be due to the fact that women received the vote in so many countries immediately after the war, when the relations between nations were of necessity widely discussed. Not only American and European women received the franchise at a moment when their countries were freshly involved in international interests but Oriental women as well; China had struggled for months with the problem of extraterritoriality and all it implied in relation to other nations; Burma and India in their demands for national independence were obliged to review not only their dominion status but various constitutional governments throughout the world in the light of their adaptation to Oriental concepts. Seven countries have included women in their delegations to the assembly of the League of Nations and two women sit as honored members of the Commission on Intellectual Coöperation. For the first term of eight years a woman was head of the Commission of the Secretariat dealing with many vexed social problems which could only be regulated by international action.

Perhaps it is because of the world situation that, as has been said many times, the clearest and most unmistakable evidence of the influence of women on modern affairs is to be found in the deliberations of international bodies.

CHAPTER V

EFFORTS FOR PEACE DURING FIVE YEARS OF WAR
FROM AUGUST, 1914 TO AUGUST, 1919

THAT the experiences in this chapter may not seem too detached from Hull-House on South Halsted Street in Chicago, perhaps I may be permitted to quote here what a professor in the University of Chicago once wrote of the connection:

Jane Addams may not have discovered the principles of internationalism through her experience at Hull-House, but it is easily within the bounds of truth to say that she could not have lived there without practising them. There were by count, a few years ago, a hundred different languages and dialects spoken in Chicago, and most of them have been heard within the last thirty years in the streets that border the famous settlement. The population maps of the district which hang in the octagon room of Hull-House record the ebb and flow of racial tides. The maps of the early 'nineties are beautifully variegated; the last of the series shows almost uniform dark blue and olive, representing Italian and Greek residents. Altogether, they remind us that Miss Addams has seen nearly all the migrant races of the world pass by her doorstep, and has lived as a neighbor among them. One of the chief functions of Hull-House has been to welcome the stranger, to smooth the path of the immigrant, to help adjust the foreign-born generations to American life. Moreover, the political relations of European peoples to each other, the problems of oppressed nationalities, even intranational party disputes, have always been a part of the intellectual background of the settlement. Hull-House naturally came to represent an aspect of this country as an asylum for European races, impartial, sympathetic, understanding, the America to which Europe instinctively turned for help, for meditation and arbitration during the first months of the War. Doubtless the trust and affection with which Miss Addams had inspired so many Europeans, many of them, it is true, of humble birth, and the recognition of her knowledge of psychological and social conditions in Europe were reflected in the invitation extended to her to become chairman of the International Congress of Women, which was the first concerted attempt to let reason and pity into the stupid and cruel chaos of a world at war.

Doubtless this identification with European peasants for more than twenty-five years had its influence, but it was equally, I think, a long advo-

cacy of International Peace, antedating the World
War by many years

At Christmas of 1913, less than eight months
before the opening of the great war, the peace
advocates made a careful summary of what was
actually being done to realize the golden prophecy
of peace on earth. Such matters were being widely
considered that year because a great palace had
been opened at The Hague to stand to all the
world as a tangible pledge of a well-planned and
continuous effort to substitute arbitration for militarism; an effort which was claiming the ever-increasing allegiance of free men.

At a huge meeting in New York, at which An-
drew Carnegie's effort was recognized, not only by
his fellow countrymen but by peace advocates
from many other nations as well, I tried to set
forth a new internationalism which I believed was
arising from the experiences of humble people—
the hewers of wood and the drawers of water, who
for the first time in the history of the world had
been able to undertake peaceful travel and to live
quietly side by side with people of many nationalities. I believed that there was rising in the cosmopolitan centers of America, a sturdy and unprecedented international understanding which in
time would be too profound to lend itself to war.
I venture here to quote from this speech given in
Carnegie Hall in 1913, a panegyric of the soldier
because it is interesting in the light of the bayonet

controversy in which I became involved during 1915.

Ruskin tells us that war alone preserves the sense of detachment, the willingness to sacrifice life for higher aims which the soldier's career has engendered; and yet it is Ruskin who reminds us that we admire the soldier, not because he goes forth to slay, but because he goes forth ready to be slain. When we get down to the real essence of war, whenever we try to find out what it is which we actually admire—that which has made men extol war through many generations—we discover that it is this high carelessness concerning life, that it is the spirit of the martyr who sets his faith above his life. . . . The soldier ready to place his life at the service of a just cause deserves the crown of the martyr quite as much as he wins the laurel wreath of the hero.

The advocates of peace in those pre-war days were not so foolish as to believe that war had been abolished because a World Court of Conciliation and Arbitration had been established at the Hague in 1899, but we were proud of the fact that the United States was the first of all the nations to use the court; that Colonel Roosevelt as President, had submitted a difference of long standing between the United States and Mexico which was satisfactorily arbitrated: that between the date of its founding and the World War the Hague Court had arbitrated many such cases and had taken care of even more, through conciliation. We believed that war would become less and less frequent, as all the nations in the world formed the habit of taking their difficulties to an international court. We compared this to the situation in pioneer states. In the early days of California, if a horse thief or a claim jumper was caught by a vigilance committee, he was in all probability executed by the committee itself because there was no organized government and men were obliged to act promptly if their community was to survive. Gradually, however as civil government was established in California with its sheriffs and courts, lawbreakers were treated as other civilized communities treated them and vigilance committees disappeared. So we believed that the nations in an analagous situation had gone to war with each other because there was no court they could use to settle their difficulties, but that after international courts were established they would use them more and more and so finally compose their difficulties without war. This gradual use of the court seemed to us a natural way in which a political institution should develop.

II

For many reasons, therefore, it was hard to believe in August, 1914, that war had broken out between Germany and France and later to receive the incredible news that England had also declared war. My first actual impression of the war came one beautiful morning in August, when a huge German liner, to our amazement, suddenly appeared at the bottom of a hill on the Island of Mt. Desert upon which our cottage was built. It was an incredible sight—an ocean steamship in Frenchmans Bay, hard to account for until we heard that she had been several days out from New York when her captain heard that Germany had declared war and he was afraid to proceed lest his cargo of gold bullion be captured. Among the passengers was a yachtsman from Bar Harbor who volunteered to pilot the boat into port, so here she was to remain in American waters throughout the war. The huge boat in her incongruous setting was the first fantastic impression of that strange summer when we were so incredibly required to adjust our minds to a changed world.

In the early autumn *The Survey* brought out a special number which dealt with the European war from the point of view of those of our fellow-countrymen who "desire some channel in which their thoughts may run toward a better world order." In this number I begged such "not to put aside, as if it never existed, the long intellectual and moral effort toward securing better international relations—the work of such men as Grotius and Emanuel Kant, continued through hundreds of years. That internationalism proved to be so feeble a sentiment as to break down instantly and completely before the sudden rise of national feeling, does not of necessity prove that it will be forever a reed too feeble to lean upon." *The Sur-*

vey quoted that early appeal Romain Rolland made in the first days of the war:

Come, Friends, let us make a stand! Can we not resist this contagion—whatever its nature and virulence be—whether moral, epidemic or cosmic force? Do we not fight against the plague and strive even to repair the disaster caused by the earthquake?

It is impossible now to reproduce that basic sense of desolation, of suicide, of anachronism, which that first news of the war brought to thousands of men and women who had come to consider war as a throwback in the scientific sense. A finer conception of patriotism had been gradually built up during thousands of years. Europe had had one revolution after another in the struggle for a patriotism in which full loyalty to the state might be compatible with liberty for the individual to obtain fullness of life. In the genuine democracies war and armed revolution were growing obsolete and inadequate, and because these democracies were developing a system of life which could only be carried forward through times of uninterrupted peace, they had become impatient with war. Whenever war is declared, however, patriotism is reduced to the basic appeal of self-defense. Thousands of men march to death because they have been convinced that they must thus serve their country. It is one of the finest instincts of the human spirit but it is unworthy of modern civilization to utilize it at so fearful a cost.

In our first horror against war we made an indictment comparing warfare to human sacrifice. It is most astonishing that the comparison at the moment was received by our audiences as befitting the situation. I recall a woman's club in Boston in September, 1914, which applauded it heartily. We instanced the fact that at least once in the history of the world in response to their own sensitiveness, women had called a halt to the sacrifice of human life, although it then implied the abolition of a religious observance long believed to be right and necessary. In the history of one nation after another it was the mothers who first protested that their children should no longer be slain as living sacrifices upon the altars of the tribal gods, although priests and patriarchs contended that human sacrifice was bound up with all the traditions of religion and patriotism and could not be abolished without destroying both. The women led a revolt against the hideous practice which had dogged the human race for centuries, not because they were founding a new religion but because they rebelled against the destruction of their own children, the waste of the life they had nurtured. The patriarch who here and there gave heed to the pleading of the mother whose child had been set aside for sacrifice, was the forerunner of the multitude who later discovered that national courage and religious zeal were on the side of those who urged the abolition of human sacrifice. There is no record that Sarah protested against the sacrifice

of Isaac. Probably she knew nothing about it until
the danger was safely past, but certainly Clymen-
nestra did not tamely accept the sacrificial
offering of her child, and the fate of Iphigenia
disturbed Greece from one end to the other. It
took the human race thousands of years to rid itself
of human sacrifice; during many centuries it re-
lapsed again and again in periods of national
despair. So have we fallen back into warfare, and
perhaps will fall back again and again, until in
self-pity, in self-defense, in self-assertion of the
right of life, not as hitherto, a few, but the whole
people of the world, will brook this thing no
longer.

To write of our efforts for peace during the five
years from August, 1914, to August, 1919, would
be to repeat what I have already written as carefully as I could in a book entitled *Peace and
Bread in Time of War,* brought out by the Macmillan Company in 1922. We were certainly not
idle! A group of social workers met with other
like-minded people in New York in the autumn of
1914, and from this and other conferences was
finally organized the Union against Militarism of
which Lillian D. Wald of the Henry Street
Settlement was chairman. It later moved the national office to Washington and under her brilliant
leadership performed its full share of valiant
service.

Early in January, 1915, a huge convention of

women was held in Washington, and organized the Woman's Peace Party, as it was then called. The fact that I was elected chairman of this new body had much to do with my later chairmanship at The Hague.

A moving poem entitled "Five Souls" which had appeared in the London *Nation,* through the efforts of the new Woman's Peace Party was set to Beethoven's music and poignantly expressed what many of us felt in those first months of war. I venture to reproduce it here because I can find nothing else which so represents the state of mind of many others who like myself knew people of many nationalities who had long lived together as good neighbors until the war suddenly set them into opposition one against the other.

First Soul

I was a peasant of the Polish plain;
    I left my plough because the message ran:
Russia, in danger, needed every man
To save her from the Teuton; and was slain.
    I gave my life for freedom—This I know;
    For those who bade me fight had told me so.

Second Soul

I was a Tyrolese, a mountaineer:
    I gladly left my mountain home to fight
Against the brutal, treacherous Muscovite;
And died in Poland on a Cossack spear.
    I gave my life for freedom—This I know;
    For those who bade me fight had told me so.

THIRD SOUL

I worked in Lyons at my weaver's loom.
  When suddenly the Prussian despot hurled
His felon blow at France and at the world;
Then I went forth to Belgium and my doom.
    I gave my life for freedom—This I know;
    For those who bade me fight had told me so.

FOURTH SOUL

I owned a vineyard by the wooded Main,
  Until the Fatherland, begirt by foes
Lusting her downfall, called me, and I rose
Swift to the call—and died in fair Lorraine.
    I gave my life for freedom—This I know;
    For those who bade me fight had told me so.

FIFTH SOUL

I worked in a great shipyard by the Clyde,
  There came a sudden word of wars declared,
Of Belgium, peaceful, helpless, unprepared,
Asking our aid; I joined the ranks, and died.
    I gave my life for freedom—This I know;
    For those who bade me fight had told me so.

It was doubtless because of the many nationalities composing Chicago that a general protest meeting against war was called there in March, 1915, under the name of An Emergency Federation of Peace Forces. The *Chicago Daily News* of March 6th, 1915, in an article entitled "Chicago Initiative in the Peace Cause" reports:

When the registration cards were gathered, about 300 men and women were found to have come from many states and cities, all the way from New England to the Rocky mountains. They represented commercial interests at the east and the national socialist party headquarters here at the west, newspapers and more than thirty colleges, fraternal orders and federations of labor, women's clubs and state and city governments, native Americans and foreign born citizens from many lands, peace societies and churches of different faiths. Chicagoans were a small but influential minority. Jane Addams was chosen to preside over the permanent National Peace Federation and Louis P. Lochner was made secretary.

The concluding paragraph of this account is given here to show that at that moment the newspapers were still friendly to peace advocates.

The petition and platform were thought by those from the east and from Europe to be worthy of the city in which Abraham Lincoln was nominated for the presidency of the United States, and were expected to lead up toward emancipation from war.

A boastful statement, in character with Chicago perhaps, but after all showing that our efforts had not been considered alien to the spirit of the city.

III

It was in the early spring of the same year, 1915, that a group of European women—Dutch, British, German and Belgian—disappointed that the International Suffrage Alliance had felt obliged to abandon its international congress, which was to have been held in 1915, set about arranging an

International Congress of Women at The Hague. Women came from twelve countries: Austria, Belgium, Canada, Denmark, Germany, Great Britain, Hungary, Italy, The Netherlands, Norway, Sweden, and the United States, the latter sending forty-two delegates.

The congress at The Hague drew up resolutions which embodied many of the propositions afterwards included by President Wilson in his Fourteen Points. Above all, it advocated a plan first proposed by a Canadian woman, Julia Grace Wales, who was on the faculty of the University of Wisconsin and an ardent delegate to The Hague congress. This plan was for a conference of neutral countries without diplomatic, but with scientific functions, to offer continuous mediation, inviting suggestions from all the belligerent nations and submitting to them all, simultaneously, such proposals for peace as should appear most reasonable.

Immediately after The Hague congress, delegates were sent to the governments of all the chief belligerents and neutrals to present this program and urge a calling of a conference of neutrals.

The delegations [to quote from our own report] were received by the governments in fourteen capitals, Berlin, Berne, Budapest, Christiania, Copenhagen, Hague, Havre (Belgian Government), London, Paris, Petrograd, Rome, Stockholm, Vienna, and Washington. We were received by the Prime Ministers and

Foreign Ministers of the Powers, by the King of Norway, by the Presidents of Switzerland and of the United States, by the Pope and the Cardinal Secretary of State. In many capitals more than one audience was given not merely to present our resolutions, but for a thorough discussion. In addition to the thirty-five governmental visits we met—everywhere—members of parliaments and other leaders of public opinion.

We heard much the same words spoken in Downing Street as those spoken in Wilhelmstrasse, in Vienna as Petrograd, in Budapest as in The Havre.

Our visits to the war capitals convinced us that the belligerent Governments would not be opposed to a conference of neutral nations; that while the belligerents have rejected offers of mediation by single neutral nations, and while no belligerent could ask for mediation, the creation of a continuous conference of neutral nations might provide the machinery which would lead to peace.

Emily Balch, Alice Hamilton and myself—the three American members of the delegations—set down our experiences as best we could in a statement,[1] which was presented to every member of the United States Senate and of the House of Representatives. There lies before me as I write a sheaf of replies to the member of Congress who had presented our book to his colleagues; all of these replies are favorable and friendly in spirit although it is well to remember that Congressmen hostile to the proposition probably did not write at all. It doubtless helped our cause that a resolu-

[1] *Women at the Hague,* (Macmillan, 1915), Addams, Balch, Hamilton.

tion favoring the neutral conference had already passed the Senate, largely through the efforts of Senator Robert La Follette.

In spite of the fact that some of the newspapers had distrusted the Woman's Congress at The Hague, our reception when we returned was a cordial one. A huge mass meeting in Carnegie Hall had been arranged for us upon our arrival in New York, and the City Council of Chicago later sent a formal committee of welcome to meet us, upon our arrival in their city. Of the New York meeting *The Survey* epitomized the reports as follows:

1. That the women from The Hague actually got through to the men in the state departments of the Great powers, not merely to drop a tract and be bowed out, but to sit down and talk the issues through. They were not accused anywhere of being "peace-at-any-price" people. Nor was peace their slogan—but some method of approach to a settlement other than the military method which is costing so heavily and is getting nowhere.

2. That these statesmen were for the most part representatives of what might be called the civil group in each country; a group which is standing out for victory no less strongly than the military group, but which nonetheless is apprehensive that under the shadow of the war, long-fought-for civil rights are being invaded; that the longer the war goes on, the less the civil parties will have to say as to its terms of settlement; and that if the military parties of the different nations settle the terms of peace, it

will mean to clamp militarism upon Europe for a generation.

3. That with the military forces dead-locked along the concrete trenches, the civil leaders would welcome an opportunity to end the war and stay the carnage, but they are themselves bound hand and foot by the feeling that if they even talk terms of peace their position in their own country and before the world will be weakened; that they would welcome, therefore, action by the neutrals which would open a way for negotiation with honor, and that the United States with its mixed peoples is pre-eminently the country looked to for taking the initiative in this emergency.

4. That while offers of mediation by the United States to the belligerents would be rejected, and while no belligerent could ask for mediation, a continuous convention of neutrals would create a channel through which some opportunity might lead to peace; that such a conference should not be made up purely of governmental representatives—who would think and act along rigid nationalistic lines —but should if possible be drawn by some more democratic process from commercial, labor, and scientific fields which have genuine international experience.

The instinctive reaction of simple women to the human factors in war had been illustrated for me at the beginning of the Second Balkan War, when about two hundred Greeks who had held a meeting in our gymnasium marched from there to the train on the first lap of their long journey to the seat of war. Only a few hours afterwards approx-

imately the same number of Bulgarians from
neighboring parts of the city, marched by Hull-
House, proud of the fact that they, too, were starting forth to defend the fatherland from enemies
which included the Greeks. A Hull-House neighbor, a shrewd and able woman, remarked to me as
the last stalwart form disappeared: "I look at
these young men here and at those who marched
by this morning. Both sets of them fine upstanding young fellows, that some mother has brought
through the measles and whooping cough and all
that, and here they are, going away to kill each
other. Why not stand up right here in Halsted
Street, and pair off as they do in Parliament—and
its the strange thing for me to be recommending
the English Parliament as a model for anybody,"
she concluded.

I thought of this incident in Europe during the
first year of the Great War when a young soldier
had sent a letter to the Woman's Congress at The
Hague in which he wrote: "Ever since I have been
in the trenches I have been wondering what is the
matter with the women. They would not be called
cowards and they need not be afraid. Why are
they holding back? It is clear why the men are
holding back, but why do not women make a statement so many of us are longing for?" In another
nation and in another language a statesman that
same year expressed his surprise that women had
been silent so long, women who are not expected

to fight and could so easily have made the protest.

In one of the earliest books issued from the
trenches, a soldier wrote that the scenes which remained in his mind as the most unnatural, most
suggestive of nightmare, were the crowds of
women surrounding the railroad trains leaving for
the front; urging their lovers, husbands and sons
into battle. Only the little children were permitted to shed the tears appropriate to separation
and death.

It was in the first years of the World War that
women had their best opportunity to make their
distinctive contribution to the situation. All the
censorship which ingenious minds later evolved
did not then exist and women came to know
authoritatively the effects of war upon the civilian
population. During those first months of the war
the French Chamber of Deputies, in anticipation
of the effect upon the nation of slaughter had
passed a law that during wartime war benefits
would be given equally to the mothers who were
married and to those who were unmarried; the
French churches restored foundling boxes, which
had been taken away by law, to afford mothers an
opportunity to rid themselves of unwelcome children but still keep them for the nation. We were
also told that every effort was made throughout
the German Empire to secure the children of their
own soldiers, for the revivifying of the nation's

bleeding vitality, although it might mean the low-
ering of moral values all along the line. All such
inevitable consequences of war militate against
the age-long effort of women to establish the
paternity of their children and the father's responsibility. In the interests of this effort, the state
has made marriage a matter of license and record,
and the church has surrounded it with every possible sanctity. Under the pressure of war, however, both of these institutions in a large measure
withdrew their protection, and it became clearer
each day that all that women had held most dear
was to be swept away.

In 1915 a world at war had not yet made itself
at home in our imaginations and we were unprepared, upon our return from The Hague, for the
opposition of the press which had become quite
irrational and virulent against all advocates of
peace. The cartoons alone had held up war to op-
probium. It may be that the lisence granted to the
king's fool, surviving in the modern cartoonist,
accords him the privilege of uttering his shrewd
wisdom without offense; or it may be, that the
more primitive graphic art in the moment of strain
had been instinctively utilized to express the horror which holds us all in its grip but which we
shrink from formulating in words.

The storm, so far as I myself was concerned,
broke suddenly and with great violence in July,
1915, when Richard Harding Davis, who had

been a war correspondent, and was naturally filled with admiration for the gallant men in France, in a letter to the *New York Times* accused me of saying that the soldiers would not fight unless they were first intoxicated. No charge, of course, in the wide world could have been better calculated to bring down upon me vials of wrath and righteous condemnation. It was founded upon a statement I had made in an address in New York City the week of our return from The Hague. I was presenting data, which to my mind indicated a revolt against war taking place in the midst of war itself. I cited the loathing against their own use of the bayonet felt by a certain type of young men, to overcome which "We were told in several countries that stimulants were administered before a bayonet charge was ordered."

It never occurred to us who heard this statement nor to those who made it, that this was done because the men lacked courage. It was taken for granted that the stimulants inhibited the sensibilities of a certain type of modern man, to whom primitive warfare was especially abhorrent, although he was a brave soldier and serving his country with all his heart. The giving of stimulants was a quicker process than that incitation to reprisals and revenge which in actual warfare so often serves as an immediate incentive.

It was of course far from my wish and intention

to add one word to the campaign of calumny, to disparage either the motives or the courage of the long line of fighting men, to repeat one tale of horror which might increase that poverty of heart ever induced by hatred. We returned from Europe in 1915 in a much too serious frame of mind to wish to utter a word which might increase the confusion and misunderstanding or which in those trying times could undermine the respect for our common human nature.

The journalistic attack continued for week after week in every sort of newspaper throughout the country, and in a certain number of them in England and France. It also brought me an enormous number of letters, most of them abusive, but a minimum number from soldiers who had actually been through bayonet charges, and these letters, I am happy to say, were always sympathetic and corroborative.

This stormy experience was at least a preparation for the raging tempest which was to come later, after the United States had entered the war, and perhaps fortified us in advance. At any rate, it was at this time that I first learned to use for my own edification a statement of Booker Washington's. "I will permit no man to make me to hate him." We realized that it would be insupportable that an advocate of peace should become embittered with those who differed, when he based his whole cause on the right to differ!

It seems strange in the light of later experiences that we so whole-heartedly believed in those days, that if we could only get our position properly before the public, we would find an overwhelming response. The year of 1916 was filled with public meetings and educational conferences, and the presidential campaign of a candidate who had "kept us out of war" gave us an opportunity to talk peace which was still permissible in a neutral country. It is also strange that we considered a spirited hearing before the Military Affairs Committee of the House of Representatives so favorable to our cause that thousands of copies were sent out franked by the "Willful Men" in Congress, a staunch friend among the number being the father of Charles Lindbergh.

II

During the months between May and November we continued to work for a Conference of Neutrals. Perhaps our desire for it became too exigent, but after the President of the United States decided that he could not take the initiative in the matter nor yet respond to one of the smaller European countries which was willing to call the conference, we fell back upon private initiative, hoping that the government would see the value of such a conference after it had become a going concern. It was well we had fortified ourselves with a little philosophy in advance, for the "Ford

Peace Ship," which sailed at Thanksgiving time in 1915 became a subject for jocosity on an international scale, and perhaps the gayety of nations in that moment of depression became a little hysterical. In order to epitomize the incident, I will again quote from an objective source:

Contrary to general belief, Miss Addams was not a member of the company which sailed on the *Oscar II* as Mr. Ford's guest. She was at the time lying desperately ill in a hospital at Chicago. She was, however, committed officially to the conference and would be the last person to disclaim her responsibility. It is true, she felt distrust of the publicity involved in the charter of a special vessel, and pointed out that it would be possible for the members of the conference to get to Stockholm by themselves. Mr. Ford, however, was used to performing miracles with publicity. He preferred derision to no "story" at all. Accordingly the *Oscar II,* with the miracle worker's promise "to have the boys out of the trenches by Christmas," carried sixty-four newspaper men, all prepared to exploit the greatest of all the Ford jokes. The joke was taken seriously and hopefully in Europe. Although Mr. Ford abandoned the enterprise, the Conference of Neutrals was held in Stockholm and drew up two addresses, one to the governments of the belligerent nations, which again directly foreshadowed the fourteen points. The Conference was reorganized as an International Commission which continued to hold sessions until the United States entered the war.

It is difficult to account for the animus which pursued these early efforts for peace. Granting that the Hague Congress and the Stockholm Conference did nothing directly effective towards securing it, nevertheless it cannot be pretended for a moment that these efforts prolonged the war. The Ford Peace Ship may have been a gesture so futile as to be ridiculous—still it was a movement of generous faith at a time when more responsible politicians were afraid to act. No one suffered by it except the participants. In any case, the peacemakers of Versailles had no license to cast their stones at the peacemakers of The Hague and Stockholm.

The Woman's Peace Party at that time numbered some 25,000 members on a count including affiliated membership. Many women throughout the country in those years before the United States entered the war, were ardent for peace and believed that women had a special obligation to withstand war as a human institution.

During these neutral years it was possible for the women in the United States to keep in communication with the international body of women organized after The Hague meeting, with headquarters in Holland.

The Woman's Peace Party at its annual meeting, held in Washington, January, 1916, became the United States section of the international organization. One of our most interesting undertakings was held in connection with this Washington meeting—a conference of Oppressed and Dependent Nationalities, to which citizens of the United States who by birth belonged to such nationalities had been invited. A rousing meeting representing half a million Ukrainians had

been held in Cooper Union, New York, two
months earlier, demanding "autonomy for all
nationalities in Europe, now the object of contest
in war." We hoped in this conference addressed
by Poles, Czechs, Slovaks, Lithuanians, Letts,
Ukrainians, Jugo-Slavs, Albanians, Armenians,
Zionists, and Irish Republicans, to emphasize the
federal form of government with which the
United States had familiarized them, and that as
Europeans of American citizenship they might be
able to make a contribution at the end of the war,
similar to that movement which has since been
called "The United States of Europe."

Quite early in the proceedings it was obvious
that each group remembered conditions as they
had existed under the old régime and it was hard
for them to hold any other conception of patriotism than that involved in overcoming oppression,
at least they felt that they could do nothing con-
structive until they had gotten rid of alien rule.
Of course men like Masaryk and Benes even then
saw the opportunity for making a state out of
the populations which later became Czecho-
Slovakia, but their amazing strategy was not then
evident nor did the first official recognition of the
new state extended by President Wilson, occur
until much later.

In February, 1917, there was held in New York
City, a conference of the leading peace societies
of America. The meeting was inevitably a diffi-

cult one, but a committee of five was sent from the conference to President Wilson. We came away from a prolonged interview quite convinced that the United States was about to enter the war. In the course of the conversation the President reminded us that he had made every effort to keep the peace and he also quoted from his recent Senate speech in which he had promulgated the Fourteen Points we all so greatly admired, and which so many thousands of people all over the world had already received with devout thankfulness. Our committee, of course, believed that as the Fourteen Points could only have been formulated by a great neutral so they could be consummated only in an atmosphere free from the rancors of war. Until that time the peace people had regarded the President as a friendly ally in spite of his St. Louis speech, but from that time on we felt officially outlawed, and the committee of five representing the national peace organizations left the White House in deep dejection.

I have written little of the many societies working for peace during this period, although I had been an officer in several of them for many years. I was continually being introduced as a "founder" of the American Peace Society established in 1826; there were the Organization Centrale pour une Paix Durable, with headquarters in The Hague, The Society for Securing International Friendship through the Churches with its representatives in all the leading nations of Europe, the League for Democratic Control in England, and the Fellowship of Reconciliation of which the United States section had been organized in 1915. I was grateful for the comradeship which service on its national committee afforded and for the meetings, especially for one which was held at a three-day session in a boarding school on the Hudson. It also offered a clearing house for the opinions of the conscientious objectors, whom we were always ready to serve. The most important of all these societies in my own experience was the Friends Service Committee, whose work among the civilian populations in the devastated war regions had been carried on since the beginning of the war.

I had seen something of its work in France in 1915 and had met there old social service friends whom I had known both in England and America who were grateful for the opportunity the Quakers afforded them. They believed that only the spirit of human fellowship could quench the lust for war, that neither horror nor dread can ever suffice to stay the hand of mankind lifted against itself in murderous folly. Fear is too akin to the motives which are responsible for war itself so that we cannot hope for an ally in fear. Two months later after war had been declared, the Woman's Peace Party adopted a "Program during War Time" at a national conference held in the

Friends' meeting house in Philadelphia. In the interests of good will and tolerance it was urged, "Let those of opposed opinions be loyal to the highest that they know, and let each understand that the other may be equally patriotic."

V

Chicago with its diversified population, inevitably displayed many symptoms of an inflamed nationalism, perhaps the most conspicuous were the deportations and trials of "Reds." Throughout the period of the war we were very anxious that Hull-House should afford such refuge as was legitimate to harassed immigrants. Organizations whose headquarters were constantly being raided brought us their libraries—pitiful little collections of battered books—to keep for them until the war was over. I always said that we would not hide them, but if they wanted to put the books in our open reading room we would be glad to lend them the use of our shelves. There would be an occasional copy of Karl Marx or Bakunin, more often Herbert Spencer, but almost always there were Shakespeare's complete works and a library of American Literature. One Sunday afternoon I received a call from a man from the Secret Service Department, who asked me if I knew that Bulgarian communists were holding a meeting in our largest public hall. I told him that I knew some Bulgarians were having a concert in Bowen Hall

—what better could "the alien enemy" do, I queried, than to spend a Sunday afternoon in a decent place listening to good music. He replied that his orders were to arrest the leaders, and he went back to the hall for that purpose. He returned in an hour to say that he couldn't find the leading communists for no one had said a word, and because he was young and perplexed he asked me what I would do in his place. I replied that I was afraid that I should return to headquarters and resign because I happened to feel very strongly in regard to arresting people without warrants. He answered that it wouldn't be necessary to resign because he "would be fired fast enough." I never heard of his fate but I was thankful that we got through the entire period of the war and post-war without a single arrest at Hull-House, if only because it gave a certain refuge to those who were surrounded by the suspicions and animosities inevitably engendered by the war toward all aliens. I remember one excited man who came into Hull-House to report that he was sure that "the Roumanians north of Madison Street were hatching a plot against the government" and who was very much disconcerted when I reminded him that the Roumanians were on the side of the Allies. "I never can get those Balkan countries straightened out" was his apology and I was in no position to remind him that it was not his geography that was at fault but his state of mind.

As to the attitude of Hull-House during the war, perhaps I may again be permitted to quote from an outside source:

The Hull-House residents were far from being unanimously pacifist. In fact, most of the residents were for the war. Eight young men who were in residence volunteered, and six of them went overseas. A contingent of the Hull-House Boys Band, with their bandmaster, went to the Front, and were afterwards taken into the occupied territory. Soldiers from the district were given their last meal at Hull-House before they left for France, with their families and sweethearts standing outside the door until the meal should be finished and they could give their last farewells in the Hull-House courtyard.

A description of Hull-House in wartime, written for the *World Tomorrow,* states the following:

But the distinguishing characteristics of this settlement, its unshakable tolerance, is the fundamental respect its members have for one another's firm beliefs. The specific thing which sets Hull-House apart from others, which has carried its name around the world as a generic title, is this atmosphere of chivalry, so hard to describe, so much harder to achieve. . . .

I should not have ventured to have written the following words myself, though I will confess to a certain sense of their fitness. The writer continues:

How is it that this company preserves its ranks so staunchly unbroken? The reason is their profound conviction of the worth and sanctity of the opinions of

other people. Few Socialists, no Communists have it;
few reformers, few doctrinaires, few radicals, few
uplifters. Only heart-whole democrats, who believe the
Kingdom of God is a republic in which the Sovereign
dwells equally within each citizen, can possess it. These
things explain perhaps how Hull-House has been able
to hold so long its great company of valiant souls,
slacking neither their valor nor their comradeship. It
is the complete respect with which widely severed convictions are regarded by every member of the group.
They differ violently but with great fellowship, like
knights who battle in the tourney but drink to one
another's prowess before and after.

The writer did not mention the professional
services given by one of the residents, Doctor
James Britton, who served in the Medical Corps
in Washington, for many months; Mr. George
Hooker who was head of the Draft Board in the
Hull-House district with a corps of volunteers
from the residential force of men and women; Dr.
Rachell Yaros carrying on the Social Hygiene in-
struction throughout the country; Mrs. Kenneth
Rich and Jessie Binford officials in protective work
for young girls in the environs of the training
camps; the inspection of munition factories for the
elimination of poisonous gases by Doctor Alice
Hamilton; the innumerable groups of women,
sewing and knitting for the Red Cross, the classes
in war cooking, canning and food saving, and
many another activity similar to those carried out
throughout the length and breadth of the land.

VI

My own activities were connected with the Department of Food Administration, and I venture to put them into the chapter on efforts for peace in wartime, because I firmly believed that through an effort to feed hungry people, a new and powerful force might be unloosed in the world and would in the future have to be reckoned with as a factor in international affairs. Some of us had felt that the failure of the many international courts and leagues attempted during the last three hundred years might have been due to the fact that there was nothing upon which to focus scattered moral energies and to make operative a new moral ideal. The enthusiasts, having nothing to work upon, were reduced to the negative proposition of preventing war, they had none of the positive incentive which arises from looking after economic and social needs.

The Food Administrator in Washington constantly conferred with the representatives of the neutral as well as the allied nations, that there might be an equitable distribution of existing supplies. He had announced that the situation was more than war, it was a question of human survival. It appeared at moments as if civilization having failed to make a community of nations along political lines was at last tragically driven to the beginnings of one along the old primitive folk-

ways because in six thousand years no other successful method had been devised. Did women in
failing to insist upon their own rôle, deprive a
great experiment in international relationships of
the fresh human motive power which was so sorely
needed, and was the League of Nations unable to
utilize these humanitarian motives, inevitably
thrown back upon the old political ones.

So throughout the months that the United States
was at war I did what I could, not only to induce
my fellow countrymen to produce and conserve
food, but so far as possible to point out that only
through such an effort could the civilian populations throughout a large portion of the globe survive. I was sent out from the Central Office at
Washington and from the Food Administration
Departments in various states. Some towns would
consider me too pacifistic to appear; others apparently had never heard of my deplorable attitude
and still others, bent only upon the saving of food,
were indifferent. In New Orleans my warmest
welcome came from a negro church, where the
congregation sang so lustily, "I want to be like
Jesus in my heart" that the preacher explained
that it was the first time he had dared to give out
that hymn since the war began. In Salt Lake City
I sat next to a man who had been active in bringing charges against a clergyman, not only because
he had talked peace but because he had seen too
much of the I.W.W.'s Upon my inquiry, if the

church did not acknowledge its obligation to the
type of man that such an organization represented,
he replied that of course the church had an obligation to every human being, but that the clergyman in question had not gone to the I.W.W. in
order to do them good, but because he liked them.
It was impossible not to remind the speaker that
the command itself to minister to every creature
had been coupled with the statement that it could
not be achieved save with affection and good will,
to which he responded impatiently, "We just can't
have that sort of thing out here." I recall an
address to the General Federation of Woman's
Clubs at a biennial convention held at Hot Springs,
Arkansas, where I hoped to find some trace of
woman's recognition of her obligation to feed the
world and of her discovery that such a duty was
incompatible with warfare.

VII

But if we were disappointed by the militant attitude of most of the club women all the more comfort came from the fact that there were small
groups of women in the other nations at war, who
like the Woman's Peace Party in the United States
were doing all they could to uphold the ideals of
a peaceful world. When the Woman's International League held its second international congress in Switzerland in May, 1919, groups of
women came from twenty different nations, most

of them having incurred great difficulty in travel. The ordinary means of transportation between countries had not yet been restored and in some instances there were such passport difficulties that the Australian delegation was able to arrive in Zurich the day before the French one did. Because our congress met while the Paris peace deliberations were still going on we were enabled to be the first international group to point out the dangers to permanent peace contained in some of the provisions of the Treaty of Versailles, and as our delegates represented nineteen countries, we were the first group from both sides of the conflict, to consider the covenant of the League of Nations. The delegates changed the name of our organization to the Woman's International League for Peace and Freedom, unwittingly approaching the name of a society founded by Victor Hugo in Switzerland, many years earlier, called Peace and Liberty.

It was after this congress that we established our International Headquarters in Geneva, when it had been decided to locate the League of Nations there. We hoped to avail ourselves of the ever-increasing data on international affairs, constantly accumulated by the Secretariat, and to share the companionship of like-minded people organized to promote every form of effort for better international service, who had also established themselves in Geneva.

Perhaps the international associations represented in Geneva will gradually form the beginnings of a wider sense of unity. The human power for action mysteriously depends upon our capacity to throw into imaginative form that which we already know, upon a generous impulse to let it determine our deeds. In such new paths as conscious international action we are curiously dependent upon our immediate neighbors.

There comes to one in Switzerland more than anywhere else those glimpses of what Plato calls "the eternal pattern." Suddenly and unexpectedly it becomes visible before one's eyes. It is as likely to be a vineyard on the bank of a lake as the shining snows on a mountain peak which all at once reveals the profound significance of life. It may be because the archaic processes like glacial erosion, which made the earth itself are still going on, that we are unconsciously reminded of the geologic ages with their prodigious length of time and so lose all sense of impatience. Advocates of peace surely needed such reassurance during those years for, as the war proceeded, we were often conscious not of self-sufficiency, of which we were accused, but of a certain sense of guilt which is sure to come to him who defies the accepted standards of society. The criminal has been defined as one who sees no reason for conforming to society's moral standards. He is either apathetic or defiant to society's notion of property, of commercial honor or of the sacredness of human life. We also shared

a certain daily experience with the criminal, for
the surveillance of secret service men and the effort
of military intelligence "to get something on" us
was not psychologically unlike the shadowing by
detectives, and the readiness of the police to arrest
him, to which the well known criminal is constantly subjected.

This sense of being apart from your fellows was
broken into at neutral Switzerland for a blessed
fortnight. A well known American journalist said
of the Zurich Congress:

The will toward peace and international neighborliness so often trampled under since the war, became
alive again in that hall. The air was the old free air
and the spirit lifted and expressed itself.

After the Zurich Congress and five days after
peace had been officially declared, Doctor Alice
Hamilton and myself went into Germany with a
committee of Quakers from England and the
United States, in order to make a survey for the
work of rehabilitation undertaken by the Society
of Friends in Germany as in all the other war-
stricken countries. Happily, we did not go in absolutely empty-handed. The English Quakers had
brought with them thirty thousand dollars, raised
under the slogan of "Gifts of Love," with which
had been bought through the Hoover Commission
thirty-five tons of condensed milk, ten tons of
cocoa, seventeen tons of sugar, and so forth, which

we actually distributed among hospitals for children and crèches, principally in Chemnitz, Halle, Leipzig, and the smaller towns of the industrial district of South Saxony, where the starvation had been especially acute. Doctor Hamilton and I wrote our impressions and recommendations in a report which was published by the Friends Service Committee of Philadelphia, and it is of course unnecessary to describe once more the thousands of school children filing past us, with their sunken chests and shoulder blades standing out like sharp wings; or the piteous old people who had barely survived because they felt they had no right to a share of the scanty food. It was a great relief to be able to renew relations with social workers in various German cities—Sigmund-Schultze was not only the head of a settlement in Berlin but a lecturer on social ethics in the university. He had withstood the war madness, and although under the surveillance of the government had retained both positions. The gifted Alice Solomon, as head of the National School of Philanthropy, had made a valuable contribution in the study of the industrial status of women, as exemplified by their war work.

Upon our return from Europe, we traveled far and wide in the United States in an effort to procure food and money for the relief of the starving German children, working of course always with the Friends Service Committee. At first it was

difficult and we met everywhere the charge of pro-
Germanism, but gradually as time passed it became
possible to secure impressive committees with the
advantages of newspaper backing. Long before
this, however, public approval or disapproval
came to seem of little consequence compared to
the tragic suffering we had seen face to face. The
United States was in a curious state of mind during
those first years after the war. Perhaps, because
nothing save love stirs the imagination like hatred,
there was a necessity for some object upon which
the hatred stirred up during the war could vent
itself. What so near at hand as the pacifists whom
the newspapers had systematically identified with
the enemy. Our unpopularity, however, was not
all the aftermath of hatred. Some of it was due to
the noblest emotions many of our contemporaries
had ever known; Galsworthy has written:

The war was a great forcing house, every living
plant was made to grow too fast; each quality, each
passion; hate and love, intolerance, courage and
energy, yes, and self-sacrifice itself, were all being
forced beyond their strength, beyond the natural flow
of the sap, forced until there came a wild luxuriant
crop.

Perhaps it was our preoccupation with actual
starvation that constantly drew us back to an examination of ultimate aims—to an interpretation of
life itself. It led us to discuss that world-wide
"tradition of a long and profound battle over what

does in truth, constitute the spiritual life of mankind." Perhaps it was mere self-justification or only a rationalization of the position which we had irrevocably taken, that led us to make the reply accepted by at least a minimum of philosophers in every age: "If history has an ethical direction, its symbol is not the clansman or the warrior, but he who passively defends an idea."

CHAPTER VI

POST-WAR INHIBITIONS

SOCIAL progress during the decade from 1919 to 1929 was conditioned at every turn by the fact that we were living in the midst of post-war psychology and that, which complicated the situation much more, these years were concurrent with the development of a revolution in Russia which filled the entire civilized world with a paralyzing fear. Men were in a panic not only lest orderly methods of government be broken up by violence but even more lest the rights of private property be abrogated in other parts of the world as they had been in Russia.

The situation was analogous to the cold fear which held Europe in its grip during the three

decades following the French Revolution, from
1789 to 1815. Free-born Englishmen, members of
Parliament, abandoned their advocacy of the abolition of slavery and even the regulation of the
slave trade because any attempt to modify existing
conditions was looked upon as revolutionary and
held up as an attack upon religion and upon the
family. A brilliant study has been made of this
social psychology by an Oxford man who lost his
life in the World War, in a book entitled, *The
French Revolution in English History*. It
remains for an American student to make a similar
study of the Russian revolution in American history. If such a student turn philosopher he might
well point out that as both religion and the family
survived the French revolution—which was indeed
the merest episode in the long history of both—so
the institution of private property may survive
the Russian revolution.

It was, however, undoubtedly a great detriment
to our national development in the second decade
of the twentieth century that our policies were
directed so largely by the panic-stricken and by
those who were skeptical of the essential integrity
of human nature itself. Any proposed change was
suspect, even those efforts that had been considered
praiseworthy before the war. To advance new
ideas was to be a radical, or even a bolshevik. The
nation forgot that nothing is so dangerous as to
prohibit social changes, nothing so unnatural to

the very structure and function of society as to forbid its growth and development.

Throughout the decade this fear of change, this tendency to play safe, was registered most conspicuously in the field of politics, but it spread over into other fields as well. There is little doubt that social workers exhibited many symptoms of this panic and with a kind of protective instinct carefully avoided any identification with the phraseology of social reform. There is, of course, a temptation to this attitude in the very situation itself. A keen observer of human nature once cautioned us against the limitation of altruism. He pointed out that a board of directors appointed by shareholders, to procure for them a maximum of profit; that an agent engaged to collect rents for an estate, are deflected from their naturally generous impulses which as individuals they would be glad to trust and so constantly respond to a professional sense of duty that in the end human relationships are befogged and deadened. Their sense of duty thus specialized and limited, is dangerous because it refers only to a small group of men and excludes the penetrating sense of the fundamental unity and interdependence of society. They lose the challenge to a wider and more human relationship— the lure of a fuller fellowship.

Doubtless some such limitations during the long years of their effort to correct maladjustment have been set to the altruism of the social worker, who tends to exalt an ideal devotion and loyalty to the lowliest, into a complete moral code. Certainly the wider movement of civilization is against limited loyalties, but to cope with this conception we need a new courage, more generous association, more freedom of expression and at the same time more candid and intimate relationships.

At a National Conference of Social Work, in 1924, I reminded my colleagues that many cities at that moment through nursery schools and nutrition classes, with the help of school nurses and dental clinics sustained by the City Health Departments were gradually abolishing toothache for the entire generation. Happily this effort is quite devoid of any social theory, but if one should be attached to it I predicted that most of the social workers would be frightened and feel that they must drop it. We are quite willing to work hard at the abolition of toothache, but not willing to discuss social theory, and if a powerful newspaper called the effort Bolshevistic, so filled with terror have certain words become, that doubtless a few social workers would be found to say: "We don't really approve of dental clinics; and, of course, we do not extend their services to adults who might be radicals; we are only experimenting with baby teeth."

II

Certainly the courage and conviction of American social workers was put to the test in the effort to secure an amendment to the Constitution, which came to be known as the Child Labor Amendment. During the war, the Supreme Court of the United States had held that the existing Federal Child Labor Law was unconstitutional on the ground that it was an interference with States' rights, and the decision was followed by a curious revival of anti-federalism. Certain business interests representing huge aggregations of capital which had been assembled without reference to state lines, declared themselves opposed to Federal interference, and used the situation to secure a definite check upon the whole process of adapting the Federal system to the needs of a changing industrial situation. In the fight against the proposed Twentieth Amendment they recruited for the struggle able and disinterested people all over the country, who because of the Consitutional argument, preferred to see the legislation for the protection of children and youth fail rather than let it prevail by virtue of Federal authority. Big business doubtless opposed the amendment, also, because it might prove an opening wedge for the regulation of industry in general if it were admitted that Congress had the constitutional power in one particular. They preferred to have industry remain in the no-man's land between state ineffectiveness and Federal unconstitutionality, unhampered by any Federal regulations.

Doubtless also the growing unpopularity even

then of the Prohibition Amendment influenced the situation. It was said that there had already been more than enough "tinkering with the Constitution."

A public discussion of all the issues involved would have been most valuable, but that was impossible because a much easier way was at hand for defeating the Amendment, the very simple expedient of calling it Bolshevistic. The entire subject of child labor was described as

a Trojan horse concealing Bolshevists, Communists, Socialists and all that traitorous and destructive brood. . . . That the pacifist and seditious crew train with them and fraternize with them goes far to support the assertion.

I recall a talk in the course of that campaign to a group of professional men, most of them with a college background, who asked me to state categorically the author of the Child Labor Amendment and the city in which it was written. To my reply that the bill had been drawn by a professor in the University of Pennsylvania, and that he had probably been in Philadelphia when he wrote it although he may have been in Washington in conference with the Child Labor Committee, they asked me whether I could make an affidavit to those statements, otherwise they would have to believe what they had been authoritatively told that the amendment had been written by Trotsky in Moscow. There was no discussion and the arguments for such a constitutional amendment could not be entered into, because all the time was taken talking about this preposterous statement which seemed to them so important. Had the public over-learned its lesson of "being good" during the war because of the severe punishments meted out to him who dared to differ?

A liberal journal has recently stated:

Within a year after the war began the old causes were gone, and we were steadily forced back from our advanced positions—public ownership and enfranchisement of labor, economic freedom, industrial cooperation, and political equality for the black man with the white man, for the alien with the citizen—these were all abandoned like war trenches on the Western Front, and we found ourselves fighting in the last ditch for the primary bases of democratic society, the civil liberties proclaimed in the Declaration of Independence and guaranteed in the Constitution.

Certainly the elementary bases of American liberties were universally challenged by 1920, and in January of that year there was formed a new organization known as the American Civil Liberties Union, "to champion in the highest courts the civil liberty rights of persons and organizations." It was organized to contest in the courts all attempts "to violate the right of free speech, free press and free assembly," adding that it was proposed to "keep the industrial struggles in conformity with the Constitution of the United States and of the several States in the Union." I was a member of its national committee throughout the first decade of its existence. Perhaps of all the wartime organizations, it was most open to attack, partly because it became identified with the people and the associations whose constitutional rights it defended, and partly because it was easy to take definite statements out of their literature which isolated from their context, had a dangerous sound. The Military Intelligence Association in Chicago, which had no official standing with the Government, but whose name gave the public the impression that it had, never ceased to use membership on the board of the Civil Liberties Union as a grave charge of disloyalty. Year after year they supplied material drawn from the publications of the Union, to whomsoever wished to attack the pacifists. I find a copy of a letter, written by a friend of mine to the *Chicago Tribune,* which explains the situation. It read as follows:

Gentlemen: Relative to the article on Miss Jane Addams which appeared in the issue of January 14th, may I draw attention to the extraordinary method the military gentlemen took to discover her views on world peace; despite the fact that Miss Addams is constantly speaking on international affairs, that she has written several books on the subject and various signed articles in magazines, they proceeded as follows:

They find her a member of the general committee of an organization with headquarters in New York known as the Civil Liberties Union. The president, Rev.

Harry Ward, professor in the Union Theological Seminary in that city, has written a pamphlet on free speech in which he discusses the Anglo-Saxon contention that the "overt act" deserves punishment.

The military gentlemen select a paragraph from this pamphlet, take it out of its context, construe it as Miss Addams' sentiments, and upon that basis they denounce her as a red. In order to give this statement color—no pun intended—they refer to the defense fund raised by the Civil Liberties Union some years ago for Wm. Z. Foster and others involved in a raid in Michigan, but say nothing of the later activities of the Union such as the defense of Mr. Scopes at Dayton, Tennessee, or the still more recent defense of the young colored physician in Detroit, Michigan.

The whole proceeding is so unconvincing, and so like an amateur detective story, that I am quite sure no one of your readers will be able to take it seriously.

Perhaps the crowning absurdity was the offer by Captain Hopkins to Miss Addams that if she would repudiate these statements made by Mr. Harry Ward in New York as to the historic basis of the Anglo-Saxon theory of free speech, that he, Captain Hopkins, "would never mention her again." Whether this was meant as a bribe or a threat, or was an effort to dictate the organizations which Miss Addams is at liberty to join, it is hard to say.

We found the most curious and widespread misunderstanding of the word "internationalism," which was doubtless traceable directly to the connection of the Third Internationale with the Russian régime, although during the summer school of the Women's International League held in

Salzburg in 1921 we found that internationalism was considered friendship for the Jews and an attack on Anti-Semitism. In the United States it took me some time to discover why "pacifism" should so often connote bolshevism, until it was gradually made clear that some people believed that the pacifist advocated reducing the armed forces of the country so that when the Bolshevists arrived in America, they should find no resistance. We were slow to understand this elaborate charge and it would have been hard to anticipate an interpretation so complicated and remote.

What I found very difficult in the post-war decade was the habit of the press who divided all the public activities which they reported and any sort of speech which they considered worthy of notice, into the broad divisions of one hundred per cent patriotism or such lack of it that it bordered upon treason. We used to remind ourselves that when the first biological discoveries were published, they were regarded as indecencies, to be put out of sight as much as possible and never discussed in polite society; when the first anthropological discoveries were made the statements were regarded as blasphemy, and it is not impossible to find contemporary minds by which they are still so regarded; when the first efforts were made to open better international relationships between widely separated people, it was perhaps quite natural that such efforts should be regarded as treason.

It is always easy to discredit those who are working out a new line of action, by applying to them opprobious epithets. The situation in regard to the press made everything more difficult. Left over from the war period was the habit of refusal to discuss those subjects which might imperil the morale of the reading public and censorship was accepted as a part of patriotic obligation. England after the war made a vigorous effort to restore freedom of discussion, but in this country no such concerted movement took place.

There is no doubt that the enlightened press might have agreed, even then, with the abstract proposition that it is difficult to give balance to our public opinion or to get the emphasis which each new generation demands unless both sides in a given situation are allowed to express themselves. The press might also have conceded that the only safe way either to maintain or to modify social institutions is by free discussion, yet any attempt at modification of existing institutions or even a restatement of well established beliefs was, throughout this decade, denounced as dangerous and Bolshevistic.

III

We felt the censorship of the newspaper most sharply when we tried to talk of the League of

Nations or the entrance of the United States into the World Court. The attitude toward the League of Nations doubtless arose from the fact that when the plan of the League was brought to the United States the nation was already so inclined to prejudge it, that its practical usefulness to the world was never discussed. Americans are said to be pragmatic in philosophy and inclined to proceed on the theory that a thing is good if it works well. When we discussed the League of Nations, however, we were met with talk about the supreme sovereignty of a nation, the ideals in our early history and other abstractions easily turned into slogans which were not subject to change. The country missed the opportunity of a prolonged public discussion on foreign affairs and our possible relation to them.

In lectures advocating the entrance of the United States into the World Court we encountered everywhere the isolation theory, which seemed the result of a national timidity—a nostalgia for the national nursery—rather than consideration of virile standards of conduct based on the merits of an adult situation. I recall an evening of spirited discussion when a leading citizen said that he would give his last drop of blood to prevent his beloved country from joining any Court to which Russia finally would also adhere. During a series of lectures given at the state universities of the Middle West I could discover in the heat of the opposition and by

the very phrases used in the discussion, those towns
which habitually read a leading Mid-West newspaper. The opposition was almost always confined
to the faculty, the students over and over again
coming to my rescue—perhaps they had less time
for newspaper reading. It was hard sometimes
not to retaliate to quotations taken from our
national documents by quoting from the very writers of those documents—Thomas Jefferson's position so often used by Lincoln, "Let America
remember that free speech and respect for the
opinions of others are measures of safety," or "Any
error of opinion may be tolerated when reason is
left to combat it," although such quotations would
have been considered unpardonable radicalism.
When the shades of the founders of the republic
were gravely utilized against our entrance into the
World Court it was, of course, possible to reply
that they were the very men who had devised and
made workable an Interstate Court new in the history of jurisprudence; and that the Supreme Court
of the United States was more experimental in its
day than the world court is now.

There were many indications at this period that
war had once more made itself at home in the
world. I recall speaking at a banquet in Washington to a cultivated group of negroes, some of
whom were attached to Howard University and
others who held governmental positions in the
capitol. There was much talk at the moment of

the colored troops on the Rhine and the American negroes had felt the general odium which resulted from the excited discussion. In the course of my address I had remarked that whatever might be said of the man who defended his own hearthstone by recourse to war, it was hard to justify taking men from remote colonies to fight on another continent for causes which they could but dimly understand. To my surprise a number of the audience heartily contended that it was an enormous advantage to these colored men from Africa to be given a military training in Europe. One of the audience went so far as to say that if five out of every ten colored men thus transported lost their lives, it was an advantage that five returned to their native country, knowing how to shoot, for it was, in the end, the most valuable knowledge they could possess. I am quite sure that my audience was not unanimous but for the moment it seemed to me one more evidence of the result of war and its insistence that nothing can be done save through the use of armed force.

At a Sunday afternoon meeting in Cincinnati, when I expressed the hope that we might in time trust such safeguards as the World Court, a man arose in the audience and stated, amidst much applause, that whatever happened in the line of arbitration among other nations, the Nordics must remain armed in order to protect the finest products of civilization as they had so nobly done in the

World War. Before I could "take the word" one
of those cranks who so often frequent Sunday
afternoon meetings arose in reply and assured the
gentleman and through him the audience, of
course, that at this moment the Nordics were
already fairly well disarmed: that the purest
Nordics in the world were in Iceland, where they
did not have a single soldier nor a single battle-
ship; that the next were Scandinavians who in
Norway had turned their navy into a merchant
marine, in Sweden their war department into one
of national defense, and in Denmark were discus-
sing the abolition of the entire army. He concluded that the next purest Nordics in the world
were in Germany, which had been forcibly disarmed; and so at last we reached England and the
United States, whose Nordics are of such mixed
variety that they were scarcely to be depended
upon to make a response to a purely Nordic
appeal.

In spite of a war-weary world preparations for
military defense increased during the decade. A
survey showed that ten years after the "war to end
war" six million men were serving in the active
forces of the fifty-two principal countries of the
world while twenty-seven million were enrolled in
the trained reserves. In western Europe, where
Germany and her former allies have been virtually
disarmed under the peace treaties, the vast majority
of countries have increased their man power above

the 1913 level. The allied countries have increased their army budgets from 1913 to 1927 by nearly $200,000,000.

As a result of the preparedness propaganda there was an astonishing increase of military training; the Reserve Officers Training Corps was established in the universities and colleges and military training was made compulsory in the state universities. The Universities of Minnesota and Wisconsin were the first to break through the illusion that military training must be compulsory in all universities founded upon the Land Grant Legislation, and although a legal opinion to the contrary was rendered as early as 1924, and in spite of the efforts of a virile organization against military training in civil educational institutions, other state universities retained compulsory training. The situation doubtless demonstrated once more that people thoroughly imbued with a belief that safety depends upon military defense cannot easily change to a belief that safety may become dependent upon political agreements.

IV

During this decade from August, 1919, to August, 1929, the W.I.L. which became the abridged name of our organization, Woman's International League for Peace and Freedom, expanded its activities. Following the Congress in Vienna in 1921 the European members were instrumental in calling a meeting at The Hague in December, 1922, which was a conference in co-operation with various international bodies, on the general economic situation. The discussion was an able one carried on by well known authorities in economic and political history who only too clearly saw the difficulties of the immediate future.

After the Hague meeting I met my friend, Mary Rozet Smith, in Paris, and in January, 1923, we started together upon a journey around the world, during which I saw many of the W.I.L. members as well as those of the Fellowship of Reconciliation and similar organizations.

Upon our return to the United States in the autumn of 1923, I fulfilled a request to send a Christmas message to the various sections and corresponding societies of the W.I.L. at that time representing thirty-two countries. The message is repeated here as an impression of the situation and of the compunction at that moment felt in various parts of a post-war world. It was probably influenced by my experience at a dinner in Geneva a short time before. An American had invited those of his fellow countrymen who represented the various movements in Europe to alleviate the conditions among the survivors of war. There were representatives of the Red Cross, the Y.M.C.A., the Friends' Service Committee, the Y.W.C.A., the Near East Relief, and many another, who gave it as their opinion that only religion could restore the war-ridden countries to anything like a normal relation to each other or to a reasonable state of mind among themselves; that only a religious revival would be powerful enough to wash away the effects of the animosity and cruelty, to melt down the barriers represented by the high tariffs and other devices separating the recent enemy countries. When I responded for the W.I.L., I gave my agreement to their hopes, but added that as religion had never been revived in an individual without a conviction of sin, so I was sure that a war-weary world would never have that beneficent experience until it was ready to declare that war had been a sin. A distinguished English scholar at once replied that the war had been a painful necessity, that it was not a matter of moral volition with England, but a response to a situation which could not be avoided. "We could not call it a sin even for purposes of repentance," he declared, to which of course the reply, too obvious to need to be put into words, was that neither had they secured the revival for which man's spirit panted as the hart for the water brooks. At any rate, here is my Christmas message which may have an interest as an impression of post-war conditions in various parts of the world:

The desire for Peace and Good Will perpetually renewed in the hearts of men on Christmas Day, in this year of our Lord 1923, is shadowed by a compunction and by a curious sense of futility. We know the

world is not at peace nor is there enough active good
will in it, to accomplish the healing of the nations.
Conscious that we have all failed in a new reach of
human understanding, in moral energy adequate to
repair the ravages of a world war, in a fellowship warm
enough to melt down national animosities, we stand
shamefaced in the midst of the Christmas rejoicing.
In the hope that this uneasiness may be but the beginnings of remorse, but the stirrings of that self-abase-
ment which inevitably precedes a great spiritual awakening, the following Christmas message recalls the
words of Him whose birthday we celebrate.

The divided nations of *Europe* in a panic of appre-
hension lest old enemies seek revenge, lest sudden social
changes destroy established governments, are constantly gripped by the fear of unemployment, of revolution, of bankruptcy, of starvation. Baffled and frightened statesmen stand helpless amid a ruined social
fabric and see no way out. It is as if He had never
uttered the words "Love alone can cast out fear," or
as if He had never given a basic command to His followers, "Be just and fear not." As these statesmen
celebrate Christmas Day may they be convinced that
only Love and longing for Justice can remove distrust
and desire for revenge, can repair the confidence and
good will essential to the comity of nations, can recover
economic security and moral stability for peoples so
recently fostered into habits of hatred and suspicion,
and at last restore Peace to a continent distracted by
long continued warfare.

The United States of America, caught in a traditional distrust and dislike of "foreign entanglements,"
abandons the solemn covenants made in her name,
restricts her immigration, increases her tariffs, and
refuses to consider her war loans as part of an interna-

tional responsibility. Although producing beyond her
own needs and increasing her national shipping, she has
failed to bring together American plethora of wheat
and European dearth of bread: she has as yet found no
way of restoring the purchasing power of Europe to the
end that multitudes of idle and disheartened men may
be employed and that millions of starving women and
children may be fed. As Christmas is celebrated across
her prosperous continent may her statesmen remember
that He once said: "Lend, hoping for nothing again,
and your reward shall be great." May the Christmas
season stab broad awake this nation peopled by Europeans and their children, lest adopting a policy of
national isolation, she some day recall in bitter regret
the condemnation of "Whoso liveth to himself."

Those nations in *the Orient* which have so recently
entered into world relationships that they could not
escape a share in the great war, have unhappily
acquired a new consciousness of the part military preparedness may play in the attainment of national
ambitions. May *China* and *Japan* with their age-long
admiration for sound ethics and their veneration for
the teachings of the sage and of the saint, profit by the
advice given to one who drew his sword in quick
defense against a military threat: "Put up thy sword
into his place for all they that draw the sword shall
perish by the sword." May they realize that that
nation is already perishing by the sword when military
authority dominates civil life, when the talk of foreign
interference is substituted for discussion of internal
reforms, when the fear of warlike neighbors is deliberately utilized to postpone the day of disarmament.

In *Africa,* in *India,* in the *Philippines,* good men
striving to establish accepted standards of government
among alien populations are disconcerted and alarmed

by a rising tide of self-determination, by an assertion
of the popular will against their control. May these
men, honestly convinced that the time has not yet come
to renounce their stewardship, remember His severity
towards the self-righteous, and at least on Christmas
Day recall His solemn warning, "Take heed that ye
despise not one of these little ones." And may the
millions being prepared for citizenship renew their
resolution to continue the policies of a great teacher
who more than any other living man is steadfastly committed to the typical Christian adventure as yet un-
tried, of non-resistance. May at least one nation of
oriental peoples actually fulfill that essential doctrine
preached by Him who was born Christmas Day on
eastern soil.

V

During this decade, 1919 to 1929, which was so
dominated by fear-control that many normal
activities were prohibited, the W.I.L. held four
international congresses, one in Vienna in 1921,
one in Washington in 1924, one in Dublin in 1926,
and one in Prague in 1929. The Washington meeting was so difficult that we very much doubted the
wisdom of having extended an invitation to hold
it in the United States. We found the newspapers,
the patriotic societies and the military, making a
charge against us of "internationalism," as if that
in itself was altogether damaging. The American
members of the organization were almost as surprised as our visitors, for we had long assumed
that devotion to international aims does not inter-

fere with love of country any more than good citizenship detracts from family devotion; rather, as Mazzini pointed out, the duties of family, nation, and humanity are but concentric circles of one obligation.

Survival of war psychology is an unaccountable thing; it constitutes a new indictment, if one were needed, of the devastating effects of war upon human character. As American citizens we were mortified that our guests, in the moment of landing, felt certain currents of intolerance never before encountered in our international congresses. In my presidential address I begged them not to take the situation too seriously, and assured them that the American delegation did not, for it knew only too well how easily newspaper attacks are manufactured and how ephemeral are the consequences of such attacks. I was able to illustrate this from a recent experience; when in the interests of our league I was in London in 1915, the business portion of that great town was placarded by huge posters, black on a yellow ground, which fairly shouted to the passer-by "To the Tower with Ramsay MacDonald," "The Pacifist to the Tower," etc. These placards had been put up by one Horatio Bottomley, the editor of *John Bull,* who was, as our English delegates knew, at the time of the Washington Congress in jail himself while at the same moment Ramsay MacDonald was prime minister of England. It seemed to prove once more that this old world of ours, which does not always progress, certainly always turns around and that night and day alternate with fair regularity. We feared most of all that the delegates might be frightened by the clamor into holding a dress parade congress, and we urged them to speak from the depths of their own experience, quite sure that they would meet a response from the churches, colleges, cities, and farms of the United States. In fact an entire nation was demanding that war should cease whatever might be true of a handful of people living in the capital where army and navy men, both those who have retired and those in active service, were so vocal in their opposition to peace that our foreign visitors might easily be deceived.

The opposition in Washington was manifested especially in connection with the current propaganda for chemical warfare, a subject on which the W.I.L. Congress had created a special committee. The Major General in charge of the Chemical Warfare Divisions in Washington was at that moment both very enthusiastic over the possibilities of this type of warfare, and confident that the chemical manufacturers would popularize his department throughout the country. He was naturally very much annoyed by this feature of our congress. It was not difficult for him to combine his cause with that of the ladies representing ancestors who fought in the War of 1812. Although the delegates to the congress were received by the President of the United States and had other governmental courtesies extended to them, the Europeans were perplexed to find so much war hysteria in a country which they had idealized as committed to the utterances of President Wilson. Delegates to the International Congress were present from the national sections of Australia, Austria, Belgium, Bulgaria, Canada, Czecho-Slovakia, Denmark, France, Germany, Great Britain, Greece, Hungary, Ireland, Italy, Japan, Netherlands, Norway, Poland, Sweden, Switzerland, the Ukraine, and the United States, besides visitors and fraternal delegates from Bolivia, British Antilles, China, Cuba, Ecuador, Guatemala, India, Liberia, Mexico, Philippines, Turkey, and numerous national organizations in the United States. Even in connection with the delegations our European friends were startled to hear that the delegates from Haiti had not come because the sailing date of the English steamer which they had intended to take had been changed, and rather than to submit to the conditions required of colored passengers on an American boat, they had preferred to stay at home.

However, there were most cheering reports showing that war inhibitions were lifting. Austria told of the bonfires made of old nationalistic textbooks, which cleared the schools for the use of classics culled from all countries and for a series of two hundred stories from twenty different nations. This report seemed almost as significant as the fact that "Austria has freely renounced a piece of Hungarian territory assigned her by the peace treaty." Czecho-Slovakia urged the establishment of chairs for peace in universities and told of the new museum of peace established by President Masaryk next door to the museum of war in Czecho-Slovakia, Holland reported the establishment of an international law school at The Hague; Switzerland was working out plans for civilian service to provide for the patriotism of the great number of conscientious objectors who now spend several months each year in prison rather than submit to military training; a Swiss group under the leadership of Cérésole cleared stones from flooded pastures and did other such works of restoration that they might thus demonstrate the possibility of substituting civil service for the military. Denmark, which had long been our largest national section, reported a W.I.L. representative in each electoral district and a woman member as the Minister of Education; Danish and German women had exchanged visits and organized public conferences in the territory ceded to Denmark after the war. These peace missions had been a constant feature of the International W.I.L. from the very beginning, when a committee of our women with the Friends and the Fellowship of Reconciliation had lived in the Ruhr during the days of the greatest difficulty there, and later, when the Polish and German members of the W.I.L. had done what they could to mitigate the situation in Silesia. The Committee on Peace Missions told of a remarkable piece of work carried on in Finland and there was a moving report of the collection of money and jewelry made by the women of our German section in order to plant trees in the devastated areas of France. England reported the decision of the British government to abandon the construction of a naval base at Singapore; and the significant change in the foreign policy of England, requiring every treaty to be laid upon the table of the House of Commons for open discussion before its consummation. The Japanese delegates reported the withdrawal of the Japanese from the Chinese province of Shantung.

Our Congress rejoiced over the practical results of the Conference on Naval Disarmament held so short a time before in Washington itself and the announcement of the President that he contemplated calling a world conference for further limitation of armaments; the peace resolutions of the last meeting of the International Education Conference held in San Francisco; the new note of decision in the peace committees connected with all women's organizations and the widespread peace movement throughout the churches.

The congress of the Woman's International

League was followed by a two-week summer school in Chicago, where no difficulties were encountered, although some arose in connection with a private car, the Pax Special, which carried twenty-five of the delegates of the international congress to and from Chicago, making an opportunity for them to be heard in many cities of the United States and Canada. On the journey westward in certain of the cities, meetings and receptions were canceled because of propaganda based not only on misunderstandings but on the deliberate misrepresentation which had first made itself felt in Washington. This propaganda in the same phrases always preceded the Pax Special, but the animosity curiously evaporated when the townspeople were brought in contact with the delegates themselves and heard their messages of good will. In one respect this opposition had differed from that which they had encountered in Europe; the ex-soldiers often led the opposition here, while in Europe these men were usually their best friends. In one city the meeting was held in the Episcopal Cathedral, preceded by a religious service, and the women from the war-stricken countries, Belgium, France and Austria, were shocked to find that the flag preceded the cross in the ecclesiastical procession. There was a certain irony in the situation, the patriots suspected the women of a lack of patriotism, the women suspected the clergy of a lack of proper religious sentiment.

It has been said of the United States that the sense of humor was so strong in our early days because humor is a result of overcoming obstacles, of which the pioneers encountered many; and that our early humor, distinguished by robustness rather than subtlety, persisted for generations. Perhaps something of the same condition made our war spirit so persistent; it had taken the country many months to be convinced that it belonged in the war, but having overcome traditional restraints and obstacles, the war spirit was also distinguished by robustness rather than subtlety.

VI

It is hard to give a chronological account of the opposition of the Daughters of the American Revolution and similar bodies to all of the organizations of every sort who were committed to securing better international relations. This opposition extended over a series of years. I had myself belonged to the Daughters because my sister, who was devoted to them, had made me a member in the late 'nineties. I am afraid that I paid little attention to the membership at the time, but when as a juror in social economics at the Paris Exposition in 1900 I was able to secure a grand prix for the D.A.R. exhibit there, they hastened to make me an honorary member. I supposed at the time that it had been for life, but it was apparently only for good behavior, for I am quite sure that during

They sent out a *dossier* against individuals found on the list, which was a curious mixture of truth and fiction, and of sinister interpretations of simple situations. It was a continuation of the same war hysteria, which had produced the Lusk report, issued by a committee of the Legislature of New York State; of the attacks made on the floor of Congress upon those who had fostered the Children's Bureau and the Shephard-Towner Bill for maternity care. Mrs. Carrie Chapman Catt, who was not a member of the W.I.L., made a gallant defense of Florence Kelley, as a defender of the rights of children, of Rose Schneiderman, as a labor leader, and of myself as a pacifist, in an able document, "An Open Letter to the D.A.R.," published in the *Woman Citizen* in July, 1927.

The W.I.L. was persistently attacked by the state chairmen of the American Legion, who were anxious to send a full state quota of young men to the summer military camps, and found that it was not always easy to secure the required number. We knew nothing of their difficulties but because the camps seemed unduly to exalt military service for one's country as over against useful forms of civilian service, the W.I.L. promoted a plan for various forms of civilian training in governmental summer camps. We were more easily able to do this because the War Department under whose auspices the military camps were conducted, did not carry them from their own appropriations but secured special funds from Congress. We felt that the Federal government might be asked to appropriate similar sums for civilian camps to be conducted by the Department of Agriculture, by the Bureau of Forestry, by the Reclamation Service or by the Coast and Life Guard Service. Because many boys on the farms who could not leave home in the summer to join the military camps, were eager for some such training at other times in the year, the agricultural papers began to promote the idea and the scheme suddenly appeared very dangerous. The American Legion denounced the W.I.L. in no uncertain terms for this base suggestion, and it was made the subject of prolonged attacks by the official organ of the R.O.T.C. in the colleges and universities. After a surprising attack upon me by one of the officers in the Illinois Legion, my friends arranged a great banquet for me in the huge Furniture Mart in Chicago, in which quite undeserved panegyrics were delivered, ranging from the kind telegram from the President of the United States to the affectionate tributes of my humblest neighbors. It was undoubtedly a case of the swinging of the pendulum.

In addition to existing organizations devoted to the war type of patriotism others were founded as emergency measures in order to control what were considered dangerous situations. There was a surprising number of such organizations and they flourished on the credulity of those still under the influence of war propaganda. A new one was attempted in Chicago as late as 1927, the American Citizenship Foundation, to control and supervise speakers at all church and public forums, lecture courses, women's club meetings, and so forth. They began by establishing a black list, both of persons and organizations. The latter in their enthusiasm included the League of Women Voters and the American Association of University Women. They planned a two million dollar fund to keep the heretics silent. This hope, however, was never realized in spite of the heroic efforts of a professional promoter, who began perhaps a year too late.

Our generation has evolved many new words as occasion demanded them; for scientific discoveries words like electrons, for new inventions words like radio, and dozens more for new groceries and automobile parts. We evidently need new words for this new panic which then seized the public mind. To apply the word patriotism to it is certainly a misuse of the word which has long connoted courage and candid loyalty to the highest achievement of which one's country is capable.

VII

The established attitude of the public which having made up its mind for war regarded any symptom of international good will as treason, reappeared in 1929. Rosika Schwimmer, a Hungarian pacifist, closely identified with the W.I.L. in its organization at The Hague in 1915, who was living in the United States, was denied final citizenship papers on the general ground of her reply to the following hypothetical situation: Would she, as a citizen of the United States, nursing a soldier in time of war who might be lying in an unprotected tent, defend him from an enemy training his gun upon him from the tent door, if she had a revolver close at hand? Her reply that she hoped in such a situation that she might have the courage to defend her patient with her own life if necessary, but that she would not shoot the man at the tent door, was deemed unsatisfactory and citizenship was denied. The opinion was reversed by the unanimous decision of the three Appellate Court judges, but was sustained by the Supreme Court of the United States, although with the dissenting opinion by three of the Supreme Court Justices, whose stirring dissent, written by Mr. Justice Holmes, bids fair to become one of the treasured documents in our history.

In that same month a Canadian professor, Doctor MacIntosh, in Yale University, was denied American citizenship because of his unsatisfactory reply to the question, "If necessary, are you willing to take up arms in the defense of this country?" He was a veteran of the World War, but said he would not go to war again unless he approved of the objects for which the war was carried on. The decision of a New Haven judge quite deliberately stated that the religious scruples of the individual must make way for the demands of the State. Another decision by a Federal judge in Richmond, Ind., concerning a Canadian Quaker made this point even clearer. At the moment it would seem that nationalism, growing over bold, was legally claiming the place of religion as Tomlinson's London vicar had predicted in the following words:

My church is done, my God has been dropped again. There is another god now, the State, the State Almighty. I tell you that god will be worse than Moloch. You had better keep that in mind. It has no vision, it has only expediency. It has no morality, only power, and it will have no arts, for it will punish the free spirit with death. It will allow no freedom, only uniformity. . . . You will have to face the truth, you will have to face it. It is nothing but our worst, nothing but the worst of us lifted up.

Was ego-compensation, formerly placed in another world, now being achieved through the identification of the individual with the State? During the months of 1919 which I had spent in war-stricken Europe I had often felt as if the minds of Europeans had been so submerged under a great emotionalism, as if the love of country had for so long a time inhibited family affection and daily interest that people had not yet returned to normal life and perhaps would not be able to return for many years. The spirit of nationalism in 1919 was very unlike what I had seen in Europe during the latter decades of the nineteenth century when it was greatly enriching the literature of the Romantic Period and feeding Wagner's mighty genius with folk-tales and ballads and also reviving dying languages like Gaelic and Czech.

Had the war forced the growth of this beneficent nationalism and given it an exaggerated place in human affairs, fulfilling the prediction of the psychologist that when a single trait is unduly developed, a form of exclusion results. Are the widespread evidences of inhibited conduct and of intimidated opinion due to such exaggerations which only kindly Time in its amplitude will be able to modify.

CHAPTER VII

CONTRASTS IN A POST-WAR GENERATION

IF we often felt that the spirit of intolerance had spread over our own time, choking free sensibilities and stunting the growth of the spirit, it was because we were able to compare it with pre-war times, and naturally we looked with anxiety upon the young who had grown up in this atmosphere and knew no other.

I am quite confident, however, that while the inhibitions of this post-war decade seem obvious to us, this interpretation will strike young people as most surprising, because their impression of this period would doubtless be its courage in the rejection of inhibitions. They would instance their sense of release and their new confidence in self-expression. Of course we realize that each generation clings with an almost romantic fervor to the aims of its own age and because we must always make a distinct effort in order to keep open the channels of communication with youth, it is very easy to misunderstand them. They not only think differently, so that their opinions are unlike our own, but they exhibit a tendency to surround these differences with secrecy, lest the old become horrified and try to destroy what they cannot understand. I will confess that what disturbed me during this period and what seemed most unlike my own youth, was the spirit of conformity in matters of opinion among young people especially among college students. In a city like Chicago this may be due somewhat to the fact that many young people who go to college and to the universities are the children of immigrants. They are anxious to appear as if their families had lived in America much longer than they really have and to conform so carefully that no one will suspect their recent coming. Conformity thus becomes a sort of protective coloring.

This situation may have been intensified beyond its normal manifestations by the fact that after the war, there was a great access of students in all the higher institutions of learning due partly to increased prosperity and partly to the new impressions which many young men had received in the army, among them being one that "the college fellows were always the officers." This increased zeal for education was all to the good of course and we are told in the young people's defense that we misinterpret their desire for conformity to their own standards, that it is really a defiance of the authority which is so often associated with obsolete standards. But this would mean that in the very assertion of independence each one feels that he must be bolstered by others, and must constantly reassure himself that he is, after all, very much like the people with whom he is identified.

It is doubtless true that in the heart of every young person lies a certain fear that he may not make good, for he is conscious of a weakness in himself that he is not sure of in anyone else. It may be that our contemporary young people in addition to this inevitable burden of youth, are carrying their share of that fear-control so apparent throughout the nation and everywhere expressing itself in a dread of change, in a desire to play safe and to let well enough alone. We may easily believe that the combination has overwhelmed their nascent strength and forced them into an undue conformity. Or are we all equally afraid of what will happen to us if we do not carefully conform, and do the young simply conform more obviously in their anxiety to do it properly quite as they are more meticulous as to their hats and shoes?

Every thoughtful traveler who came to America during the early post-war period remarked upon our excessive conformity, and explained it in various ways. One well-known philosopher said:

Although machinery makes man collectively more lordly in his attitude toward nature, it tends to make the individual more subservient to his group. Perhaps this is one cause of the fact that the herd instinct is so much more insistent in America than in England, and that individual liberty is less respected, both socially and politically. I think, however, that the more important cause is the mixture of races and nationalities in the United States which makes herd instinct a necessary, unifying force.

Whether or not we accept these explanations we must agree that the opening of the windows to vigorous thought, to pungent criticism which "the man from the soil" was long supposed to bring into academic halls, at present has lost ground in American colleges. There is no doubt that this conformity and lack of independence current among American students are often incomprehensible to their fellow students in other countries.

In Calcutta, where I was once addressing an audience composed largely of young men, I found myself briskly heckled: it began when a young man with a very Oxfordian accent asked me if the people in the United States still believe that all men were created free and equal. I discovered that I was being grilled because the day before the United States Supreme Court had sustained a decision that a Hindu could not become an American citizen. These Hindu students all thought this decision a great unfairness for it not only hurt their race pride but they considered it a blow to their nationalistic movement. But what bewildered them most of all was that no protest came from the student body in the United States who they felt should be defending the basic doctrines upon which the new nations, including the United States, had been founded. They believed that the young throughout the world were united in upholding these doctrines and they could not understand indifference when this breach of principle had been made.

II

Because the effect of war on our social institutions was responsible for a period of political and social sag, did the young people attempting to recapture life just when democratic advance had been discredited, when political and social changes were inhibited, inevitably push forward their own experimentation into the more intimate areas of life? The new psychology had stressed the importance of those subconscious deep-lying strata of personality, which profounder than reason are a direct product of racial experience. In addition, the Freudian theories as to dangers of repression, were seized upon by agencies of publicity, by half-baked lecturers and by writers on the new psychology and finally interpreted by

made a cult of frankness. They derided especially the doctrine that "there is no conduit to the mastery of the world other than the mastery of self." Many of them were amused at the appeal to what they called "The priceless mid-Victorian notion of duty." Nevertheless, it seemed at moments to their elders as if the prophecy in Wordsworth's *Ode to Duty,* although couched in the jingling rhythm the young so heartily despise had been fulfilled. "Serene would be our days and bright, And happy would our natures be, If joy were an unerring light, And love its own security." The last line states the question, is the joy of self-expression an unerring light and is love its own security. Upon the assumption of an affirmative reply these unresisting believers in the power of the subconscious easily arrive at a denial of the value of self-criticism and of self-discipline. In their refusal to be tied to conceptions of duty they threaten to become abject followers of blind forces admittedly beyond their control. In a moment of exasperation Epicurus is reported to have exclaimed that he would rather be a slave to the old gods of the vulgar than to the forces of Destiny evoked by the philosophers of his day. The fear of missing some emotional stimulus may well become a tyranny worse than the austere guidance of reason.

On the other hand, if all that makes for self-expression and self-development and the determination to secure a new freedom in sex relations

seems at moments to absorb the entire reforming
energy of the young, it is also obvious to them
that the previous generation was too exclusively
concerned for the masses, too intent upon the
removal of what seemed unfair restrictions for
the man at the bottom of society. Have these contemporary young people inevitably gone back to
liberty for the individual? Does the pendulum
have to swing back and forth from individual to
collective effort and does it always seem inconsistent as the two advocates pass one another? Of
this I recall a striking instance; we had tried to
interest a group of people who, through their own
journal, had long stressed individual liberty, in the
political liberty of the inhabitants of Haiti, which
at the moment was occupied by United States
Marines. A committee in which the Women's International League had been represented had
visited the island and came back to urge public
opinion in favor of self-government of Haiti.
Political liberty, however, seemed of no consequence to this journal, so committed to the liberty
of the individual, and as we talked to them about
it, we seemed to be speaking two different languages. Apparently, to this set of people as to
many another, freedom meant unlimited opportunities for self-development with the recognition
on the part of society that such freedom was important and the next step in social reform. This
desired freedom and self-development was always

were self-supporting and devoted to their chosen fields of activity. I asked one of the finest of them, my friend Emily Greene Balch, who for twenty years had been head of the Department of Economics in Wellesley College, and who through years of study in Europe and as the first secretary of the Woman's International League knew the women in many countries, to give me her impression of the situation. I quote the following from her illuminating reply:

Men had normally given hostages to fortune in the shape of families. Professional women were far freer in general to risk their jobs for the sake of unpopular principles and tabooed forms of activity. They had, too, a quite special spur in the desire to prove incorrect the general belief that they were congenitally incapable. They found a tingling zest in discovering that it is not true, as woman had been brought up to believe, that she was necessarily weaker and more cowardly, incapable of disinterested curiosity, unable to meet life on her own merits. Much good feminine energy went astray in proving that women could do this and that which had been marked taboo, when perhaps this or that was not the most desirable thing to do. There was also another incentive in the sense of opening the way to others and the sharing of an interesting experiment. Is it compatible with the modern theories about sex that two generations of professionally trained women lived, without vows or outward safeguards, completely celibate lives with no sense of its being difficult or of being misunderstood? Some of them later married; most of them did not. Now they are old or oldish women, how do they feel about it? They are rather a reserved lot, but quite willing to admit that it has been a serious loss, certainly, to have missed what is universally regarded as the highest forms of woman's experience but there is no evidence that they themselves or those who know them best find in them the abnormality that the Freudian psychoanalysists of life would have one look for. They are strong, resistant and active, they grow old in kindly and mellow fashion; their attitude to life is based upon active interests; they are neither excessively repelled nor excessively attracted to that second-hand intimacy with sexuality which modern science and modern literature so abundantly display. It is, however, strange to them to read interpretations of life, in novels, plays, and psychological treatises that represent sex as practically the whole content of life; family feeling, religion and art, as mere camouflaged libido, and everything that is not concerned with the play of desire between men and women as without adventure, almost without interest. If the educated unmarried women of the period between the Civil War and the World War represent an unique phase, it is one that has important implications which have not yet been adequately recognized by those who insist upon the imperious claims of sex.

If this period in which the unmarried woman played her part was marked by an undue interest in social and economic reform it was perhaps natural that the next generation should choose other objects for its endeavor.

Possibly the whole difference between the generations rests upon a basis quite outside of personal experience. Certain authorities contend that the attitude of an age toward the great problems of life tends to become symbolized in catchwords which are often associated with its own scientific discoveries. One of the younger generation himself has written of this: "Evolution was the watchword of rebels against social injustice; relativity is becoming the watchword of rebels against the tyrannies of absolute moral judgments and too inflexible rules of life." He further explains: "Relativity soon ceases to be simply a doctrine of higher physics and becomes a way of looking at things which is valuable in the age-long fight of the younger generation of the moment, against the tyranny of tradition." As our generation endeavored to ameliorate untoward conditions and to abolish unfair restrictions because we believed that each human being had a right to develop to his utmost capacity, so the next generation in turn is bent upon the same quest. The motivation is undoubtedly similar although the field of activity is changed. It is not all a struggle of opposing interests. There is also "the battle of the angels."

IV

The current endeavor of the new generation is characterized by a widespread and sustained effort in the fields of education and public health but above all by a marked increase of interest in world affairs. There is a new awareness of other people, a lively interest in foreign matters and at least the stirrings of a will to organize this politically cha-

otic world. In the midst of the new militarism
there is a conscious demand for political action
looking toward a peaceful world; an insistence
that although governments were originally evolved
for competitive fighting and are hard to move in
any other direction, nevertheless the time has now
come when governments must move on to effective
action for world organization.

If the formula is trustworthy that a behaving
organism reacts to the stimulus of its entire environment, certainly the young people of the post-
war generation who have so enormously enlarged
their environmental interest, are facing the possibility of discovering and utilizing new motiva-
tions. They are out for an honest, frank and effi-
ciently hard world. In approaching life by a new
synthesis they evince a fine sense of social adventure and of course utilize the tireless energy of
discovery, which belongs so preëminently to youth.

Typical of the directness and efficiency put into
international relations by the younger generation
is the No More War Movement in England with
its scathing descriptions of the shattered world
which has been handed over to the contemporary
generation. Such fresh statements on the part of
post-war youth broke into the self-righteousness
which so persistently dogs the feet of the sober
middle aged and the elderly and which has always
wrought its share of havoc. Our self-righteousness was pretty well disabled when we were

reminded by the Youth Movement that of all the generations of men who have lived upon the face of the earth, our generation has the least claim to advise the next. The responsible adults living in the world in 1914 had been unable to avert the great war which resulted in the annihilation of ten million young men. The occurrence of such a catastrophe must have been due to the lack of adequate political arrangements between the nations so that when difficult international situations arose the statesmen were unable to compose them. It must inevitably appear that the commercial and industrial development of the world outran the political arrangements, and above all, that there was no morality vigorous enough and sufficiently international in outlook to forestall such a disaster, nor to keep it within bounds when it did occur. The next generation will never know what its own world would have been, had the millions of young men killed in the war survived, and had they been able to bring to its tangled affairs their experience and understanding. One of the young soldiers, a survivor, has written:

And that is just why they let us down so badly. For us lads of eighteen they ought to have been mediators and guides to the world of maturity, the world of work, of duty, of culture, of progress—to the future. We often made fun of them and played jokes on them, but in our hearts we trusted them. The idea of authority, which they represented, was associated in our minds with a greater insight and manlier wisdom. But the great war shattered this belief. We had to recognize that our generation was more to be trusted than theirs. They surpassed us only in phrases and in cleverness. The first bombardment showed us our mistake, and under it the world as they had taught it to us, broke in pieces.

At least the insufferable assumption that the older generation is *per se* wiser, has been cleared out of the way. All of us, of whatever age should therefore find it easier to work together and have the resulting enormous advantage. Because of the sense of struggle between them, the two generations inevitably face a period of conflict unless they are open to that conception of the social forces which comes from integration in the sphere of activities rather than in that of ideas. What we want is not mere argument, certainly not suppression of any sort, but the release of energy and the evocation of new powers in common action.

V

All diversity, Miss Follett assures us, in that remarkable book of hers, *Creative Experience,* if wisely handled may lead to the something new which neither side possesses, whereas if one side submits to the other or a compromise is made, we have no progress in the end. She makes it very clear that integration "occurs in the sphere of activities, of desires, of interests, not in that of mere ideas or of verbal symbols." This necessity

'will' and to leave us unequipped as to actual practice." Of course, I should have been only too happy to tell him that our young men of the West in the theological schools and elsewhere were ardently working upon such a technique. In the absence of this possibility and owing to my difficulty in making him understand why the college youth did not seize upon this tremendous task, I refrained from telling him that China's best hope for help in the West would come more naturally from the older generation from whom they obviously did not expect it. Did the difficulty arise from that curious lack of synchronism between the ideals and devotions of the members of the same generation? Would those of us fed upon Victorian ideals see more clearly and sympathetically the significance of the political aspirations of these young Orientals than their own Western contemporaries did? Was this because both China and India are basing their demand for political freedom and independent citizenship upon those earlier political concepts which had established the independence of many existing nationalities and had freed the slaves throughout the world? The particular demand the young Christian preacher made at that moment was for help in a definite line of action in which our generation of the West had most completely failed. In finding a substitute for violence and in the actual use of so-called "soul force," India had outstripped us by years, although it was our own particular generation in the West who had had a chance to profit by Tolstoy's teaching. We could not expect the youth in Europe or America surrounded by military training and nurtured in the doctrine of the efficacy of war, to care for the ideal of non-violence as we might have done. Mere discussion with that little group of earnest young Christians was obviously useless, Gandhi alone in all the world could offer them integration in the sphere of activity.

Another instance of a call for mutual action came in connection with a tense situation during the months following the war when the British government was dealing with the uprising in Ireland by methods too well known to need recapitulation here. The Irish in America were relating in grisly detail the atrocities of the Black and Tans and inflaming not only their traditional hostility toward England but also influencing to a very marked degree American opinion in regard to the League of Nations on the ground of Great Britain's six votes and by many another jibe. In the midst of this situation the New York *Nation* held an election for membership on an Irish Commission who might sift the charges and if possible recommend negotiations between the contestants upon which I was, perhaps unfortunately, elected a member. The Irish Commission sat in Washington where many witnesses were heard who came from Ireland for the express purpose. The chairman of the commission, Hollingsworth

Wood, was a well-known Quaker, who had been in communication with the Quakers in Ireland and we fortunately had as members two United States Senators, one from each of the leading political parties. No British responded to our urgent request except two English women, one of them now a member of Parliament who had gone into Ireland on behalf of the British section of the W. I. L. and came over to tell the commission of their findings. One of the interesting aspects of the hearings, for me at least, was the fact that in the midst of the actual warfare there had been a very large amount of passive resistance. The Irish had so far refused to use the British courts of justice that some of the court houses were actually closed. The Irish were of course obliged to set up their own courts, held in secret, but administering a rough-and-ready justice. There was in it apparently not only a gesture of revolt but a desire for a non-resistant demonstration against the existing government.

The commission in Washington opened its hearings soon after the death of Terrence Mac-Sweney which was the result of a hunger strike in an English prison. His sisters appeared before us and others of his intimate friends and followers reflecting the glory which martyrdom always carries and opening up the question of how far it is possible to use it as strategy.

Although the commission was forced to hear

only one side of the controversy which was exactly what we had not wished to do, the published report of conditions in Ireland in its essentials was never contradicted, and at least brought a new sense of understanding for an amazingly complicated situation to thousands of people previously limited to partisan statements. The accident that the 1926 Congress of the Woman's International League met in Ireland gave to this work with the Irish Commission an additional and unexpected value. It added to the warm welcome which we received there, where, as the Irish humorously said, a peace meeting had never been held before. The "integrating" value of a common effort was illustrated at the very first public session of the Congress held in the hall of the National University which had been placed at our disposal for the Congress, where both Mr. Cosgrove, the President of the Irish Free State, and Mr. De Valera, head of the Republicans, appeared as guests; while the two men did not meet, that they remained under the same roof made the adherents of both say that there was something in this peace idea after all, little suspecting that they both came because the League members of the differing factions had been able to work together on the committee of arrangements and each group for the first time had invited its own friends to come to the same place.

There was something about the meeting in this

new nation that gave us a direct touch with the spirit of youth with whom all things are possible, and this in spite of the serious difficulties which Ireland was facing. Within the W. I. L. itself as in other international undertakings two things gradually became evident, that youth was determined to make a new world in which it might live in safety and that our generation was able to understand their efforts only when we were actually working with them, that a mutual purpose coalesced best through action and that there was no other basis for genuine understanding.

Another illustration of the interaction of expansion of interests with new developments of activity was the movement for Exchange Fellowships resulting in a great accession of foreign students to the United States. Ten thousand is the estimate made for the current year with perhaps half the number of American students in Europe on the exchange fellowship basis. These migrant students come to Hull-House each year, sometimes only for a visit of inspection, sometimes to remain for weeks or months. Among the latter have come those from France, Germany, Czecho-Slovakia and Switzerland: absorbed in academic studies or in the Fine Arts, in social work or in methods of industrial organization; whatever their special interest they were all enthusiasts for the new relations developing between different nations and eager for a clear basis of actual knowledge upon which a new world might be built. They were conscious of the gain in the sheer fact that in the decade after the World War the great powers had tried again and again to adjust their conflicts by the method of general conference, and it seemed to those who liked to quote "the historian of the future" that this effort was comparable in world affairs, to the birth of representative government or any other of the great historic advances. They predicted that they would be able some day to boast that in their youth mankind made its first practical step to establish human society upon a world basis. A very real and matter-of-fact world was being evolved before their eyes and they took it for granted that men and women of all ages were committed to it.

I had much the same impression of interest centered in actual achievements during the summer of 1929 when our W. I. L. Congress met in Prague. Perhaps it was because a remarkable list of peace-loving men at the moment held high governmental office, and that to President Masaryk were added Briand, Stresemann, MacDonald, Hoover, and Stauning of Denmark. Without claiming that these men were pacifists, the young women in our congress reminded us that it would not have been possible in any other period of world history to cite such a group of responsible statesmen so determined to find political expression for better international relations.

The emphasis upon achievement was further demonstrated by the fact that among the delegates who came to Prague were five members of Parliament; Emmy Freundlich, the first woman M. P. in Austria and a representative of her government at the World Economic Conference; Ellen Wilkinson, M. P. from England; Agnes MacPhail from Canada; Helga Larsen from Denmark; and Milena Rudnicka, Ukrainian member of the Polish Parliament, all of whom had vigorously advocated the cause of peace in their legislative capacity.

We heard reports showing that our League had led a very active life during the three years since we had met in Dublin; reports of the very successful mission of two of our members to the women of Indo-China and of China; of journeys made into the new Baltic states and into the Balkans in preparation for an East European Congress held in Vienna. We also had a report of the brilliant congress arranged by our League in Frankfurt on Main on modern methods of warfare in relation to the civilian populations. The technical as well as the ethical side of the situation had been ably presented and well-known scientists had agreed with the military experts that no adequate means of protection for the civil population in time of war is now possible; the only way to safety lies through policies leading to disarmament. But always there was this stress upon achievement and I more easily understood this spirit abroad in Europe when a report was given to our congress from a remarkable gathering of five hundred young people representing the Youth Movement in thirty-one nations, which had been held in Holland in August, 1928. In spite of diverging views and heated discussions Youth had solemnly decided that they could not afford to ignore the opinions of those with whom they disagreed and they indicted a certain section of the older generation, because they would be ready to go to war whenever national finances permitted and they also accused them of gross stupidity because they made no serious attempt to understand their adversaries. It was evident that they did not trust their elders even yet, in regard to war. I recalled what an upstanding young man at a meeting in Washington had said:

We are throwing our lives into a venture of trust in men . . . youth is not discarding old traditions, but assuming authority in behalf of the people who come after . . . we are out to abolish treason to the human race . . . we take our stand against bombs on homes! We are through with killing children. We will give as a pledge of faith in mankind an outlawry of war in ourselves.

This speech although delivered by an American, had in it something of the spirit of the Youth Movement which has arisen in one European country after the other since the war for it is perhaps inevitable that those nearest to the World War should feel most impatient for immediate action.

VI

Possibly the younger people are more naturally sensitive to a nascent world consciousness than the older ones. Perhaps the outgoing generation is only too aware that war as an institution blasts the hopes of mankind, and is apprehensive that if cherished social movements should be again well under way, they might again be destroyed and scattered to the winds by another war. There may be a poetic justice in the fact that our generation will be crippled forevermore by the effects of the war which we failed to avert, so that we must humbly depend upon the untrammelled hopes of the young.

Certainly the most successful efforts to secure more adequate international arrangements are carried on in the United States by citizens of all ages and degrees of education. In this new urge to know the world the two generations are heartily united, as a brief review of their common undertakings will indicate.

The enormous increase of interest in foreign affairs, in what was happening in other parts of the world, was registered in the United States the very day before the Armistice was declared when the Foreign Policy Association was founded in New York City. It was designed to aid in the solu-

ing efforts of the few Americans who remained
members of the Secretariat, rendered valiant service to their fellow countrymen by presenting a
clear understanding of the League and its functions. I sat in the gallery of the Assembly when
Germany was admitted to the League. It was a
great moment and in a sense the consummation of
a long moral effort, which was capped by the
speech made by M. Briand on behalf of France.
He said that for many centuries the men on either
side of the Rhine had met in combat—they were
sometimes called Gauls and Teutons, sometimes
French and German—but at least once in each
century and sometimes in each generation, and
twice within the memory of living men. But he
ventured to predict that though the old causes of
war might remain—though the strata of coal and
iron would continue to lie in such unfortunate directions, and all the rest of it—never again would
these two nations engage in war, because a League
had been established wherein these situations
might be considered and conflict averted. M.
Briand made a very eloquent speech. It is easier
perhaps for a Frenchman to lay his hand on his
heart and talk of the future than it is for some
other nationals—but at any rate, he carried with
him the unanimous consent of the entire Assembly.

It was the fashion in the United States just then
to call the Assembly a mere debating society, to
say that the actual responsibility was vested in the

Council with the big powers in control. It seemed to some of us that even if this were a correct estimate such a departure in international affairs was in itself most significant. We might all be grateful that there should be a small area on the earth's surface to which governments might send their representatives to debate upon questions of worldwide importance and where the big powers should be challenged by the smaller ones. In line with this, I recall an incident in which a humble man made a moral appeal to the 1923 Assembly to which the delegates enthusiastically responded. He himself was a delegate from Haiti—a small republic of colored men in which the United States at the moment was maintaining marines— who got up to protest concerning an incident which had happened in Africa in one of the mandated territories, when the South African Free State had bombed villages from an aeroplane in order to secure a prompt payment of taxes from their inhabitants. The Haitian submitted that this was no way to collect taxes, and on that ground made an appeal to the moral sentiment of the Assembly. Almost immediately three very distinguished Englishmen explained, no nation ever apologizes, that the incident had been reported to Parliament and the man responsible had been recalled; that the British Empire was far-flung and occasionally unfortunate things occurred which no one regretted so much as the government itself,

slave traffic; and Doctor Alice Hamilton, a member of the Commission on Health and Public Sanitation, was greatly interested in combating epidemic diseases.

All over the world there were many non-governmental efforts to secure better international relations. Immediately after the Peace Conference in Paris—perhaps because it was seen that the position of official representatives was almost impossibly difficult—Englishmen and Americans attached to their respective delegations, feeling the need of freer and more thorough study, organized the Royal Institute of International Affairs in London and the Council on Foreign Relations in New York City. Later there was organized through the efforts of the Pan-Pacific Union an Institute of Pan-Pacific Relations which has come to be considered almost official in questions affecting the countries of the Pacific area. While the United States has through Congress attempted to preserve its traditional isolation, we have been unable to ignore the interlocking character of world politics and the rapid extension of financial and political interests has forced the country to take part in this new conference method. Several universities have developed institutes for promoting discussion of international relations; among them the University of Chicago, the University of Virginia and a dozen others. Perhaps the most significant approach to international affairs from the

scientific standpoint is the Walter Hines Page
School for International Relations established at
Johns Hopkins University in 1926. The founders
acknowledged that:

The very nationalist feeling which strengthens democratic government at home is, in itself, a barrier to the
discovery of facts in the international field, particularly
when these facts turn out to be unpleasant or unpopular
to the electorate.

As a result of this, the primary purpose of diplomatic intelligence is to promote national interest. We
have what might be called an industry of foreign relations, but we have no science; we have a trade, but no
art. And so far no definite effort has been made to train
scientists in this important field.

The Page School, which is to be established at Johns
Hopkins University, will concern itself with investi-
gating world problems and conditions by study of
original sources. Non-political, with no motives other
than accuracy and the desire for truth, the men engaged
in these researches will become experts in international
problems. They will become true scientists in that they
will stand outside of the circle of diplomatic or political
interest.

VII

Those of us who are eager for better international relations can ask for nothing more than
this fine scientific approach, and that such opportunities should be offered to the post-war generation.

The proposition to outlaw war by international
agreement was first made by a well-known attor-

ney in Chicago and after a campaign exhibiting great devotion on the part of the originator and of its first adherents. Outlawry of War became a popular cause throughout the United States and finally resulted in the Pact of Paris more popularly known as the Kellogg Pact. This Pact eclipsed all former treaties by outlawing war itself as an institution, by making war as such, illegal; the signatories to the treaty pledged themselves never to use war as an instrument in international affairs. This comprehensive treaty illustrates, as nothing in all history has done, the genuine movement for peace taking place all over the world. It has been endorsed and ratified by government officials and voted upon favorably by hard-headed, even by hard-boiled politicians. The difficulties ahead lie in the enforcement of this high resolve and unless it is to prove an example, like the Prohibition Amendment, of government action outrunning public opinion every effort for popular backing must be made along both educational and empirical lines. Ramsey MacDonald has said in connection with these treaties that the mentality of the people must be transformed from a dependence upon military security to a dependence upon political security, the latter "rooted in public opinion and enforced by a sense of justice in a civilized world."

This is the task awaiting this post-war generation. It will require all their efficiency to accom-

CHAPTER VIII

A Decade of Prohibition

'A NEIGHBORHOOD such as ours affords an epitome of the results of general unenforcement of the prohibition regulations in Chicago, as in other American cities. Very interesting experiences in the last ten years at Hull-House center about the Eighteenth Amendment. Our neighborhood has sheltered the bootlegger in his earliest activities, witnessing his rapid rise into power. It knew the adventurous hi-jacker and can trace the humble origin of the political liquor rings. It was filled with pride when Diamond Joe entertained the United States Senator.

In a very brief review of the situation previous to 1919 it is perhaps sufficient to record the fact that the neighborhood was largely composed of southern Europeans, with whom excessive drinking has not been habitual. The Italian saloon, as it was somewhat incorrectly called, was used largely as a legitimate club, as were the Greek drinking houses, frequented by men who had immigrated in great numbers without their families. Such places sold much more wine than hard liquor, and are continued, so far as their social utility is concerned, as Italian trattoria and Greek coffee houses. The regular corner saloons were largely patronized by the Irish and other Americanized immigrants. Some of these saloons, notably one opposite Hull-House on Polk Street, had no crime and disorder ever connected with it, although others in the neighborhood were notorious centers of dubious activity. Most of the saloons had no seats and the patrons were not allowed to loaf. One square mile on our side of the city numbered four hundred saloons. To the north of Hull-House, Halsted Street boasted several saloons to each block, but to the south, which developed into a Jewish neighborhood, the social gatherings were largely in cigar stores or soft drink parlors, which are still continued in all parts of town. The boss of our ward controlled numerous saloons in the ward and owned two saloons down town. His control was partly established by lending money to the saloon keepers and by securing them special patronage because he made these saloons the bases of his political operations. He distributed favors

there and all the appointments with himself or his
henchmen were made in these saloons. The enter-
tainments given by the politician to his constituents
and friends in halls of various sizes and degrees
of elegance, largely depended for their success
upon the amount of liquor which was distributed.
All dances given either by the proprietor of a hall
or by a club or association which hired the space,
depended upon the sale of liquor to pay the
expenses of rent and music. Whether these dances
were political or merely social, they therefore
urged drinks upon their own members and even
more insistently upon strangers.

In the winter of 1911 the Juvenile Protective
Association of Chicago made a very careful investigation of three hundred and twenty-eight public
dance halls, and found that 86,000 people frequented them on a Saturday evening, of whom the
majority were boys between the ages of sixteen and
eighteen and girls between fourteen and sixteen—
the very ages at which pleasure is most eagerly
demanded as the prerogative of youth. One condition they found to be general; most of the dance
halls existed for the sale of liquor and dancing was
of secondary importance. One hundred and ninety
halls had saloons opening into them, liquor was
sold in two hundred and forty out of three hundred and twenty-eight, and in the others, except
in rare instances, return checks were given to facili-
tate the use of the neighboring saloons. At the halls

where liquor was sold, by twelve o'clock practically all the boys, who in many halls outnumbered the girls, showed signs of intoxication.

Peculiar dangers were to be found in connection with masquerade and fancy dress balls where the masks encouraged undue license, and where the prizes awarded for the best costumes were usually a barrel of beer to the best group of men, a dozen bottles of wine to the best group of girls, and a quart of whiskey for a single character. At one hall it was found that a cash prize of one hundred dollars had been offered to the girl who at the end of the month had the largest number of drinks placed to her credit. As the owner of the hall lived and thrived by the sale of liquor, the dances were short—four to five minutes; the intermissions were long—fifteen to twenty minutes; thus giving ample opportunity for drinking. There was but little ventilation; apparently on the theory that the hotter it was, the more thirst would be superinduced and the more liquor would be sold. In dance halls which did not have a connecting saloon the method of selling liquor was as follows: the dance-hall keeper procured a government license for which he paid twenty-five dollars a year; when an organization applied for permission to rent the hall the dance-hall keeper went with the officers of the association to the federal bureau or loaned them his government license, and with this they secured a special bar permit for which they paid six dollars each.

to appear in the prevailing mode of dress and to keep conventions. Only in moments of recreation does their sense of individuality expand; they are then able to reveal, as at no other time, that hidden self which is so important to each of us.

The owners of the dance halls were themselves sometimes touched by the helplessness of these young people who came to them in such numbers. They asked for help from the Juvenile Protective Association which at the request of individual dance halls, appointed social workers who with the aid of specially designated policemen endeavored to watch conditions in the halls. Not until after Prohibition was established in 1919, however, was it possible to do this for all the public dance halls within the city-wide Association of Dance Halls. The proprietors have come to pay the chaperon or investigator through the treasury of the J.P.A. The Association has also designated the person to be employed. Thus under Prohibition the large commercial dance halls in Chicago have come to be well chaperoned with a standard of conduct enforced by the dance-hall managers themselves. Every boy and man who pays an entrance fee is examined by an officer for a flask; if a flask is found, it is taken away from him and in his presence the contents are poured down the sewer. At one of the large dance halls a few months ago, in one evening, out of forty-five hundred persons examined, only three were found carrying flasks.

Such a regulation of course would have been impossible unless the entire liquor business had been made illegal.

The entire dance-hall situation has been affected by it. Since there is no profit to be made from selling liquor, most of the public dances conducted by private organizations have been discontinued; therefore public dancing is more and more conducted in large halls by professional dance-hall promoters. This change has affected also the tactics of the politicians; some of them, since the abolition of the saloon, have hired vacant stores or other spaces, especially at election time, and established therein political clubs, paying the rent and in many ways putting the club members under obligations. They have even established such clubs for boys under voting age, in order to keep them in line. These organizations, however, since the abolition of the saloons, are not too successful, and political favors are gradually assuming other forms. One of the worst features of the pre-prohibition dance halls was drunkenness among the patrons, men and girls, who left the festivities late at night and whose condition was utilized by "runners" for houses of assignation. In many cases the men on the dance floor itself were procurers who had as far as possible placed their intended victims under the influence of liquor.

Drink was of course a leading lure and a necessary element in houses of prostitution, both from a financial and a social standpoint. Many students of the subject believed that professional houses of prostitution could not sustain themselves without the "vehicle of alcohol." Although the red light district of Chicago has been abolished, there are still of course many well-known houses, and it would be interesting to know how far their existence even now is dependent upon the liquor sold and consumed in them.

But if alcohol was associated intensively with these gross evils, it was also associated with homely and wholesome things. A certain type of treating had a social value which has disappeared, and doubtless large family parties have been less frequent, with the lure of drink and the consequent element of hilarity removed. Callers were then regaled with beer brought from the corner saloon, often illegally sold to a child who was hurriedly sent to get it for the visitor. Impecunious neighbors it was said sometimes called for the sake of the beer hospitality, and neighborliness has doubtless declined in those houses in which drink has disappeared. The Italians consider a wedding at which there is no wine for drinking the health of the bride to be an absolutely unnatural affair, and the substitute of "soft drinks" to be most unsatisfactory. Nevertheless, Bowen Hall, belonging to Hull-House, is used almost every week-end for a large Italian wedding party, although no alcoholic drinks are allowed there.

of the years of general prosperity following the war. Doubtless there is a great change in the standards of living, and many of our old neighbors have left the vicinity of Hull-House in search of better houses. As we meet them from time to time, they are obviously buying better clothes and enjoying more recreation. The Forest Reserves, which have been recently thrown open, are made use of by immigrant families in surprising numbers. The excursion implies the use of an automobile, but it is an unusual family who cannot boast of a brother-in-law or a cousin who owns a car. If this was true of the more prosperous family who had moved away and of those whose business as merchants, kept them in the neighborhood, the noticeable well-being of the others may have been due to the fact that the mothers' pensions are more liberally administered and that a more generous relief policy has been inaugurated by all the charitable organizations who have adopted and accepted a higher standard of living for the families under their care. Certainly since 1919 the usual family has received the envelope of wages more nearly full than was possible under the old treating system. The man coming home from work with his own crowd, would stop in a saloon and treat six or eight or even ten men, each one of whom would in turn treat him with the others. It would end in each man drinking more than he really wanted and paying much more than he could afford.

I recall a characteristic and striking example of improvements in family conditions during the years between 1919 and 1921—when the Prohibition Act was in force or at least it was assumed it would be in force. A widow in our neighborhood, the mother of grown children, who had long been an habitual drunkard, pulled up during the first year of prohibition, at which time she married the man next door who had also been temporarily benefited in his drinking habits. The children's wages, thus released, painted the house, bought furniture including a victrola, and the entire aspect of the family became more respectable than it had been for years. The next year, however, the mother and her husband established a still in the basement. They both returned to their drinking habits with added periods of violence. The husband died after two years. All the children have left home except one daughter whose conscience does not allow her to desert. Her wages are the sole means of support for her mother and herself and although they still own the house, it is impossible to keep lodgers because of the mother's habits. The daughter is gifted musically, and looks back with keen regret upon her two years of release from sordid care when she could "really give attention to music."

Italians have not markedly changed their actual habits, for they always drank sitting in small groups, with much talking and often petty gambling. They all possess the land hunger of the European peasant, and the high wages since the war have enormously stimulated thrift. Many of them find it possible to make at least the first payment upon a house and lot, although the necessity of saving often holds down the standard of living for the entire family. However, the Americanized children more or less take care of this latter situation, and in spite of grumbling fathers and frightened mothers there has been an enormous purchase of automobiles, radios and victrolas.

During these first two years, beginning with 1919, we were all elated by the marked decrease in so-called disorderly conduct. A large section of the City House of Correction was closed, and the well known tremens ward of the County Hospital. It was said by temperance enthusiasts that the doctors complained they did not have enough cases of delirium tremens for clinical purposes. The local drink cure establishment closed for lack of patrons. Our neighborhood registered a general lack of street disorders and also of family quarrels, which had so often put a mother and little children into the streets, turned out by a drunken father, sometimes in the middle of the night. From our first years at Hull-House, we had had such forlorn families seeking refuge behind our brick walls.

In those halcyon days of the early prohibition period, factory managers said that industrial accidents were doubtless fewer but their statement was

into court under the Contributing to Delinquency
Act because the home had become a distributing
center for bootlegging products. The charge did
not include drunkenness, but merely disorderly
conduct on the part of the purchasers. The mother
came to the settlement offering to make any
arrangement for the care of her children, such as
boarding school or living with relatives, which the
settlement thought best, saying that she couldn't
possibly abandon her business and that she was
making enough money to care for the children
properly. She had, of course, no intention of giving them up, and was devoted to them. I could
easily cite dozens of similar instances, which
increased in number and variety as bootlegging
increased in volume and extent. The building conditions of our neighborhood easily lend themselves
to this traffic. Along the south branch of the Chicago river the property owners are waiting to sell
their old houses and barns, disused stores and small
factory buildings, believing that the sites will be
used for railroad terminals, garages and ware-
houses, which are already displacing the old buildings. Previous to 1918 the neighborhood was one
of self-respecting immigrants although there was
a tendency for the houses to grow less desirable
because it was near the river just back of the down
town districts, where real estate values were constantly rising. The landlords, unwilling to put
more money into erecting tenements, rented the

old wooden houses which survived an earlier period. Many of these houses were bought by the immigrants themselves and portions of them sublet, sometimes without adequate repair, with the result that as the more prosperous people moved out, the newly arrived immigrants, seeking low rents, crowded into their places. Since the enactment of the quota regulation for European immigration, the houses are being slowly filled by Mexicans. The district is well known as the largest winter resort for Gypsies in the United States, although curiously enough, they seem to prefer to live on Halsted Street itself, perhaps because the stream of people passing by affords so much more opportunity for fortune-telling and automobile trading, or because it is easier to secure an empty loft or large floor space upon which they camp in family groups, as if they were still living under the open sky. Twenty people were found in one such room, with an old man dying of tuberculosis.

These dilapidated houses and somewhat casual population afford good hiding places both for the manufacturing and storing of liquor and for the hi-jackers and others who openly prey upon the illicit industry. A hi-jacker is one who holds up a truck of booze, frightening the driver with his gun until he induces him to desert his load. The driver dare not call upon the police to protect his illicit freight, and when he is obliged to abandon it, can only telephone to his gang and try to intercept the hi-jacker later and in turn terrify him with guns in order to recover the precious stuff. If the original owner of the "booze" later calls upon the police at all, he can make a charge only for the stealing of the truck without daring to mention what was loaded upon it, for of course "booze" is not legitimate property. From time to time we have found abandoned trucks in the alley back of Hull-House which have evidently been left there because it was dangerous for the hi-jacker to keep them near his own house. Of course the profession of a hi-jacker is highly lucrative. He obtains his booze with all the profit it stands for without even the difficulty and expense of manufacturing it. He sometimes operates directly upon the manufacturing still and empties the storeroom of its contents. Such places are also easy victims of the regular hold-up men, and this accounts for the fact that many of them are equipped like a small arsenal. Naturally the owners of places which have been robbed are filled with vengeance and unending raids are thus started. There is in all this warfare an element of old-fashioned business rivalry, what used to be cut-throat competition. Bootlegging, in its economic aspect, is a great industry. Production, formerly carried on in factories, if we may thus designate the distilleries and breweries, has become decentralized and has gone back into the home industry stage. This is just the reverse of what has happened in other industries.

We find the exploiter trying to get control of all the stills within a given area, creating a situation comparable to that in the Pennsylvania oil fields years ago. Almost any man who had a piece of land where a well could be dug, could produce oil after a fashion, but for selling it he was dependent upon rival companies. Unless one company could gain control of a given section, it was a great disadvantage because the mere collection of the oil meant crossing and recrossing a given territory and because of the necessity for focusing the oil at a given point for final transportation into the outside world. As one company gained control of a certain section, and impinged upon the territory belonging to a rival, the competition became more and more intense, until one company won the field. The bootlegging situation came to resemble that in the early Pennsylvania oil fields not only in its economic structure but in its ruthlessness and widespread terrorism. The production of alcoholic drinks, by going back from the factory to its domestic beginnings, quite naturally first fell into the hands of those who had never gotten very far from the domestic type of industry. These actual producers exhibit many of the characteristics of simple people, but the new industry, in the selling end, from the very first attached to itself shrewd business men, trained in an age of complicated commercialism, who also understood the necessity for political protection.

We had grown accustomed during the last decades to the idea that great vested interests connected with the manufacturing of alcoholic drinks were bringing to bear continuous pressure on Congress and very often on the state legislatures as well. We had at one time our own whiskey ring in Illinois with headquarters at Peoria. But the pressure formerly brought to bear on Washington and upon state capitals, has now been transferred to the simplest unit of government, the patrolman on his beat. The Federal officials detailed to enforce an unpopular law are subjected to temptations of the most flagrant sort. The development of political corruption in connection with the manufacture and sale of liquor follows a direction the reverse of that of the industrial change from factory to decentralized small-scale production. The old national whiskey ring came first, for it was in General Grant's administration that the Secretary of the Treasury unearthed frauds in the collection of internal revenues for certain distilleries which were operating in collusion with high officials, who throve upon the profits. The wholesale corruption of petty government officials came much later with the decentralization of the industry when business opportunities on an unprecedented scale had been opened to simple peasants who have an opportunity to make money such as they had never even dreamed of before. It is not difficult to understand that the barrier of illegality was a frail one and easily went down before this onrush of avarice.

In the first days of the home brewing and kitchen distilling, rival bootleggers found it essential to control a given area, and they made to anyone discovered operating within that area, a fifty-fifty proposition. They gave police protection and selling advantages in return for half the output. If a man resisted, his still was broken up, and if he was persistent, he would suffer personal violence. But he was in the end obliged to conform or to go out of business. In fact, however violent his opposition to the monopoly, he could not go on without protection and there was the added danger that his neighbors would "squeal to the police" if he were selling to a rival. From the beginning these home producers realized that it was the transporting and selling end of the business which was difficult and perilous, and so there inevitably developed a hostile rivalry between two sets of men who were not producers, but sellers. They were not, of course, carrying on a purely economic rivalry, for the situation was enormously complicated by the fact that both the manufacturing and selling were illegal and absolutely dependent upon successful corruption. Even if the federal official did not collect money for protection, some one would probably do it in his name, and if the policeman on the beat was perfectly honest, politicians who pretended to control police organizations, collected for him.

The law breaker, of course, always subjects himself to an unending series of blackmail. There is also the grave situation when bootleggers come to count upon immunity from the very people whose business it is to report them. In a very real sense, the people who represented the administration of the law become as much a part of the criminal situation as do the so-called criminals themselves.

In the very earliest day of the 1920's, the illicit making of liquor entered the stage of the small factory or shop, although small copper stills were piled high for sale in the outdoor markets of the neighborhood, strictly family manufacturing was going out. The larger stills were owned by groups of bootleggers who employed men from the neighborhood. The enterprises housed in old barns and basements used gasoline for heating the mash and operating the still, the whole outfit was expensive and required a man capable of running it as well as one who would be courageous if the police appeared. There was also a real danger from escaping fumes if the matter were carelessly handled. Sometimes the volume of business was quite large—a still recently raided in our neighborhood was producing two hundred gallons a day. It was housed in a comparatively small barn for the vats were in the basement sunk into the ground itself. The "stuff" is moved sometimes in a dilapidated old grocery wagon, sometimes in a motor truck. In our neighborhood it is usually

handled in two gallon cans. The inhabitants of a
street near the settlement were accustomed to seeing a man sitting on a front seat beside the driver
on an old Ford truck with a shotgun wrapped up
in newspaper lying across his knee; another armed
man would walk casually along the pavement.
This was to secure protection from hi-jackers as
well as from police interference. During one half
year our neighborhood was filled with bootleggers
coming from various parts of the city, added to
those from our own vicinity, because the local
police captain had the reputation of being easy to
deal with. As there have been several changes in
the precinct since, it is perhaps useless to repeat
the stories then afloat of the amount of money
exacted for such immunities.

This political protection produces great cynicism among the immigrants who say quite openly
"you can do anything in America if you pay for
it." What must be the effect of an incident like the
following? An Italian drinking with his gang one
evening came home late at night and was shot in
his own kitchen by a drunken companion. There
was sufficient proof to indict the wife for com-
plicity in the murder. She acknowledged that she
was "fed up" with the abuse of herself and her
family, and had promised to divide the insurance
money with anyone who would get rid of her husband, who was himself supposed to be something
of a gunman. Although it was shown in court that

the insurance money had been divided with the
gang, she was acquitted through the political
power of the gang in a determination to save itself
from exposure. A year later, the city was astounded
when an assistant states attorney was shot and
killed in an automobile in company with a man
whom he had tried for murder but who had been
acquitted. The assumption was that the states
attorney had been collecting from the gang of
men with whom the criminal was connected. Two
juries failed to convict the murderer. It was said
that the official had been "bumped off" for political reasons totally unconnected with bootlegging.
Without a verdict, it is impossible to know the
situation but there is no doubt that the incident
gave an increased consciousness of political power
to the bootlegging community.

The Sicilians in Chicago have an unsavory reputation for desperate measures in connection with
bootlegging, partly because of the dramatic history
of six Sicilian brothers, three of whom lost their
lives in a prolonged war with a rival gang. The
story, which in many respects is a typical one, may
be outlined as follows:

Jim, the oldest of the six brothers, who came to
the United States fifty years ago, operated a res-
taurant and a speakeasy; Angelo quickly reached
the heights of an extortionist, and when Sicilian
turned against Sicilian, in an aldermanic election,
he killed his man, and thereafter had a standing as

a gunman. Sam, more diplomatic, in training and temperament, acted as a political agent for his brothers. Antonio was the gentleman of the family, the opera patron, and man-about-town. Peter was a saloon keeper, and Michael was well fitted to do the rough bidding of his brothers. They formed a united family and gained a foothold in the alcohol business. They put stills in the home of every Sicilian whom they were able to dominate. In a short time they controlled much of the home-made alcohol in the city and were able to undersell all competitors. The combined credit rating of the family at one time was five million dollars, each one of the brothers almost a millionaire. Indeed, it was necessary to have capital in this business. In the fall of 1923 it was discovered that one Italian bootlegger had a payroll for chauffeurs, truckmen, bootleggers, guards, killers, and lawyers, of twenty-five hundred dollars a week.

The troubles of the brothers came at length from a savage outbreak with the rival gang, in which three of their men killed the hated leader of their competitor. Swift vengeance followed. Angelo was the first of the brothers to be killed, and Mike was next, although he was actually shot by the police as he was running away from the rival who had tried to kill him. Then, a few weeks later, Tony was shot down as he grasped the hand of a supposed friend who lured him "to the spot." These brothers had the reputation, even in the Old

Country, we were often told, of being able to live without working, a remark very sinister in its implications. A certain type of Sicilian for centuries had a training in taking care of his own affairs outside of the law. The island was full of banditry and the vendetta survived there longer than in any other part of the world. A man so trained easily goes over into the selling of booze, ready for all the desperate measures which may be involved. If a rival "muscles in" as the bootleggers laconically phrase it, on the territory and trade of his gang, he is ready to punish him. His very training in illegal activity and in dealing with his enemies for himself, becomes economically useful in the peculiar situation obtaining in Chicago in "the third decade of the Twentieth Century," as our newspapers put it. If he can go through the form of a trial and "walk smilingly out of court," so much the better. These two gangs of Sicilians almost exterminated each other, and the entire Sicilian population of helpless immigrants, living in Chicago, suffered in the process.

But in the last analysis, it is big money that makes Chicago gang wars so murderous. The city holds the key to the rich trade of the West and Northwest in whiskey, wine, gin and beer, exactly as it does in wheat, hogs, furniture and more staple commodities. Bourbon now comes from Canada and is cleared through Chicago, arriving on motor trucks, steamers, freight cars, and aeroplanes, from

Success depends upon who shoots first, for shooting is inevitable and a matter of self-protection on both sides. How general the carrying of arms by boys, for one reason or another, has become, is shown by the recent killing of a police officer when he was arresting five boys who had been drinking and were evidently out for mischief. They told him to let them off or they would shoot him, and they finally succeeded in doing it because they outnumbered him in firearms.

Bootleg liquor is integrated with vice and crime quite as liquor always has been. Roadhouses where liquor is sold are notorious for their prostitution, and automobiles make it possible to quickly transport patrons to these disorderly roadhouses—also affording concealment for the intoxicated young people returning together. In addition to a boy's natural love of automobiles is the association of banditry. An automobile bandit is more successful and more dangerous than the romantic wild west robbers of fifty years ago, or the bands so recently to be found in remote parts of Sicily, of Spain or of Mexico. While much of the amateur city banditry was developing previous to bootlegging days, the liquor situation has given it a tremendous impulse and a certain warfare between the constituted authorities and the outlaws has become a recognized factor in the situation.

A boy in the State Reformatory tells how easily he and his gang, who owned a Ford, used to hold up young people who were returning from the roadhouses, finding it easy to take their money because they were always more or less intoxicated. Another boy convicted of burglary had been made unconscious by liquor obtained outside the city. His two companions took him in their automobile to a drug store at the edge of the city for treatment. When the clerk had obtained a drug useful for an unconscious patient, they shot him in the arm and proceeded to rob the drug store. They then fled, leaving the unconscious boy behind them. He was of course arrested as an accomplice in the robbery, although the two others with the automobile were never found.

How inextricably this new type of crime and indeed the whole prohibition question is involved with the development of the automobile it is impossible to describe. Chicago, with only one third of the population of New York, covers four times as much territory—prairie territory opening by hundreds of outlets into the country on every side—and this too affects the local situation.

The Juvenile Protective Association in the summer of 1929 made an extensive survey of the so-called roadhouses surrounding Chicago, which increase in numbers as the automobile grows in popularity. A digest of the report, placed by the able superintendent—Jessie Binford, a long-time resident of Hull-House, before the law enforcing agencies of Cook County, states:

If legitimately conducted, the roadhouses might provide most attractive and safe recreation, but the vast majority as operated in Cook County at the present time, constitute a decided menace, offering untold temptations to young people and not only moral but physical hazards.

The drunkenness encountered during the survey was appalling, so that driving along the highways, particularly late on Saturday nights and early Sunday mornings was exceedingly dangerous. . . . Liquor is undoubtedly the greatest contributing factor to conditions which involve crime, demoralization, immorality, bombing, murders, racketeering, prostitution. In 142 of 171 resorts visited, apparently alcoholic drinks could be purchased. One proprietor said that he paid $56 a barrel for beer and $125 a case for whiskey and netted a substantial profit on his re-sale. The wholesale prices that he paid, he said, were set by the "syndicate"; he might get it cheaper elsewhere, but he had to buy from them.

A syndicate, in Cook County road-house parlance, is a closely organized and powerful group of beer and liquor barons backed by various politicians who have divided and allotted the territory among them, control the sale of liquor and beer, dictate prices, and see to it that the road-houses buy only of them. If they should try to buy elsewhere, several proprietors explained, they might expect to be blown up or "taken for a ride." The syndicates are also declared to be the purveyors of a real degree of protection according to the circumstances of each individual case in which they become involved. A portion of the profits of the resort may be expected to pay for protection. One syndicate is supposed to supply the district to the north, another to the west, and still another the south.

The report concludes:

There was a time when city dance-halls were as dangerous to boys and girls as the roadhouses of to-day through a tie-up with the vice and liquor interests. They have been brought under supervision, by and large, but through the automobile their old problems have been widened out beyond the cities where control by parents, authorities and public opinion is even more difficult than in the cities themselves. Supervision is scattered through the little municipalities, which find the license fees from the roadhouses attractively lucrative. And behind the network of shabby and gaudy resorts lies the ruthless power of organized interests, for in the roadhouses, as in the dance-halls and *maisons de joie* of older days, the one essential for success seems to be a ready supply of liquor. The present study is based on Cook County alone, but there seems every reason to believe that its chief findings could be duplicated in the environs of large cities from coast to coast.

It would seem,

concludes the association moderately,

that we could no longer afford to ignore these conditions.

V

The most optimistic citizen, however, could scarcely be proud of the rôle the police play in the Chicago situation. Years ago it was customary and considered necessary for the head of the police force in any large city to maintain certain useful contacts with the underworld. Today, and for a different reason, officialdom, from the chief of

police to the neighborhood cop, evidently still
maintains such contacts, and perhaps never before
have they been so lucrative. This connection
between the police and the gangsters is clearly
revealed from time to time; the *Chicago Tribune*
of February 28, 1929, reported the following statement in connection with the effort to discover the
slayers of seven men who were massacred on
February 14, having been stood against the wall of
a garage in an inner court and shot with the preci-
sion of an exectuion. During the effort to capture
the murderers, and under the stress of almost hysterical excitement, the police talked so freely that
they naïvely revealed a connection between themselves and the bootleggers. Suspicion fell upon
them because

it was learned that about December first of last year,
after a change in police commanders, M—— claimed
the right to all beer sales in the Cragin district. This
district had been abandoned by its former beer purveyors, whose political prestige had waned, and under
the new police régime the Capone beer flowed in that
northwestern section. Encouraged by the easy conquest,
M—— and his crew, with others of the neighborhood,
moved eastward over the river to where Moran and
his gang held sway.

This marauding was evidently punished, possibly
by a rival gang, although that has never been made
clear.

Some months later the community was startled

when a squad of policemen pursuing an automobile in which four gangsters were escaping, shot them all because they refused to halt, the automobile landing in the ditch when the dead hands of the driver dropped from the wheel. Later it was whispered about that the automobile had been accidentally ditched and that the police had shot the helpless men in reprisal; that the police had pursued the gangsters into the country because the latter had refused to pay the police who had been protecting them; so lax were they in their obligations that they actually owed money to a hundred and thirty policemen. The police squad had gone after them to demand a show-down and if everything else failed to make an example of them that would throw terror into the hearts of any other gangsters who were delinquent in payment to the police. Naturally such whispered reports are not capable of proof but they are horribly demoralizing to the thousands of simple people who believe them. Such stories of the police doubtless gained credence because the Chicago force are constantly associated with their own deeds of violence. When the chief of detectives wishes to be most impressive he sends out an "execution squad" of city detectives who boast that they have each killed at least one gangster. The chief very much admires the record—one lieutenant has killed eleven men, another five, still another six and so on, their names, each credited with his executions, are given to the press. Often in the past the newspaper editors have allowed themselves to be impressed by such feverish energy of the police in rounding up miscellaneous unfortunates. Now they have become wiser. The *Chicago Daily News,* for instance, made the following comment:

Gangsters grow rich on mere vocal reproof. They care nothing for sensational hunts for murderers. Indeed, these serve the gangsters' purposes. Such hunts help to distract attention from the damning facts that the murder gangs are permitted freely year in and year out to distribute their truckloads of beer and their cases of booze, to run their gambling houses and their houses of prostitution unmolested.

Citizens must cease to participate in the childish game of the police who make a futile hue and cry over past killings while continually inviting fresh killings because of illicit privileges accorded by them to murderous gangsters.

It is said that throughout the year of 1929, the gang murders in Chicago have averaged one a week. For the most part the gangsters kill each other or are shot by policemen. Doubtless this has an important bearing upon the situation. The good citizen does not bestir himself and considers that he is not involved so long as the killing is confined to gangsters. Perhaps thus making a distinction in the value of human lives may account for the lack of effective action or it may merely be due to the gangster's power in politics. It is said that gang life in New York tends to dovetail into one political machine and thus avoids the waste and duplication of the struggles for territorial control. In Chicago every election is a battle in which the power of the gangs may determine the success of a political party.

In pre-Volstead days happiness and release from reality were associated with drinking, and much of the social life for men centered around drinking together. There is no doubt that more wholesome outlets are gradually being substituted in spite of the fact that many young men are very eager to demonstrate their superiority to law, and consider this demonstration a very sporty thing. We know indeed that a great many young people are drinking at the present moment solely from a sense of bravado. Each generation looks for a method with which it may defy the conventions and startle its elders. The present generation seems to have settled upon the obtaining and consuming of illicit liquor. The motive is so cheap and superficial that it is almost impossible to place the situation in the area of morals or any other human field. Unhappily their elders often imitate and abet them, although they live in homes in which liquor was never used in the pre-war days.

There is a general impression, however, that this braggadocio movement is spending itself and that a reaction has set in among the young people themselves. Many flappers are afraid to drive with men who carry hip flasks. Automobile accidents are multiplied, not only by the man who is intoxicated but even more by the man whose few drinks have made him recklessly eager to take chances and have evoked within him a certain exhibitionism of dare-devil courage. If it ever comes to a forced choice between automobiles and liquor, there would be little doubt, I imagine, as to which would be preferred.

If one needed any further proof of the power of propaganda and of the almost hypnotic influence of the slogans of the press, the Chicago settlements found it when they collected the opinions of all sorts of people throughout their neighborhoods about prohibition. It was amazing to find how the very identical phrases were used in the different parts of the city, phrases easily traced to the propaganda of the liquor interests who have such a large business stake in the sale of liquor on the old system. Although over 99 per cent of the persons interviewed were very positive in their opinion that saloons should not return, the majority of them favored beer and light wines. They constantly used the stock phrases: (a) There are more people drinking than ever before; (b) The disregard for the prohibition law is lessening the respect for all laws; (c) Conditions have become increasingly worse; (d) Prohibition is an infringement upon personal liberty; (e) The law was put over at an unfair moment. Added to them were the well-worn statements, given as opinions, although it was impossible to secure figures or even

many examples, that there was drinking among
women and adolescent boys more than heretofore;
that the entire prohibition law is considered a
farce and a huge joke; that lack of enforcement is
leading to police protection and graft.

Doubtless all bootleggers would oppose a
change in the law and would adduce their own
lines of argument, for such is the inevitable reaction of men whose vested interests are involved.
But the bootleggers have not yet mobilized their
public opinion, and their siogans are still surrep-
titious.

VI

This attempt on the part of the Federal government "to interfere with the drink situation" has
certainly not met with the same vigorous opposition which an earlier one did, when, in 1791, the
United States government passed the first legislation connected with the imposition of a Federal
Revenue Tax on manufactured liquor. The Whiskey Rebellion, which occurred in 1794, was a most
dramatic incident in the long warfare. But there
were many lesser ones. This earlier interference
of government with personal liberty in regard to
the liquor traffic is so seldom referred to that I
venture to quote here a description by a well-
known historian:

* To aid in meeting the increased charges caused by
the assumption of state debts, Congress in 1791 after

* The Rise of American Civilization—Beard, Vol. 1, 357-8.

a savage debate passed an excise law laying, among other things, a tax on spirits distilled from grain—an act especially irritating to farmers of the interior already marshaling under opposition banners. Largely owing to the bad roads, which made it hard for them to carry bulky crops to markets, they had adopted the practice of turning their corn and rye into whiskey—a concentrated product that could be taken to town on horseback over the worst trails and through the deepest mud. So extensive was the practice in the western regions of Pennsylvania, Virginia, and North Carolina, that nearly every farmer was manufacturing liquor on a small scale; the first of these states alone, according to the reckoning, had five thousand distilleries. The excise law, therefore, provided in effect that government officers should enter private homes, measure the produce of the stills, and take taxes for it directly from the pockets of the farmers.

As soon as the news of this excise bill reached the interior, an uprising followed—an outbreak of such proportions that Congress, frightened by the extent of popular dissatisfaction, removed the tax from the smallest stills and quieted the farmers of Virginia and North Carolina. In Pennsylvania, however, the resistance stiffened. Some of the distillers in that state positively refused to pay the tax; while rioters sacked and burned the houses of the collectors just as Revolutionists thirty years earlier had vented their wrath upon King George's agents for trying to sell stamps. When at length a United States marshal attempted to arrest certain offenders in the summer of 1794, a revolt known as the Whiskey Rebellion flared up, resulting in wounds and death.

The defiance of the Internal Revenue Tax is still carried on in remote mountain fastnesses and in such hidden places, the two types of bootlegging running concurrently, as it were. The Internal Revenue Service has developed a staff of fine men, devoted to their duty, and while it has been most unfortunate that the Federal officers charged with the enforcement of the Volstead Act were exempt from civil service examination, it is hoped that the Prohibition Reorganization Act, which became effective April 1st, 1927, giving the commissioners power to reorganize the field forces under classified civil service rules, will mark the beginning of a more reasonable and effective enforcement.

It is easy to find another historic precedent in which the Federal government was obliged to administer a law in the midst of a population averse to enforcement. During many years thousands of former slaves, legally freed by the Fourteenth Amendment to the Constitution, found themselves in the midst of a population who were theoretically and practically averse to their freedom. Some of the former slaves were scarcely more free than they had been before, some of them fell into a sort of peonage and many of them were gradually deprived of the franchise given to them for their own defense. And yet, could anyone say that this amendment was not to the great advantage of the citizens of the United States, nor deny that after two generations of even pseudo freedom the negroes have had an enormous advantage over their forebears?

Another point of analogy between the abolition of slavery and the abolition of alcoholic drinks, lies in the fact that in both cases large vested interests were involved, and that the property was expropriated by the government without indemnity for losses. Both sets of men, the ex-slave owner and the brewers and distillers, felt honestly aggrieved and issued a vast amount of propaganda against this governmental action.

To come back to the city of Chicago, it is safe to assume that the actual situation in regard to the police administration in relation to the prohibition of alcohol is like that which formerly obtained in Chicago and other large cities in regard to the police in relation to open gambling or the illicit sale of narcotics. This latter situation was not permanently changed, although sharply pulled up by the public opinion resulting from the publication of the Vice Commission report in which it was stated that the commissioners had full proof that "A criminal conspiracy existed between certain commanding officers and certain gamblers, whereby money had been paid to secure protection for illegal games of chance." And yet we were informed later that nine hundred and ninety-nine arrests and two hundred and forty-eight convictions for the moment wiped out public gambling in Chicago.

In one month's time, at a cost not exceeding $1,000, the commission's investigators broke up a large part of the sale of cocaine, opium and other drugs, in violation of the law. It was incidentally discovered that one illicit dealer paid $3,000 per annum for protection. If such a situation could be changed through an aroused public opinion, certainly the present one, connected with the illicit sale of liquor, can also be changed. To give it up now, or to modify seriously the Eighteenth Amendment, would be to obtain not even a negative result, and would mean that we never could be clear as to the real effect of national prohibition.

Whatever the final decision, of one thing I am quite clear; that what the prohibition situation needs, first of all, is disarmament. If this necessitates Federal control of the sale of firearms, so much the better, but whatever is necessary for the final results, the Federal agents should promptly be taught some other methods than those of gunmen. It is their business to bring lawbreakers into court and not to punish on the spot. That the police of the Irish Free State, established immediately after the evacuation of the English troops, and after Ireland's civil war, could go unarmed in the midst of a population still carrying concealed weapons, encourages me to believe that brave and conscientious men may be found to make arrests without firearms, as the English police have done for so many years. There is an obvious need for a tireless intellectual effort, as well as for a sympathetic interpretation of the situation.

I am setting down these experiences for what

empirical value they may have, and the reflections they have evoked, while sometimes disconcerting, are at least genuine.

VII

Out of my own experience I am convinced that our experiment in the United States is being watched all over the world, both by the few people who believe that the governmental prohibition of the indiscriminate use of alcohol marks an upward trend in civilization, and by those who crave for their own country the economic advantages which prohibition entails, believing that the increased speed and mechanization of life, not only in transportation but in our daily living, requires the protection it affords.

Lillian D. Wald and myself were once given an interview with Calles, then the newly elected President of Mexico. He wished to talk only of prohibition—how well was it operating in the United States; what were the difficulties encountered; what were the substitutes which the workingmen were finding to give them the joy of life and the relief from deadly monotony which liquor had afforded them for so many generations. He himself had been governor of one of the Northern Mexican states which had tried the experiment of prohibition, and felt that dry legislation had added one more to the many advantages which the United States possessed. He believed that with the

reform which the Mexican Labor Government
was then planning, nothing could be more important and useful than the abolition of the use of
pulque, which would be less needed as an anodyne
as the standard of life was raised. This conversation took place in the early days of Calles' administration, when all reforms seemed possible, but it
was, at least, a sincere tribute to our great
experiment.

I once held a similar conversation with several
members of the government of the Irish Free State
in 1926, one of its early years. They too were full
of plans for reforms and social experiments. I
had been invited to see the great engineering work
which would so canalize the River Shannon as to
secure enough power to electrify the industries
throughout Ireland; it was hoped that the Irish
people, through this distribution of electric power
from a central source, could keep to their old village organizations in industry as in other affairs.
I had been taken to see the new houses, which were
being erected not only in the towns but in the
smallest hamlets as well, and was invited to inspect
the governmental efforts to increase the efficiency
of the coöperative dairies. But every single member of the Government with whom I had a chance
to really converse asked at once, sometimes wistfully, about the working of prohibition in America. How did the Irish-American take it? What
difference did it make in the politicians and in

their attitude toward life; did the abstainers seem puritanical and insufferable, or were they the same old boys? These officials always closed the conversation with the pious reflection that if they could eventually utilize the full man power of Ireland as they hoped in time to utilize her full material resources, all would be well.

CHAPTER IX

Immigrants under the Quota

THE distinct change in national policy represented by the Quota Act initiated in 1921, has been defined as the nation's massive attempt to draw its traditional forces together and to exclude the people and the influences that seemed to threaten the fierce loyalties and solidarities evoked by the war. There is no doubt that the immigrant population in the United Sttes suffered from a sense of ostracism after the war, which, in spite of their many difficulties, their sorrows and despairs, they had never before encountered in such universal fashion. They had grown accustomed to the clashes between diverse cultures, but this post-war attitude deliberately complicated and doubtless increased the planes of psychical friction.

Although many good Americans had for years joined with the labor organizations and other public bodies in an effort drastically to restrict the amount of immigration into the United States, such acts, even when they passed Congress, had been vetoed by three American Presidents, and the stream of immigrants by the outbreak of the European war, had approximated a million a year. After the war, the demand for serious restriction became widespread, arising doubtless from many causes, although the emotional content in the demand was obviously due to the fact that as a nation we had become during the war overconfident of our own nobility of purpose and had learned to distrust all foreigners as "unworthy." We unwittingly reverted to a former attitude expressed for instance in the first issue of the *Panama Star,* published in Panama and brought by ship to San Francisco in 1852:

If foreigners come (to California) let them till the soil and make roads, or do any other work that may suit them, and they may become prosperous; but the gold mines were preserved by nature for Americans only, who possess noble hearts.

The sense of repression suffered during the war and after under the Quota Act was dramatized in the Chicago mayoralty campaign in 1927 when a

admission of Latins and Slavs and Congress in no uncertain terms told the entire country why such immigrants were considered "undesirable."

That old question, recorded in the very dawn of human ability to record anything—"Is the Universe friendly?"—never presses so hard upon the bewildered human creature as it does upon a stranger in a strange land when his very mother tongue, his inherited customs and manners, his clothing and his food, are all subjected to ridicule and considered *per se* un-American if not indeed dangerous, and subversive of American institutions. But at last a champion arose for the diverse groups living in Chicago. The abuse of King George—naturally pleasing to the Irish and inevitably highly entertaining to the Germans— embodied for the Slav, the Greek, the Latin, the Turk and all the rest, an assertion that the Anglo-Saxon was no better than he ought to be or at any rate that he would no longer be allowed to dictate what Chicago should teach its school children, whose racial background was as good as anybody's! The day of retribution had arrived! No one was ever hailed more devoutly as a champion of the misrepresented and of the oppressed, than was this valiant knight tilting at royalty. It was a curious revelation of the wide-felt need for championship that this revolt against the dominant race included the two hundred thousand colored people living in Chicago. Perhaps no one so wistfully feels the

long before normal conditions were restored thousands of people who were members of these separated families had sold all their belongings and were waiting at points of embarkation often remote from their homes. Without warning, they were placed under the operation of the Quota Acts, which often meant years of living in a strange land and country. During the first months of its operation in 1921, hundreds of distracted relatives came to Hull-House begging for information as to this new governmental regulation, and the stream has scarcely ceased since. This is largely because the Immigrants' Protective League occupies a Hull-House building and the fine superintendent, Mrs. Kenneth Rich, a Hull-House resident, and her staff, are constantly ministering to their wants; it is also partly due to the fact that many of the Poles and Russians had been coming to the settlement during the years immediately following the war, when Hull-House had become one of the distributing stations for the issuance of food orders under the Hoover Commission.

A class of cases for which the Quota Act made scant provision where the husbands and wives, parents and children, who were being supported by members of their families living in this country but who were unable to come to America. When a group of social workers petitioned Congress to suspend the restrictions for these so-called "fireside relatives" their number was found to approximate one hundred and seventy-three thousand.

Many of the immigrants in America have faithfully sent money to their families throughout the eight years since the quota regulation was enforced, but inevitably many of them grew discouraged and others shirked their obligations altogether. From the crowded files of the Immigrants' Protective League I have selected two letters illustrating this situation. One from Poland reads as follows:

My husband Bazyli left Poland in 1912 and since then has lived continuously in United States. He has never sent any support for me and the children. I have three children: Andrzej 17, Pelagja 16 and Szymon 15. Andrzej and Pelagja help me on the farm and Szymon takes care of the cattle. The two older children are in normal health but the youngest son is a cripple, his right leg is withered and I have no money for treatment. All three children did not attend school because during the war there were no schools, and when schools were established after the war, I had no money for clothing nor for shoes for them. My support is from my farm of which I have three hectars. I have a small wooden house, straw covered, but it is almost in ruin because of old age. I have also one horse and one cow. I live alone in the house with the children. My parents died and I was an only child. I never lived with my parents in law because I own the farm I live on and I inherited it. My husband never writes to me and never sent any money until in August when I received

$25.00 probably from him through the intervention of your Bureau. I am sending you a letter to my husband because I have not his address.

The Immigrant's Protective League at once found the husband living in Chicago. He was really trying desperately hard to overcome his illiteracy that he might become a citizen and have his wife and children come in under the Non-Quota provisions. He knew as well as the League did that it was hopeless to expect them under the Polish Quota. He had assumed that his family could support themselves in Poland on the little farm and he was saving his money for steamship tickets and for buying a home here. He had all the peasant's hunger for land, but also the peasant's untrained mind which made it almost impossible for him to master the meaning embodied in the Eighteenth-Century phrases of our basic government documents.

Too often when a great effort is made to secure citizenship papers that the families may be admitted and the applicant naïvely states the fact, the naturalization officials assume that his motive is therefore self-seeking and unworthy, and by skilful manipulation of the questions the applicant is easily thrown out. Discouraged and bewildered, he either returns to his hard study or more often sets up another family in this callous land of ours.

A letter from the Czecho-Slovakian Red Cross is typical of thousands of cases which fall under the caption of "support of relatives abroad":

Mrs. Frantiska ————, the wife of Frank ————, of Chicago, Illinois, received a permission to travel in the II preference class. However, the American Consulate did not grant her a visum because she could not answer the given questions. However, it is to be hoped that she will be granted a visum within a year if she will only study a little.

The above named has two children, Frantisek five and a half years old, and Ladislav eight years. Mrs. ———— lives in very sad conditions because her husband ceased to support her and is angry that she does not come to him.

Please locate Mr. ———— and notify him that the wife is not to be blamed for not being able to travel, because she lives in a very poor part of the country where in a long time she has no chance to meet intelligent people, and that it is necessary that he would support his family financially, and the more so to enable her to ask a teacher to help her a bit, which of course she has to pay for.

Mrs. ———— is an industrious woman who is taking a good care of her children.

Sometimes it is possible to make an appeal to a man's sense of responsibility and even to rekindle his old affection, but it cannot always be achieved.

We have learned that life is never logical and apparently not even reasonable, at least a surface reasonableness is often misleading as to the profounder trends underneath. Take, for example, the Cable Act. The women's organizations throughout the United States early endorsed this Act and did much to secure its passage because it enabled an American-born woman citizen to retain her citizenship after her marriage to a foreigner.

What could be more logical and patriotic? And yet those of us who have much to do with immigrants are constantly filled with profound doubt as to its advisability for women from other countries. I know a charming Roumanian woman married to a prosperous American. For three years she has wished to go back to visit her aged parents. The Roumanian Consul will not give her a passport because under the laws of his country she is an American. She is not eligible to an American passport because under our laws she is a Roumanian, and once out of the country she could only return as a part of the Roumanian quota. She cannot bring her parents here because only full citizens of the United States can bring parents outside the quota. The family are as completely separated as if steamships had never been invented, and afford one more corroboration of the dictum that our political concepts lag far behind our material achievements. A curious inconsistency of the Cable Act is that it takes away the birthright of an American-born woman if she marries an ineligible, i.e. a man from a country whose people cannot be made citizens, although it is precisely under such circumstances that a woman most needs her citizenship. At present she literally becomes a woman without a country.

One good result the Cable Law has produced is that the women most valiantly prepare themselves for securing their own citizenship papers. All over

Chicago the Board of Education arranges afternoon classes for these women. They are held four times a week in the Hull-House dining room, and nothing is more touching than the desperate efforts made by widows whose husbands were not citizens and who can secure mothers' pensions only after they have "obtained their papers." Although many do triumphantly and proudly acquire citizenship, thereby "proving to their children that they are not 'greenhorns', I will confess that I am often filled with a dark foreboding as to the final situation of the unsuccessful. As they make their way to the front door, after the lesson is over, collecting their little children who have been cared for in another room, I sometimes talk to the discouraged ones, conscious of an inner question in regard to these children who have been born in the United States and are here for the rest of their lives. Isn't it all to our advantage that they should be properly fed and given home care under the Mothers' Pension Act, in spite of the fact that their mothers may be unable to answer certain questions about the Constitution of the United States. Have we failed to revise our tests of citizenship to meet the current situation? Are these tests out of date and ill-adapted to our actual needs for a properly nurtured childhood? The situation smacks too much of the old literary tests of the entrance of immigrants when we discovered that after all literacy is neither a test of character nor of ability; it is

in which they move. There is something, is there
not, in the integrating of conflict? To make a synthesis between the differences that confront one in
two given situations is certainly an opportunity for
the development of character, at least of the emotional life, which, instead of being oppressed by
the old loyalties, insists that loyalty shall encom-
pass the new as well. Although the young all strain
against the standards of the Old World as exemplified in their parents, sometimes their mature judgment comes to approve these standards. One of
the members came into our Boys' Club one day
and boasted that he had three thousand dollars in
the bank. Although he was sixteen years old, he
looked much younger, and when the director made
some remarks about the folly of boasting, the boy
went home and brought back his bank book to
show that he did have three thousand dollars in
the bank. He had gotten it driving a "booze
wagon" from Joliet to Chicago, and because it was
a dangerous job with great menace from hi-jackers
and others he was paid $200 or $250 a trip. He
had accumulated this money before the hi-jackers
became suspicious of him for they had easily mis-
taken him as a young lad, driving a shabby old
truck for his father. He took the money and went
to a distant university. The first letter he wrote
home told of the drinking he found there. He
said that the men at home made booze, but they
did not drink it. He did not at all like the type of

upon railroad construction and repairs and then
went home to spend the winter. Forty years ago
when I first came to Hull-House, many Italians
went home every winter to save coal bills. All this
rough adjustment of immigration to prosperity has
now come to an end. Under the quota, an effort
has been made to proportion the arrivals month by
month throughout the year. The natural adjustment having been broken, some wise people are
doubting whether there is not something to be said
for more mobility of labor and for increasing use
of highly developed transportation facilities in
contradistinction to the method of shutting the
gates. The economists, it seems to me, have never
sufficiently stressed the fact that the great number
of immigrants formerly arriving represented an
enormous mass of consumers, who needed food,
clothing and shelter on a constantly rising standard of living. We are told that in this country of
ours every person on the average eats about five
bushels of grain a year. How far is our annual
plethora of foodstuffs due to the fact that we were
long accustomed to have markets come to us, so
that we are slow to learn how to overcome the difficulties in disposing of our products in foreign
markets? For many months during the post-war
period I gave public addresses under the auspices
of The Friends' Service Committee, who were
sending food to various starving peoples in
Europe. It was at a moment when the western

farmers were suffering from overproduction, and at one time many farmers in Kansas and Nebraska were using corn for fuel, partly because they could not sell it and partly because they had no money for buying coal, which at that moment was selling for fourteen dollars a ton. Three tons of corn—to be sold at the best for about four dollars a ton— made the heat equivalent of a ton of coal, so it was on the whole a very sensible thing to do individually if not socially.

I recall a meeting of the farmers of Kansas held at the State Capitol, with the governor presiding. A speaker from West Virginia told them that the only thing to do was to cut down production, as had been done in his state by the cultivators of tobacco. He made a strong plea, and begged them to determine what proportion of their land could advantageously be cultivated, and then to stick to it, even if the committee had to use shotguns. When my turn came I told about the shortage of food all over Europe and urged them to give all they could to the Quakers who were doing relief work in parts of the world where it was impossible for people to get enough to eat. The Quakers had rented a grain elevator at Wichita and were asking the farmers to fill it with their surplus of corn, which was transformed into corn syrup, corn oil and white corn meal, before it was sent to Poland, which at that moment was the object of our solicitude. Finally an old man in the audience arose and very impressively demanded that we have a "show-down" on this thing. He said, "These two speakers tell us two different stories, and what are we to do about it? Let's find out whether or not there is too much corn in the world and whether or not we ought to stop growing it." The audience shared his anxiety, but I am afraid that no adequate reply was forthcoming.

If the immigrants to the United States seem to discover immediately that which appears harsh and unfair, they are equally quick to find out friendliness even in remote places if it pertains to their problems. In 1921 a conference was held in Geneva, Switzerland, by the International Labor Office, having to do with the problems of migratory labor. I was surprised to find how many Italians in Chicago knew that I had been in Geneva at that time and through the kindness of a fellow countryman there, had been able to listen in at some of the sessions. Upon my return, the Italians came to see me and talked over the matter with real enthusiasm. In the old days many Italian farm workers came to the United States by way of South America. These workers very cleverly followed the ripening crop from the Argentine south of the Equator quite up to North Dakota, and then they went home to Italy for two or three months of relaxation, and came back to do it all over again, starting in to the south of the Equator during the months which are winter months in Italy. Naturally, many of these Italians, working their way North, from time to time would fall into difficulties in South America, Central America and the Caribbean countries. They would be miles away from an Italian Consul or anyone who could help them. This whole question of migratory labor upon which the harvesting for the people of this hemisphere has come to depend, is an important matter in the economic structure of the United States. Some of these Italians who could not read our newspapers, had yet heard that the difficulties of migratory laborers were being discussed in far-away Geneva, and that there was an organization interested in this very useful business of harvesting the grain of the world. They felt reassured that such a friendly thing could happen to them, and that it was on an international scale seemed quite natural. Personally, I believe that the immigrants, with their parents in the Old World and their children in the New, could give us a fresh line of hope to the vexed problems of juster relations between nations. We might, through these immigrants, make a fresh attempt away from our preconceptions, to approach our international relations with some sort of human standards, such as we have long tried to apply to our relationships within the nation. The exchange of Bulgarian and Greek populations under the auspices of the League of Nations, with which many hundreds of people in our neighborhood were poignantly familiar, demonstrated to them, at least, that there are certain things which cannot be taken care of except by a body of men from outside the country or countries involved, who act with the most righteous judgment of which they are capable toward men of varied nationalities.

V

One immediate consequence of the quota regulations was the withdrawals of the Latins and Slavs, who for years had performed the unskilled labor in America's industrial centers. This resulted in the arrival in the United States of a large number of Mexicans. One of the earliest colonies in Chicago was in the immediate vicinity of Hull-House. It was interesting to watch their reception in the neighborhood. At first the Italians received them almost as a group of their own countrymen. We had, for instance, a large Latin Club of young men at Hull-House, a membership fairly representative of both nationalities, but as the Mexicans in their innocence mingled freely with the negroes from the South, who had come to Chicago in large numbers about the same time that the Mexicans themselves had come, and because many Mexicans were dark of skin they gradually became discriminated against, even by the people of Latin origins, who in Europe at least do not discriminate against the dark-skinned man. At the end of three

years of a gradually less-cordial relationship between the groups, and long after the Latin Club
had split upon nationalistic lines, a committee of
Italians came to Hull-House with the threat that
if we continued to rent Bowen Hall to the Mexicans, the Italians would discontinue to use it for
their wedding receptions and other festivities. It
was not that they would necessarily meet the
Mexicans but that the hall would lose its prestige
if it were being used by people of color! The incident afforded an example of one sorry aspect of
the Americanization of immigrants, for it was
quite evident that the Italians had copied their
standard of social excellence from their American neighbors.

A similar example was afforded in connection
with the race riots which unhappily occurred in
Chicago in the summer of 1921. A colored man
had been lynched in an Italian neighborhood,
about half a mile from Hull-House. I had been
in Europe that summer and upon my return I
one evening consulted an association of Italian
physicians who occasionally held their professional meetings in one of the Hull-House rooms.
When I asked them why, in their opinion, such a
shocking incident was possible in the United
States, when the friendly attitude of the South
Italian to his African neighbors is well known,
the professional men replied with the utmost sincerity: "Of course this would never have hap-

pened in Italy; they are becoming Americanized."
This was said in an honest effort to interpret a
puzzling situation, and perhaps it did interpret
it.

Our national tendency to lawlessness has been
ascribed to our uncurbed and extra-legal violence
toward two races; to the frontiersman's general
habit of killing Indians, which was of course
against the law but for which he was never punished but on the other hand was often praised by
his own community; and to the cruel business of the
slave trade. Even after the latter was outlawed,
ten thousand negroes a year were brought into the
country from 1820 to 1860, and no court even punished a man for the crime until 1862. Perhaps this
historic background suggests an explanation of
our general attitude toward aliens as well as
toward law.

It would be impossible to talk of the social consequences of immigration acts without referring
to the Japanese situation. The Japanese people
naturally felt discriminated against by the Quota
Act of 1924 directly excluding them. It was the
greater rebuff in that had Japan with others been
placed under the quota, they would have sent less
than a hundred and fifty people a year. Because
I had recently been in Japan and because I was
identified with a group of women there, organized
into a national section of the Women's International League for Peace and Freedom, I re-

many of them from the sheer instinct of self-preservation had stolen food and other necessities; they had been tried by a Chinese court and committed to the one penitentiary which alone was considered worthy to house Europeans. They were certainly cared for with an elaboration I had never seen in any American or European prison, each cell containing a shelf of books and a samovar! Other Russian refugees were being fed at a public kitchen instituted by the foreign population of Peking, but they were all anxious, almost without exception, to cross the Pacific Ocean to the United States. Many of them were men of education and ability, some of them had been land owners, others represented mining interests and a multitude of professional occupations. They were obviously not Bolsheviks, because they were fleeing from the government which the Bolsheviks had established, and yet it was impossible to get them into the United States because of the quota regulation in general and of the attitude toward Russians in particular. Had they been fleeing from religious persecution it would have been difficult to refuse them asylum, but now that fear and persecution have taken up homes in the State rather than in the Church, and although they were in need of refuge if ever a group was in dire need, it was impossible to make arrangements for their entrance into the United States. Some of them of course entered surreptitiously. A friend of mine

in a Western University once invited a famous
consulting engineer, lunching at his house, to say
a few words to a Russian student from the Department of Mines, who was at that moment sweeping
his yard. The famous engineer came back, pale
with astonishment, to report that the student was
the son of an opulent mine owner whose mines
he had once been summoned to Russia to survey.

Another aspect of the Quota Act is that it refuses to be static, and an effort is constantly made,
by making it more drastic, to use it as a disciplin-
ary measure. There was a long debate in Congress over the proposed legislation for the deportation of alien gunmen, believed to be terrorizing
Chicago and other large cities. In a Conference
Committee the Senate conferees refused to accept
the very severe deportation provisions coming
from the House, contending that the bill created
unjustifiable inequities. But the discussion added
one more difficulty to a situation already sufficiently irritated.

We constantly make the charge against immigrants that they are responsible for our oversupply
of unskilled labor, although no comprehensive inquiry has ever been undertaken which could demonstrate this. We have no national system of
labor exchanges which might show how much of
the apparent unemployment is maladjustment of
the supply to the demand and how much is over-

supply. The immigrant is continually blamed for conditions for which the community is responsible. There is no doubt that America has failed to make legislative provisions against those evils as other countries have done, partly because the average citizen holds a contemptuous attitude toward the "foreigner" and is not stirred to action on his behalf. This may account for the fact that the United States has been so unaccountably slow in legislation designed to protect industrial workers. For instance, if we compare our country with others in regard to Old-Age Insurance, the record is most astonishing. Some form of pension legislation for the aged has been enacted in fourteen countries since the beginning of the World War, and still a larger number secured such legislation in the two preceding decades. If we ask why the United States has been so slow in this world-wide undertaking, may we not fairly say it is because we are less concerned for the old age of our immigrant laborer than the other countries are for their own kinsfolk, and we thus overcome the stronger democratic tendency we are supposed to possess. Is our understanding slower for those whose background is alien to our own, so that we have allowed ourselves to become indifferent to old people, surrounded too often by poverty and neglect, while Europe, out of its more slender resources, takes care of them?

An able English writer has recently contrasted

the lack of economic security for the wage-earners
of the United States with the unemployment and
old-age pensions surrounding European workmen.
He comments:

If anything like similar conditions prevailed in Europe, experience indicates that the lack of economic
security, accompanied as it is in the United States by
the customary expectation of a high standard of life
among the wage-earners, would lead to a prevalence
of lawlessness and violence and to a degree of vagrancy
and criminality which Northwestern Europe has not
known for a couple of centuries.

VI

Possibly another result of our contemptuous attitude toward immigrants who differ from us is
our exaggerated acceptance of standardization.
Every one wants to be like his neighbors, which is
doubtless an amiable quality, but leading to one of
the chief dangers of democracy—the tyranny of
the herd mind. Possibly the intolerance for differing opinion during the war and after, which
blazed more fiercely among Americans than
among any of the European belligerents, may
have had its obscure origin in some such habit-
forming daily experiences. This semi-contemp-
tuous attitude of the Americans toward the immigrant is the more remarkable because the most
successful experiment in industrial democracy
ever made in America was inaugurated and car-

ried out in Chicago by successive groups of immigrant workers.

Following a great strike in Chicago's largest clothing establishment, an arrangement was made greatly to the credit of both the contending parties, between the representatives of Hart, Schaffner & Marx, and their own workers. Through the establishment of a joint board of control, the beginning of an industrial arrangement was made which continued from year to year and is constantly growing in usefulness. It is a matter of pride to the residents of Hull-House that the first meeting which resulted in the organization, later designated as "The Amalgamated Clothing Workers of America," should have been held in one of our rooms, offered as a refuge to a number of Russian Jewish men and women who had split off from a Trades Union meeting on the North Side of Chicago. The strike of the clothing workers in 1915 had been a long bitter one, with several unsuccessful attempts at adjustment. The clothing workers did not win all their demands, but their retreat was far from being an unconditional surrender. The strikers, in the words of their president, returned to work as Union men and women, with faith in their organization and full of hope and courage for the future. Several residents of Hull-House were identified with the strike activities and with the almost city-wide effort to provide milk for the children of the strikers. The final financial report of the Secretary-Treasurer accounting for the distribution of the strike fund, printed a note directly under the grand total as follows: "From outside individuals, Ellen Gates Starr of Hull-House was the hardest worker I knew. Nothing was too hard for her; she gave and solicited funds, secured clothing, relief and shelter for individual families, was on the picket line, addressed meetings, wrote articles, interested others in our behalf. In a word, Miss Starr was one active in all phases of strike activity." This high praise is perhaps the more significant because strikers are always rather sensitive in regard to the assistance of outsiders.

The achievement of the Amalgamated in what has come to be coöperative production is the more remarkable in that great cities tend to dissolve almost as by chemical process the customs and social ties which were nurtured in rural and provincial society, so that the very cement which held groups together seems to disappear. If the individual and smaller peasant groups are to be realigned and united in common purpose, there must be in addition to the economic advantage which comes from association of mutual undertaking, a moral appeal with a sense of responsibility and a clear understanding that at moments the individual's advantage must be sacrificed to the good of the whole. This welding together into an active group has been achieved, not only by the men who composed the joint committee, some of whom were continually connected with the Northwestern University and another of whom had a background of settlement experience, but undoubtedly much of it has been done by the national president of the association, Sidney Hillman. His slogan, "self-government in industry," was drawn from the original arrangements entered into with good faith both by the employers and the men, by which the grievances arising among the fifteen thousand men who now compose the labor force of the great establishment, could be adjusted. These arrangements have further included a lengthening of the working year, and also—perhaps even a greater achievement—a securing to the workers themselves of something of the profits resulting from technological improvements as well as the finding of work for the displaced men elsewhere in the huge establishment. Quite recently the Amalgamated has been put in charge of the factory in Milwaukee. The actual day by day management rests entirely with themselves, although the material already cut into garments is sent from the Chicago establishment and the business management is also vested there. So far as this one factory is concerned, "self-government in industry" has already been achieved.

This solution for protecting the American standard of life from the menace of raw immigrant labor is in marked contrast to a suggestion made at the time of the prolonged textile strike in Lawrence, Mass., which because of the emergence of the Industrial Union, provoked a sharp divergence of public opinion as to wherein the difficulty lay, although no one could contend that the wages paid were sufficient to maintain what we like to call American standards. One suggestion was never followed up, although it remains in my mind as a valuable one; that all immigrants who, because they are not yet citizens, are wards of the Federal government and must be paid a designated living wage, as a minimum, if they were employed at all.

Paul Kellogg, editor of *The Survey,* who made the suggestion writes that he had Justice Brandeis' endorsement that the plan was legally feasible.

It is a device which might conceivably be employed in changing our restriction laws, affording as it would protection to our native laborer; because obviously if corporations were prohibited from employing an immigrant at less than a stated minimum, preference would be given to resident workmen. The scheme would set a sort of bulwark about our congested industries, so that the incoming flood of greenhorns would not undermine the foot-hold of the resident group. The whole history of the Pittsburgh district, for example, has been of one wave of immigration used to undercut the foot-hold of the preceding wave.

The immigrants themselves have never forgotten a court decision given by a Federal judge in a district comprising the mines of West Virginia.

An Italian workman had been killed and the Judge awarded the death indemnity to his family in Italy, on the ground that having taken out his first papers, the man thereby became a ward of the Federal government, who in this instance had failed to protect him.

Perhaps this great industrial experiment in Chicago, founded upon an agreement between the workers and the employers, was easier to bring about among immigrants than it would have been among native-born Americans. If an Italian is forced to make friends through the very exigencies of his work, with a Polish Jew representing another nationality and another religion, the experience cuts into all his most cherished prejudices but it is not so hard after that to make a larger synthesis and to include everybody with whom he comes in contact. All succeeding efforts will be less fundamental, for it is much harder to utilize your prejudices after they have once failed you than it was to break into them the first time. It requires less effort to be friends with your employer than it required in the first place to be friends with your alien fellow employees. Immigration by its very variety is providing its own education.

Last year I attended a banquet at the opening of the Chicago headquarters of the Amalgamated Clothing Workers of America. The handsome building—an investment of a million dollars— housed a most attractive library, a well-appointed gymnasium and business offices in which could be deposited the savings of the members (these were afterwards transferred to their own bank, down town), and all the other equipment not only for a going concern but for a concern which had been going for a long time.

No group of Americans of my acquaintance has achieved a similar success in what we like to call the American method—that is, reaching our own ends through voluntary action with fair play to all the interests involved, refusing to admit the irrepressible conflict between capital and labor in a country where a man can pass so easily from one side to the other, and where thousands of them do so pass every year. And yet in spite of such achievements on the part of immigrants our old contemptuous attitude toward them too often remains unchanged, although this successful experiment in industrial democracy has been achieved by adult immigrants, hundreds of them from Russia, hundreds others from Italy and many others from those very countries in Southeastern Europe whose ideals Congressmen declare are so inimical to our inherited institutions. The newspapers, which more and more tend to measure events not by their real importance but by their value as entertainment, have reported comparatively little of this important industrial experiment, perhaps on the whole Chicago's most significant contribution to one of our vexed social problems—a contribution in large part from our immigrant population.

VII

A European observer has said that as Spain in the sixteenth century was obsessed by the necessity of achieving national unity, above the variety of religions, so Twentieth Century America is obsessed by the need of national unity above all else; that the expulsion of the Moors and Jews from Spain corresponds with American immigration laws. It may be this touch of fanaticism which accounts for the new emphasis on the expulsion of immigrants from this country since the quota principle of limitation went into effect. Following the deportation drives in the United States in 1919 and 1920 which the then Assistant Secretary of Labor characterized as a "Deportation Delirium," smaller drives have taken place periodically. In 1926 for instance, the West Side colonies of foreign-born peoples in Chicago, some of them in the neighborhood of Hull-House, were terrified by the sudden descent of uniformed Immigration Inspectors and Chicago Police, who broke into their homes, sometimes without warrants, carried off patrol wagons full of people to the police stations and to the county jail. Out of the approximately two hundred persons who were apprehended, less than twenty-five were found to be deportable. Some of them were discovered to have been born in America, some to be citizens by naturalization and others to be perfectly law-abiding aliens who had already filed applications for naturalization. The total number of deportations shows an enormous increase during the last ten years. The old rate approximated several thousand a year but since the drives were instituted the number has increased each year until it reached eleven thousand six hundred and twenty-five in 1928.

The sentiment which prompts this policy was embodied in the last deportation law passed on March 4th, 1929, which makes re-entry into the United States after deportation, a felony; an entry without inspection a misdemeanor with heavy penalties. It also bars forever from the United States anyone who has ever been deported, for any cause, at any time, whether before or after the passage of the Act. The position of such deportees reveals extreme hardships; students who perhaps changed schools from one on the accredited list, to schools not so recognized by the Department of Labor and were therefore deported, can never return. Wives or husbands who came on a visit to their families here, who overstayed their permits and were deported, can never be reunited in this country. Aliens so unfortunate as to have become insane and to have been deported from state institutions to their countries of birth, although they may fully recover mental health, will never be able to come back. Foreign born who became public charges at one stage in their struggle toward economic security, and were compelled upon deportation warrant to leave the country—no matter how sturdily self-supporting or even affluent they may have become in the future—can never reenter. The following case which became known to us at Hull-House is fairly typical.

A man was deported to Belgium, the country of his birth, in September, 1929, leaving in this country his wife and child, both citizens of the United States. He had not been in Belgium for many years, having come into the United States from Canada in 1927, uphappily without inspection, and had married here in April, 1928. When he earnestly desired to regularize his status he thought that by going back to Canada he might apply there for a visa and wait for his turn in the preference quota from Belgium. He was arrested on the United States side of the border and promptly deported. His wife has lived in the United States since childhood and feels that this is her natural home. She has gone with her American born baby to live with her parents, hoping for her husband's return or for the remote possibility that he may be able to establish a home in Belgium. Except for his record of deportation he is thoroughly admissible to the United States but unless there is an amendment to the Deportation Act of March 4, 1929, he is forever exiled from this country.

Every settlement knows many pitiable cases of those who fall under the list of L. P. C.—liable to become a public charge. A very sad case is reported by the Department of Immigration and Foreign Communities of the National Y. W. C. A.

That of the Italian child of ten who within three years after having entered the country to join her parents who had been here some years, was sent to a public hospital for a tonsilotomy. Her parents were unable to pay for private treatment. Thus she became a "public charge" for having become dependent and cared for at the expense of a public institution within five years of entry, and therefore she was deported to Italy to live with her old grandmother.

Many hardships arise under the provision of the law which requires that deportation be effected from port to port, that is, from the United States port where the immigrant last entered to the foreign port from which he last sailed. We have known at Hull-House a Pole from the interior of Poland who sailed from La Havre, a Slovak who sailed from Naples, both when deported were landed far from Rome. We knew an Armenian who had entered the United States from Cuba to which he was returned. These cities of which the migrant is neither a citizen nor resident often refuse to take them, and some of these unfortunate people literally sail the

high seas for weeks. Another case reported by the YWCA is Vladimir I——, a Russian aristocrat of the old régime who having escaped by way of Siberia from the Revolution finally landed in Shanghai, China. From there he came to the United States to join a cousin, but within two years after entry he became insane. Having become a charge at a public institution he was automatically reported to the immigration authorities and before a social agency or the cousin could intervene he was deported back to Shanghai without any safeguards as to his protection and care after arrival there.

The Mexicans who so long crossed over the border under the old tradition of the Open-Door Policy easily grow bitter over the situation as is indicated by the following quotation from a recent issue of *El Mexico* published in Chicago:

The problem of the lack of work in the American Union (U.S.) continues to grow and it is for this reason that the Immigration authorities have received instructions to round up the Mexicans for according to reports, the Department of Labor of the United States considers it absolutely indispensable to expel from the territory all those workers and preferably the Mexicans so as to protect the Nationals and the Europeans. . . . It has been observed that they deport those Mexicans who find themselves completely without funds. . . . From this it is deduced that the North American authorities have the plan that the Mexicans do not leave the United States before spending in the United States all the product of their savings.

Of course the Mexican deportations have nothing to do with the Quota Act and are based upon the old provisions of the Immigration Act. Such interpretation, however, as the one just quoted, while obviously unfair, yet reflects the spirit of the deportees.

As the United States compared to more homogeneous countries appears strangely indifferent to remedial legislation for old age and unemployment is there a danger that we may grow harsh and unfeeling in our governmental dealings with those who are foreign born, until it reacts if not upon our own national character certainly upon the conception of our national character held by other nations. Self-righteousness has perhaps been responsible for more cruelty from the strong to the weak, from the good to the erring than any other human trait.

VIII

In the twenty years considered in this book, the first five saw immigration at its flood; then came the interruption of the war years when practically no new immigrants reached our shores, and after that the eight years of the Quota Acts. The old policies were marked by a sweeping reversal in 1921. We may well ask what these latter years have shown us as to the limitations of the new régime? In the old days we had a rounded program of assimilation to offer as an alternative to restriction but now that restriction is enforced it is only fair to question whether the great experiment of industrial democracy in the garment trades would have been feasible without it. The experiment would certainly have had much harder sledding and there is no doubt that whatever its evils the shutting off of immigration has given the immigrant groups already here, a breathing space.

This of course is a separate point from that of

continuing indefinitely an iron-bound quarantine against newcomers, of being so afraid of them that we applaud the immigration officers and the naturalization agents for every device which makes more difficult the entry of immigrants and the procuring of citizenship papers. The man who is deported because he broke down under the bewilderment of new experiences and was placed in a hospital for the insane for two months or because in the innocence of his heart he had accepted public charity for his suffering family or because out of his untrained memory he gave the name of the steamship he tried to come over on instead of the one which actually brought him, can but carry bitter resentment back with him to whichever country he may return.

During the last decade there has been much interest in demographic studies in an endeavor to ascertain how far community life is influenced by the diversity in the populations composing it, and how far its social composition is affected by the processes of amalgamation and assimilation.

In the United States we cannot assume a single norm, even for the height, weight and growth of children in our public schools, because they vary from Japanese children in California to Scandinavians in Minnesota. It is an obvious demonstration of the great variety of customs, habits and convictions in the nationality groups which make up our big cities. To be intelligent about them requires constant acquaintance and research. "The Polish Peasant in Europe and America," "The Race Relation Study of the Pacific Coast," the investigations made by the Immigrants' Protective League of Chicago in connection with the School of Social Service Administration at the University of Chicago are all examples of an attempt to keep the social worker informed, although possibly the mass of recent literary work concerning the European peasants both at home and in the pioneer colonies of the United States, may prove equally valuable. Understanding is coming from so many directions that we venture to hope for wisdom at last in our national immigration policy.

CHAPTER X

Efforts to Humanize Justice

WE have been impressively told by one of our
contemporaries that the love of justice which
exists in the heart of man is the distinguishing
mark of his humanity and should be respected as
such. He also regards it as the supreme obligation
of each generation to find the means by which it
may be purified and still further increased. He
warns us that this undertaking is made difficult by
all which we do not perceive, or perceive incom-
pletely, and by all that we question too super-
ficially. It is at the mercy of every error of reason
and of every ambush laid by personal interest.
Hedged around by the most insidious dangers, it
falls a victim to the strangest of oblivions and the

most inconceivable blunders. Of all our spiritual efforts, it is the one that we should watch with the greatest care and anxiety, with the most passionate eagerness and solicitude.

During my last twenty years at Hull-House it is possible to trace at least three different trends in the direction of a wider justice. The first, obtaining a more intelligent justice, is illustrated by the establishment of a clinic in connection with the Juvenile Court in Chicago for the psychiatric study of delinquent children. The second, which might be called an enlargement of the field of justice, is illustrated by the extension of legal protection to prostitutes who were for so long a time regarded as outlaws. The third, which could be described as a determination to be just to those "to whom we do not wish to be just," is illustrated by attempts to extend justice to various alien groups, although, unhappily, some of these attempts were negative.

In 1909, the opening year of the second twenty years at Hull-House, the Juvenile Court in Chicago, which at that time was housed opposite the settlement, became the scene of the first psychopathic clinic ever established for the systematic study of children in an effort to discover the causes of their so-called delinquency. Certain of the Hull-House rooms facing on Halsted Street have long been occupied by the Juvenile Protective Association, an organization founded by the first Juvenile Court Committee in the hope of lessening the number of children brought into the court. One of our trustees, Louise de Koven Bowen, who has long been identified with the nurture and protection of Chicago's poorest children, has for thirty years served as chairman of this association and during most of that time the superintendents have been residents of Hull-House.

There was much heart searching among the trustees of the association in regard to children who were brought before the Juvenile Court over and over again, and who later often joined the ranks of juvenile-adult offenders. We all felt that in addition to the study of conditions responsible for the delinquency of the child, there should be added the study of the child himself, not only that a scientific estimate of his abnormality might be placed at the disposal of the judge, but also that the child's full coöperation might be secured in the task of his own rehabilitation. Ethel Sturgis Dummer, one of these trustees much interested in child study, placed a goodly sum in the bank to guarantee the first five years of an experiment which from the first was rather overwhelmingly designated as the Psychopathic Clinic for the Study of Delinquent Children.

The county commissioners at once gave space in the Juvenile Court building, and supplied the necessary clerical service. Almost from the very first the able psychiatrist, Dr. William Healy, with the corps of probation officers, convinced the public that in many cases it is possible to discover some underlying cause for so-called bad behavior. At the end of five years, when Dr. Healy was called to a similar position in Boston, the county itself took over the entire clinic. Later the state of Illinois founded the Institute for Juvenile Research, carried on in one of the Chicago buildings of the University of Illinois but holding schools and clinics in various parts of the state. It is also responsible for the psychiatric study and suggestions for treatment of the inmates in various state institutions. The Institute was enlarged and its usefulness increased by a research fund, subscribed later by public-spirited citizens of Chicago. Social workers come from every part of the United States to add a practical study of psychiatry to their equipment.

Partly as a result of this increasing study throughout the country, and partly because several prominent criminal cases had been tried in Chicago which were most obviously the result of abnormality, I think we have all become more or less conscious that it is possible to trace in all of our courts at the present moment, what has been called "dual philosophies in the treatment of crime." Acting upon one theory, the crime itself is punished, according to a well-established code, so many years in the penitentiary for this crime and so many years for that. On the other hand there is a growing tendency to individualize punishment, to find out what is fitted to a given criminal in order to deter him from further crimes and if possible to reëducate him.

There is much evidence that we are caught at this moment between these two theories and that the situation is so unformulated in the courts themselves that when the psychiatrists are called into a case and the attorney and judge get a very careful analysis of the mental condition of the prisoner, they encounter embarrassment by the extra-legal material upon their hands. No provision has been made for it and it is difficult to use it with dignity and decorum.

While this challenge to existing court procedure was in an earlier stage of development and in the first years of the psychopathic clinic, we were already conscious of a curious reaction sweeping over the country in favor of severity of punishment, leaning even to the revival of old punishments which had been largely given up because of their brutality. The public as well as the officials were alarmed by the startling increase of certain types of crime, and convinced that something drastic must be done immediately. They ignorantly believed that severity of punishment was in itself a deterrent to crime. One of the most glaring examples of belief in the efficacy of severe punishment occurred in Chicago in 1911 when the city was horrified by a very brutal murder committed by six young men and boys, apparently without

flinching"—a picture which is a thousand times more intriguing than a prosaic life in prison. A careful investigation by Harriet Vittum, Head Resident of Northwestern University Settlement, made clear that these boys had all been brought up in Chicago's most congested area, where the housing is the worst in the city, and where the only amusements within walking distance were connected with saloons and designed primarily to lure their earnings from them. The challenge they met at home from the overworked, harassed parents was, "How much money on Saturday?" The father of two of the boys said, less than a week before the day set for the execution: "I don't care what they do with them; it is nothing to me"; adding, with a shrug of his shoulders: "Neither of those boys ever brought home a penny." In one of the other homes, where eleven people lived in two dark, unsanitary, rear-basement rooms, the old father, who was a ragpicker, discussed the probable hanging, saying that if Philip "swung," John, a younger brother, would have to bear alone the expense of the insurance on the life of the mother, and "she might die any day." The mother of the youngest boy, crying over the tub as she bent to the family washing, said that he had "always been a good boy at home." She was much distressed that his little sister, twelve years old, who was suffering from tuberculosis, had become so excited over the news of her brother's fate that she had

bid but very real attraction in the horrible, a sort of unescapable hypnosis. In any case, there are many reasons for questioning the simple assumption, which seems so obvious to uninstructed common sense, that the more severe the penalty, the greater its deterrent effect. The situation would be all too easy if that were true, and crime would have been eliminated in the very centuries in which it was most rampant. One result of the reaction in favor of severity of punishment was to arouse a great admiration for the use of drastic measures on the part of the public officials; a state's attorney received great acclaim and many votes when he could boast of the large number of men he had "sent over the road" or "sent to the chair."

In the midst of a period of shocking lawlessness, the Chicago chief of police announced that he was ready to promote an officer who killed a criminal resisting his arrest. The chief is quite willing that the police officer should be judge, jury and executioner all in one, and he evidently has public opinion back of him, for the leading newspaper of the city gives prizes to policemen on the same basis, and the Bankers' Association of Illinois, thrown into a panic by the large number of bank robberies in the state, has offered rewards to anyone who brings proof that he has shot a *bona fide* safe cracker. They say nothing of what becomes of a good citizen who with the best intention in· the world shoots the wrong

operation." I think there is no doubt that the older boys in our neighborhood who are openly "bold and bad" are almost always secure in the conviction that if one of them should get caught he will not be severely dealt with, that local politicians to whom he and his family are attached will take care of him; and the surprising thing is—that they usually do take care of him. In addition to the sense of safety which comes from the consciousness of political pull, is a willingness to get out of trouble in any way that is possible, because the whole thing is a legal game and acquittal for any reason is a victory. The lawyers who defend Chicago boys love to give them the impression that their clients can always get out of difficulties, that acquittal is merely a question of the cleverness of the lawyer. What startles me many times about these boys is their amazing lack of moral feeling. They seem to have no habit of considering their acts in relation to any standards, but are controlled absolutely by the spirit of bravado. They like to perform the courageous act, to pull off something that the other fellows do not dare to do. Stealing a tire in itself is a technically difficult performance and increasingly so as new devices to prevent it are developed. Its illegality adds enormously to the hazard of the feat and makes its challenge the more alluring. The unnatural state of boasting in which the young criminal lives seems to inhibit his higher faculties. It is as if the spirit of thwarted adventure and the bravado of cheap achievement were the factors which carried him into a life of criminality. Other motives are tapped later when the boys gradually find that stealing is an easy way of supporting themselves. They begin at tires and go on to automobiles. Many of them are getting away with it, but when a young man is exceptionally successful, the rest shrewdly suspect that there is police connivance somewhere. This suspicion is quite often correct, although the facts are difficult to expose. A policeman on the Chicago force quite recently was arrested for shooting a man in the throat as the result of a long, drawn-out quarrel. The policeman had weeks before agreed to indicate to the wounded man parked automobiles which their owners had left unlocked and which therefore might be easily stolen with the connivance of the policeman on the beat. The quarrel arose as to the division of the spoils, and without the incident of the shooting the arrangement between the two men would never have been discovered, although one of the Municipal Court judges had drawn attention to the fact that the Municipal Pier which reaches far into the lake held an astonishing number of automobiles, brought there by the police to be sold when the unnotified owners failed to claim them. The policeman himself—promoted according to the number of arrests he has made—embodies the use of violence although he might be the greatest

"Sure, I don't need it around here. Why bother with the thing?"

That our present methods are ineffective is obvious since all the surveys show a large number of repeaters in the penal institutions. It was shown that in the correctional institutions of St. Louis two out of three inmates were recidivists and that recidivism had increased 100 per cent in twenty years. If our legal procedure cannot do better than that in dealing with criminals we certainly have a right to challenge the whole process for there is rank failure somewhere.

The number of men and boys who are arrested and sent up over and over again are comparatively few. A larger number are protected from arrest because they have reached an understanding with the police. It is as if the members of the police force, denied the natural pride in the good conduct of their beats and an understanding of the gangs which are so often merely a group of boys looking for amusement and adventure, took it out on being good to those boys and youth whom they illegally "protect" from the results of wrong-doing. This is most often done at the request of a politician, a friend of the boy's family who has higher-up connections. Certainly a good-hearted policeman must at moments feel relieved that he can be a good friend to at least these designated boys.

Is the entire conception of the police founded

upon military discipline? Is the policeman in reality a survival of the soldier in the midst of a civilian population, and does the official conduct required from him conform to standards alien to the rest of the community? Certainly his professional advancement becomes dependent upon acts which the normal men and fathers all about him regard as harsh and unfeeling.

We are of necessity dependent upon the police for the first steps in humanizing justice so far as these boys are concerned. Because in our American system several political units are responsible for the same case, it is easy for the officials involved in a given case to "pass the buck" and to hide their inefficiency or corruption. The police who make the arrest are of course municipal officers but when the case reaches the county, the state's attorney who presents it to the grand jury may have only such evidence in hand as the police, who are often not competent investigators, have secured. With all the complicated machinery the officials all along the line have failed to reach back into the social surroundings of the criminal nor have we any idea of the crime-producing factors in his experience. The evidence of the policeman who first arrested him, gives a slant to all the legal processes to which the accused is later subjected. The policeman on the beat ought to be a valuable source of evidence as he is naturally the only man who has been exposed, as it were, to the habitat of the criminal and who gives the neighborhood standards and temptations somewhat in the humbled ways of a father whose son has disgraced him. Instead of this we get the triumphant spirit of a thief catcher determined to justify himself for having made an arrest. This attitude of self-justification is perhaps more responsible for third-degree methods than we realize.

Is the attempt to secure a more intelligent justice which the psychiatric study of delinquents typifies, still in its very beginning because we are so entangled with the older theories of crime and punishment? An English philosopher has recently stated that "the retributive element in punishment, which is based upon a rage inspired by fear of the criminal, prevents the criminal law itself from becoming an effective instrument in the prevention of fear." Does this analysis throw light upon the reactions of the community as a whole, of newspapers, officials, and the average good citizens? What we all really demand is an immunity from fear. Is the incessant insistence upon more severe punishment a result of a state of panic which inhibits our intelligence?

III

The next development in the humanizing of justice, as I have seen it in Chicago during the last twenty years also had its roots in a slowly changing public opinion. The determination to give the measure of justice to the prostitute to which she as a human being was entitled, had its beginning in England in the middle of the Victorian era through the long effort of Josephine Butler on behalf of those women whom government itself had set aside for the basest uses. Her indignation was aroused by the injustice and unfairness of the situation, and her championship centered upon the women themselves. Who can read unmoved the death of the gentle young creature in the guest chamber of the country rectory, the prostitute's stern father who had ridden hard in response to the summons, standing in his riding boots before the fire with his back to the touching deathbed scene, conscious only of his own rectitude in having summarily cast her out when she "went-wrong"? It required years of unremitting effort on the part of the national and international organizations, inspired by the "God driven" Josephine Butler, to finally break through that hard shell of self-righteousness which had for so long a time enabled good men and women to treat the prostitute with rank injustice. The record of their success may be read in the abolition of one after another of the licensed districts throughout the great cities of the world.

To review the movement as it gradually developed, so far as my own observation is concerned, is not difficult. I recall that in a study of the records of the first decade of the Juvenile Court made in

1909 by the School of Civics and Philanthropy it was surprising to find that so many of the girls were brought in for sex delinquencies. This review was carried on at Hull-House under the auspices of two of the faculty who were then residents there. I remember one of the investigators saying at our dinner table, "I had a very happy surprise in my records today. I found a girl who had actually been arrested for flipping cars."

At that moment throughout the United States there was much agitation over the White Slave Traffic Act which was finally passed by Congress in 1910, the result of an investigation made in 1908 and 1909 by the Federal Immigration Commission "on the importation and harboring of women for immoral purposes," establishing the fact that a large number of girls were being brought into the country for such base uses. In the years preceding the passage of the law, Illinois passed the first pandering law in this country, changing the offense from disorderly conduct to a misdemeanor and greatly increasing the penalty. And as a result of this vigorous action, Chicago became the first city to look the situation squarely in the face and to make a determined businesslike fight against the procuring of girls. It was evident that the entire situation was closely allied to immigration, for if a foreign girl who spoke no English and who had not the remotest idea in what part of the city her fellow countrymen lived, could be decoyed immediately upon her arrival, she was almost as valuable to the white slave trafficker as a girl imported directly for the trade. An entire decade was spent, first in collecting definite information and then in securing and enforcing legislation designed to control and finally to abolish this monstrous social evil. Minnie F. Low, of the Jewish Social Service Bureau, bore a valiant part in this effort, as did many another, while the Juvenile Protective Association was unremitting in its efforts to save the victims of this traffic, many of whom were piteously young.

I recall that in the spring of 1911 a young girl was brought by a police officer to Hull-House directly from the railroad station. She was a charming girl of fifteen whose childish face surrounded by old-fashioned curls reminded me of the playmates of my earliest memory. She had been rented at the age of twelve by her mother to a notorious man in a neighboring state, with whom she had remained for four years, ostensibly as his daughter. Her mother later sent her to Chicago, to a white slave trader, who agreed to meet her at a given spot in the large railroad station. Although she had been brought across the state line in an automobile to avoid the Interstate Pandering Laws, which imply the use of a common carrier, the careful plot failed somewhere. The girl's story, which she gave most reluctantly and which was later corroborated by government officials, revealed that she had been subjected to unspeakable experiences but she was still so simple and childlike that she lay awake until midnight to see how differently she would feel when the clock struck and she would become sixteen years old. She reported her disappointment the next morning with the gravity of a little child.

The local situation in Chicago was at last effectively reached by the work following the report of the Chicago Vice Commission. This commission was appointed by the mayor at the earnest solicitation of Walter P. Sumner, then Dean of the Episcopal Cathedral in Chicago. The cathedral, on the west side of Chicago, not far from Halsted Street, had become the neighbor to a red light district. Dean Sumner was first enlightened as to the injustices under which prostitutes suffer at the hands of the police when a girl came to complain that a policeman who had run her in had retained a bracelet which belonged to her and which he had no right to keep. A prolonged investigation of the incident revealed a flagrant and untenable situation of regulated vice, and Dean Sumner did not drop the matter until the Chicago Vice Commission, the first in the country, was organized. The final recommendation of this able commission was for a complete abolition of the segregated district. It was followed by Vice Commissions in other cities, the reorganization of the American Federation of Sex Hygiene Association, of which Charles W.

Eliot was chairman, and a widespread effort to abolish regulated vice.

Any probe into the vice conditions of the city made by a grand jury or an efficient public commission uniformly discovered that prostitution was a root source of political corruption. Although laws declaring it illegal had been placed upon the statute books, laws which even the hardiest politician dared not repeal out of respect for public opinion, nevertheless the police, backed by universal cynicism, openly considered the laws too impracticable to be enforced, and not only deliberately decided not to enforce them but actually defined the conditions under which lawbreaking was permitted. This police connivance at prostitution inevitably created a necessity for both graft and blackmail. The graft was easy, because the owner of an illicit business expects to pay for it, and all the politicians—sometimes those at the very top of the city administration—received their share of this illicit fund; in connection with this a system of municipal blackmail was also established, which just escaped legal recognition. Prostitution protected by a thick hedge of secrecy, imperceptibly renewing itself through changing administrations, was the unbreakable bank to which every corrupt politician repaired when in need of funds. The men who considered it a legitimate source of revenue fleeced in a thousand ways the decent taxpayers who refused to acknowledge its existence. In the end, the assertion of the Vice Commission, "If the Police Department of the city did its sworn duty to enforce the laws of the State of Illinois and the ordinances of the City of Chicago, there could be no open houses of prostitution," followed by the insistence that the segregated district be abolished, had its effect, and the recommendations were finally carried out.

This was indeed part of a world-wide movement, largely led by the researches of the Rockefeller Foundation and greatly accelerated by the publication of the report by the Special Body of Experts of the League of Nations on the White Slave Traffic, in 1927. The report not only gave careful facts regarding this great blot on modern civilizations, but it also exposed the futility of state regulation and of the false hopes founded upon compulsory medical examination of prostitutes. The request for such a careful gathering of statistics was made at the first meeting of the League of Nations Commission on Traffic in Women and Children, by Grace Abbott, Chief of the U. S. Children's Bureau, who was sent by the United States government to attend the meetings of the commisison. Miss Abbott not only asked for the facts, but offered to secure in America the funds needed to carry out the searching investigation. Miss Abbott had lived in Hull-House for some years, during which time she had been superintendent of the Immigrants' Protective League, and during four years when the State of Illinois took over the matter of protecting its own immigrants, she had been the state official in charge of the State Immigration Bureau. A concern for the welfare of the immigrant girl had inevitably given her information on the white slave traffic.

The Committee of Experts of the League of Nations in their report had covered Europe and the United States, but had not investigated the Oriental countries. It was a matter of much interest to me, therefore, when in the summer of 1928 I presided at a conference of Pan-Pacific women in Honolulu, to find that the women of the Orient were ready to bear their share in the spreading effort to abolish vice regulated by governmental authorities. Many of the women were conversant with the report and its declaration that the traffic in women and children could never be controlled so long as there were segregated districts ready to receive the victims of the traffickers. A Japanese delegate eagerly united with the rest of the conference in requesting an extension of the League of Nations' investigation to the countries of the Pacific. She gave an account of the segregated district in Tokio, which at the time of the earthquake and great fire had been the scene of a horrible tragedy. The district was barricaded literally with a high wall, with only two gates which

were constantly kept locked in order to prevent the
women, who represented valuable property assets,
from escaping. And because the gates were locked
at the time of the disaster hundreds of women
perished without a chance of saving their lives.
The small W.C.T.U. organization of Japanese
women, although sharing to the full the reluctance
of good women everywhere and especially in the
Orient to be in any way identified with the public
prostitute, arranged an impressive public funeral
for these women, hoping thereby to draw public
attention to the situation and to at least evoke
through the tragedy a public sentiment which
might result in the abolition of the district and
render belated justice to that "most tragic figure
in all history."

The attempt to do justice to the prostitute,
although it may be traced in various parts of the
world, is still so uncertain that it breaks down in
most unexpected places. It is possible to cite a
contemporary instance of this in Chicago; in spite
of the Illinois law that persons suspected of vene-
real disease shall be examined and isolated, it is
only women who are ever brought under the provision of this law and it is they alone whom the
judge sends to a designated hospital for treatment
during a specified length of time. This court procedure inevitably suggests the system of the old
"lock hospital" to which men of course are never
sent although men may have been arrested in the

very same raid with the women and brought into court under the identical charge.

The belief that righteous men and women may treat the prostitute without any regard to just dealing is rooted deep in a superstitious past, and has become a great stumblingblock in the contemporaneous efforts in humanizing justice. There is always one person or one situation which tests advancing moral standards more piercingly than any other.

IV

The third line of the efforts to humanize justice it seems possible to trace through the attempts, successful and unsuccessful, to secure a larger measure of justice for aliens.

Every one who has lived in an immigrant neighborhood must at times share the belief of Maeterlinck that a more robust and simple conception of justice may spring from the people themselves. This belief has a curious confirmation in that many good and simple people, when justice seems to have miscarried, insist that the lawyers and judges had fixed their minds upon the purely legalistic aspects of the case and therefore had failed to discover the equity and justice involved. Such people meekly recognize the imperfection of all human institutions, but they still believe that justice is attainable. "Of course the judge meant to do right, but the lawyers mixed him up." This firm conviction, this unending craving, is perhaps the more remarkable in that justice has no archetype in nature. Love exists in the sub-human species as well as in man, but the demand for justice cannot be copied from any observed thing outside of man, although a child makes his demand for fair dealing surprisingly early.

In a cosmopolitan city like Chicago, traditions and primitive demands of all sorts—some of them perfectly legitimate and indeed inevitable—thrust themselves into the situation and make more difficult the administration of justice. We have, for instance, a constantly increasing number of Mexicans in Chicago. The relations between the United States and the country of their birth have been complicated by the differences in legal tradition between the Latin and the Anglo-Saxon system of jurisprudence, and this inevitably influences many Mexican immigrants in their relation to our courts. I was in Mexico for a few weeks very soon after the establishment of the Labor Government, at which time there had been some friction between Mexico and England and rather prolonged difficulties between Mexico and the United States, some of them both doubtless due to differences in standards. The Mexican government asserts that our Secretary of State, when a difficulty arises between an American citizen and the Mexican government, always insists that the case shall be tried according to the traditions of Anglo-

Saxon law. For instance, one Secretary after another has refused to recognize the Latin tradition which is followed not only in Mexico but in France, Spain and Italy as well, that the subsoil belongs to the state just as it at one time belonged to the crown, and that the state therefore has a right to the oil and ore which come out of the earth. It is the point of view which makes all the difference. The American corporations interested in Mexican oil say that they are developing the resources of a country much in need of capital, that they are building decent houses for the workmen, paying good wages, and generally advancing the standard of living, that the export tax which they pay of thirty cents on every barrel is all that the industry will bear. The Mexican version is to the effect that there is no special advantage to them in that the country's resources of oil are so rapidly being drained away, that the process does not give even a great deal of work to Mexicans. They claim that it takes only about twenty-five men to sink a well and connect the flow with the pipe line, that the oil is thereafter rapidly pumped out of the earth, conveyed in pipes to Tampico directly into the ship which transports it out of the country.

Another point where differences of theory were sharply felt—a source of constant friction—was in the carrying out of the Mexican land policy through an Agrarian Commission which was restoring to each Indian village the communal

land which had been held undistributed during the
three centuries of Spanish occupation. An objec-
tion which we often heard was, that the Indians
would not work for the land owners unless they
were pushed by necessity; that the very fact that
each family could secure its actually needed food
from the village land, might result in an absolute
refusal to work for the landlord and create a serious situation for large estates, where it was already
difficult to secure sufficient labor. On this point,
however, the Labor Government of Mexico was
determined not to repeat the European situation, where a landless proletariat is driven by the
fear of starvation, nor did they wish a colonial policy such as has been pursued in Africa and elsewhere, where the natives are forced to labor under
the guise of payment of taxes. The government
believed that its experiment might prove a valuable solution of a vexed question and indicate how
cordial relations between the Europeanized form
of government and a simple population of so-
called native races might be secured. Of course
it is quite possible that ulterior designs were thus
disguised in altruistic trappings; it is difficult however to prove the charge so often made.

I sat one night at a dinner in Mexico City next
to a man who bore a Spanish title and who told
me of his mother's recent experiences, to prove that
the Labor Government did not really wish to
benefit the Indians, but that their land policy was

designed to secure the votes of an agricultural people for labor policies. He said that his mother, wishing to anticipate the action of the government, presented to each village on her estate the required amount of land, and in order to be certain that all was done properly she requested the Agrarian Commission to survey the land and make out the deeds. A great fiesta followed and all seemed well, but about six weeks later a member of the Commission came to say to the Indians that it had been very kind of the Marchesa to make them this present and that they had thanked her properly at the time of the fiesta, nevertheless, all that had nothing to do with the lands which the government meant to give them, and they proceeded to give each village its requisite amount. I repeated this story next day to a humble member of the Agrarian Commission who came to show us an agricultural school. He replied that he had never seen the land on this particular estate, but he was quite willing to assert "sight unseen" that the land given by the Marchesa had been the worst on the estate, too poor to grow a cactus, to use his own phrase, and that the Labor Government had no intention of trying out their experiment on land such as that.

All such matters are being at least discussed between the United States and Mexico by the present Ambassador to Mexico, and one is encouraged to believe that not only open diplomacy but one

founded upon human understanding is slowly
being inaugurated. It is said that the actions of
nation itself, depends to an enormous extent; but
by public opinion, upon which morality within the
nation itself depends to an enormous extent; but
certainly thousands of humble Mexicans in this
country are unwittingly making a public opinion
which in the end must influence governmental
action and which in the meantime doubtless influences their own attitude toward all the branches
of the government which they encounter in the
United States.

V

Another illustration of the way in which questions of justice affect the formation of public opinion between nations was afforded on a very much
wider scale in the summer of 1927 by the well-
known case in Massachusetts; the trial for murder
of two Italians, Sacco and Vanzetti. To live in an
Italian neighborhood when men of that nationality are suspected of being treated unfairly makes
one realize that fair dealing with the immigrants
who come to this country is of primary importance.
It requires an understanding of their background
and a genuine intellectual effort to obtain the justice which seems just to them as well as that which
seems just to us. The case of Sacco and Vanzetti at
length came to seem, in many parts of the world, an
acid test of our capacity for this type of justice. I

was in Europe the year before their execution, when I was continually interrogated about them, the questions showing a detail of information which only a few people in the United States then possessed. I had been in Paris twenty-five years earlier, serving as a juror for the United States, on Social Economics at the World's Exposition, when the city was full of horror about the Dreyfus case. Many Frenchmen felt that Dreyfus had not had a fair trial, that no one knew whether he was guilty or not, because he had not been tried on the preferred charges but on his racial affiliation. I found that many Europeans felt during that summer of 1926 that the same thing was happening in the United States of America in regard to these two Italians; that their affiliations were so unpopular that the trial did not get down to the actual facts of the case. Evidently once again people all over the world were to be aroused because they believed men were being tried on their religious, political or racial affiliations, which they instinctively realized has been the historic basis of intolerance. Because the trial of Sacco and Vanzetti had been in progress for six years and had thus afforded ample time for discussion, in the summer of 1926 many Europeans were challenging the courts of Massachsuetts as once before they had challenged the courts of France.

Apparently such cases occur from time to time and take shape in men's minds as an epitome of the problem of justice itself. I had no doubt in the summer of 1926 that able defenders would arise in America to defend the two Italians as Zola and other gallant Frenchmen had obtained the release of Dreyfus after he had suffered ten years of punishment although I well knew that the desire for equity between man and man is too often confused with a determination to maintain law and order. I speculated uneasily as to whether our American conception of justice was still too near the frontier type and to the feeling that punishment must be severe in order to preserve the very existence of the community, so that brutality and even the possibility of error became of secondary importance to our early settlers in America.

I was in the midst of these uneasy cogitations in that summer of 1926 when our automobile passed an empty house in Ireland, with one window fearfully pointed out to us as of horrible significance. The house had been occupied by a righteous and stern judge named Lynch who had passed sentence of death upon his own son brought as a criminal before his court. When Judge Lynch realized that the duly accredited officials were unwilling to carry out the death penalty and were hesitating beyond the time that the law allowed, the Judge himself hung the wayward boy "by the neck until he died" from the second story window in his own house. Judge Lynch performed this stern duty with his own judicial hands, because he was anxious that justice should prevail and that no softness should intervene in carrying out a righteous decision. And yet so penetrating was the final verdict of the people, that the name of Lynch has become ineradically associated, not with the stern, uncompromising carrying out of judicial procedure, as might have been anticipated, but with the violence which ignores all legal processes and it is now the accepted designation of the acts of a mob which takes the law into its own hands. It seems on the face of it unfair that the word *lynching* should have sprung from the name of one who so sternly respected the law.

It may have been the grisly story itself which gave me a chill sense of disaster as we drove away from Judge Lynch's house, or I may have been subtly influenced by one of those patches of black which so suddenly overlay the green of Ireland; either the massed shawls of a group of women or a broad line of peat-bricks piled on the edge of a village as if underlining its poverty. I realized with an almost sinister foreboding that this test case in the United States would be tried in a New England court where, ever since the days of Anne Hutchinson, the bog of self-righteousness has so often mired fast the feet of good men.

Did the simple people among whom this first use of the word originated, instinctively understand that self-righteousness is responsible for the most subtle forms of lawlessness; that law and order, when preserved at the expense of just dealing, often defeat the very purposes for which courts were established.

For twelve months after my return in the fall of 1926 popular appeals for clemency for Sacco and Vanzetti were made from all over the world wherever the names of the two men had come to embody a sudden warning that the universal sense of justice was imperiled. I vaguely recalled what a poet had written, that the mass of men are unconsciously impelled in certain crises to act in sheer defense of their most precious spiritual possessions and that they spring to the task as to a trumpet call.

During the summer of 1927 as the date of the execution of Sacco and Vanzetti drew nearer, hundreds of American citizens felt impelled to do all in their power to commute the death sentence to life imprisonment, that at least the case should not be irrevocably closed. People from all over the country and from many parts of the world sent petitions to the governor of Massachusetts to this effect, reminding the governor that the right to commute a sentence and the pardoning power has been vested in the executive as an integral part of our system of jurisprudence and as a recognized safeguard against the miscarriage of justice. And yet these fundamental facts were so ignored, that I was told, for instance, that my own appeal was unconstitutional as well as unpatriotic when I sent an open letter to the chairman of the Foreign Relations of the United States Senate urging him to endorse a similar request to the Massachusetts governor on the ground that to put through the execution in the face of such universal protest might quite easily embarrass our relations with other nations, especially with those of Latin America. The very day that I sent my request there had been a demonstration of twenty-four thousand Italians near Rio in the Argentine. The Senator's reply was so confident that our national judgment was supreme and that all the protests were sheer interference, that there could be no doubt in my mind that he, like the officials in Massachusetts, had grown confused between justice and the machinery of the law; between love of country which would ardently preserve her from committing an injustice, and the orthodox form of patriotism, which unhappily assumes that one's own country is always in the right and the other countries uniformly in the wrong—a sort of national self-righteousness.

It was impossible in the period of depression and heart searching which the tragic outcome of the Sacco and Vanzetti case had induced in so many people, even to derive comfort from the statement that the injustice of nature to the individual sometimes ends by becoming justice for the race. We know that "Nature has time before her; she can wait; her injustice is of her girth. But for us it is too overwhelming, and our days are too

few." Some of us felt that the outcome of the
Sacco and Vanzetti case threw away an opportunity unique in the history of the United States for
demonstrating that we are here attaining a conception of justice broad and fundamental enough
to span the reach of our population and their kinsfolk throughout the world. Is the great idea of
justice which has undergone many transformations
since history began, being passionately challenged
now in the United States by a new generation of
many national origins? Do they instinctively realize that the test is of primary importance, that out
of the very composition of our national life we may
approach a universal type of just dealing which
alone is stable and secure?

The one novel* written about the war which
most nearly approximates an epic, turns upon the
clash between two conceptions of justice. The fate
of a humble Russian who had been condemned to
death by a German court-martial on the Eastern
front becomes an episode of tragic significance
because the men of one nationality are responsible
for just dealing to a man of another nationality
with whom they are at war. While millions of
men were being killed and the fate of nations was
in the balance, the life of this one man is thrown
into relief as a test case of justice between man and
man; it is carried on in the white light of *"specie
eternatatis"* which may break through into mundane

* *The Case of Sergeant Grischa,* by Arnold Zweig.

affairs at any moment whether in time of peace or war. The situation is reduced to a dramatic struggle between two sets of men of the same nationality; those who feel that discipline and the findings of a court must be maintained, and those others who envisage the execution of a wronged enemy as a moral catastrophe. The contest is led on one side by the commander-in-chief who honestly believes that "the state creates justice" and must maintain its own prestige; the protagonist on the other side is a divisional general who holds that nothing in the world can justify a state in setting in motion the mighty machinery of law against the innocent and so destroying the nation's very sense of justice. He regards such destruction as the supreme disaster and the final dishonor.

VI

Does the sense of justice and fair play spring up anew in each generation for the healing of its own ills, and must we learn that this can be depended upon as each generation depends for the care of its young upon the wellsprings of tenderness born anew with the birth of each child? Must our problems be solved in relation to that marvelous longing for juster relations which is not only new in each generation but increasingly more insistent?

Fortunately legal scholars themselves are becoming more and more conscious that law must be regarded as a social instrument. The Yale Law School has begun to coöperate with economists, psychologists and others in the new Institute of Human Relations. The Harvard Law School in order to study the problem of fitting punishment to the criminal rather than to the crime, has founded an Institute of Criminal Law. Most ambitious of all, perhaps, is the new Institute for the Study of Law at Johns Hopkins University, which is not a law school at all in the old sense, for it does not produce practicing lawyers but will engage in projects of fundamental social research which aim to develop coöperation among legal scholars and those working in related fields. It is to be hoped—if it is playing the game to hope in relation to research—that these various experiments will confirm the growing opinion that justice is not obtained by withdrawing the judge from contact with life, as the old wig and gown intimate, but will be achieved in proportion as the judge is cognizant of life; that justice between men as between nations can only be obtained through human understanding and good will.

The most striking institutional expressions of this unending effort were established in 1899 by the opening of two courts, each the first of its kind in the world. The first Juvenile Court was opened in the conviction that the existing court procedure was not fitted to a child's needs; and a court was established at The Hague in Holland dedicated to the conciliation and arbitration of all difficulties arising between nations. These widely separated courts are not so unlike if we take the point of view of mankind's long spiritual struggle to maintain and purify the reign of justice in the world, with the obligation laid upon each generation to find the means by which justice may be extended into new fields.

After the World War, as part of the instrumentalities designed to keep the peace of the world, the World Court, much more juridical than its predecessor and dealing with a larger range of cases, was established at The Hague. It is very impressive to see the court in session and one's hopes incautiously leap forward to the possibility of uniting Latin logic, Slavic idealism, Asiatic quietude and Anglo-Saxon common sense into a World Court with the outcome of a wider conception of justice than any one nation has as yet been able to obtain.

Obviously both of the international courts were attempts to augment the conception of justice itself and to widen its application in response to the demands of a new world consciousness which will in time brook no other conception of justice than that which is world-wide.

CHAPTER XI

The Play Instinct and the Arts

BECAUSE the modern industrial city is so new, we are as yet ignorant of its ultimate reactions upon human life, and we know little of the impressions and even of the scars which this new type of living makes upon that most highly sensitized material, the body and mind of the young at the moment they are most acutely alive to their surroundings. We only know that young people, with their new-born instincts, whether walking in crowded streets or in the open fields, continually test the achievements and shortcomings of the life about them by standards of romance new to them but as old as the world.

Because the youth of Chicago have been brought

343

together from all parts of the world into one cosmopolitan community, in sentimental moments certain lines of Swinburne seem so appropriate that we can almost imagine them chanting together:

> We mix from many lands
> We march from very far
> The light we walk in
> Darkens sun and moon and star.

We realize afresh that it is the business of youth to reaffirm the beauty and joy in the world that such spontaneity may become a source of new vitality, a wellspring of refreshment to a jaded city. It is easy to fail to utilize it, the artists are preoccupied trying to recapture it after the first bloom has escaped them and only occasionally do the educators demonstrate that each child lives not only in an actual environment visible to all, but in enchanted surroundings which may be reproduced by the child himself.

The early School of Education at the University of Chicago, founded by Dr. John Dewey, demonstrated that a child after an historic period had made itself at home in his imagination would wholeheartedly live in it for weeks at a time. He energetically dug, built, wove and cooked, sometimes according to his need in a primitive hut, at other times in a medieval castle surrounded by a moat. But because this fresh imaginative life with its instinct for play is in a sense the mission of art itself we have found at Hull-House that our educational efforts tend constantly toward a training for artistic expression; in a music school, a school of dramatics, classes in rhythm and dancing and the school of the plastic and graphic arts. In the last which we call the Hull-House Art School the children are given great freedom in the use of color and clay and other media through which they may express those images which are perpetually welling up from some inner fountain, and which suggest not only their secret aspirations, but, curiously enough, something of their historic background.

Because Hull-House is in an immigrant district, we have the great advantage that children in the art school are of many races and nationalities and to a surprising degree they are familiar with the backgrounds of culture which their parents represent. The other day in one of our pottery classes where the children were trying historic subjects, the Scandinavian boy made a Viking bowl, the Mexican an Indian hut, the Greek the capital of a Corinthian column, the Italian the dome of St. Peter's. The variety was interesting, but not nearly so significant as the fact that each boy recognized what the other boy had made and called it by name. They were disconcerted only by an Egyptian pylon which a sophisticated elder was modeling, and they excused themselves by saying that they didn't have any Egyptians in the school, but they hoped after a while that one would come. This school gives the children space, time and tools, and is sure that they will find their own way, although of course the teachers help them over difficulties of material and push them toward a clearer expression. There is apparently in each material new suggestions and a new joy in manipulating it, as each child finds a chance to make his own contribution. One of the younger teachers considers it her chief business to discover and remove inhibitions, because she finds that joy is the most important factor in freeing the child's expression, she has apparently discovered with Count Keyserling, that an inhibited artist is of no use in the practical world. Norah Hamilton, the head of our little art school, says that if such artistic children have no early outlet for their gifts they may never find a real place in the world about them and their possible contribution will be lost. She further adds:

The children seem to find in their inner lives a world of color and beauty in which they are perfectly at home. They work with freedom and endless facility, with faith in their own way of seeing, and with faith in hands and material to carry out their vision. They give their best, and take it for granted that what they give is good. They are free from our inhibitions, use their full selves and make use also, perhaps, of an instinctive self. They give the reality as it comes to them but the reality is living and filled with the spirit of play, that "other seeing" that finds the play world as real as the material world "peopled with psychic beings kin to them," as were the hills and streams to the Greeks, the kings of all artists. To sum up the charm of the children's work, they give us a new world seen with new eyes. Perhaps, with the great primitives, they follow nature's very ways, are close to her rhythm; perhaps obey some law inherent in things as they are.

Included in the art school program are talks given with photographic reproductions of the early Italian painters shown to the pupils by Miss Starr when they spend an evening in her bookbindery. She is often impressed by their quick recognition of the message which the picture would convey and by the admiration bestowed by her young visitors upon the ability of the artist "to get it over." Excursions are often arranged to other parts of the city. It is both travel and adventure for the children to visit a museum and they refer to these trips years afterwards as to great events, also the sense of contrast apparently makes them see their own part of the city with a new sense of romance. Sketching classes are held every summer at the Bowen Country Club and almost every member of the school spends at least one week-end there every year. They vie with each other as to which season was found to be the most beautiful and defend certain aspects of light and color with genuine enthusiasm. Most of them also have two weeks vacation there in the summer and recount not only the excursions and sports of country life but tell a great deal about its beauty as well. It may possibly be easier for Italian children to talk openly about such matters because the life of an artist is familiar to them and they know that it is a national asset that thousands of people come to Italy every year to admire the beauty so lavishly found there.

II

The Joseph T. Bowen Country Club consists of seventy-two acres of land overlooking Lake Michigan. It is cut through by transverse ravines filled with wildflowers each spring and with flaming sumacs on their banks in the autumn. The Club was given to Hull-House as a memorial and the donor, Mrs. Bowen, is an enthusiastic gardener who has developed on the coast of Maine one of the most beautiful gardens in America. She has permanently endowed a club gardener so that the place throughout the season may overflow with flowers, fruits and vegetables. From the elderly women who sit in the old-fashioned arbor in the middle of a formal garden, recalling the flowers of long-ago childhoods in many lands and demonstrating once more that color and fragrance have a unique ability to evoke reminiscence, to the city-bred little children who have never seen flowers actually growing and swaying in the moving air and who lower their voices, as if speaking of a sacred matter, to ask whether it looks like this in heaven, the garden is an unending delight. A constant effort is made to cultivate accurate observation, photographs are made of the trees and flowers and the children make blue prints of all the kinds of grasses and weeds they can find, they weave baskets and mats of the indigenous materials, they gather the cherries and the small fruits. The Boys' Camp on the other side of a ravine is in the midst of the tallest and oldest trees. When the boys can be induced to reveal their most intimate impressions of the summer, it is always of the wind in the trees that they tell for it is their first acquaintance with that mysterious murmur. Perhaps the very novelty in these experiences makes both young and old more sensitively alive to the unending charm of the outdoor world, but the year by year continuity is an important factor. Many of the young people have been coming to the club through eighteen years, they remember when the tall trees by the garden gate were little, the summer when we had no raspberries because the rabbits had eaten the bark from the bushes during the winter of incessant snows; all of the natural landmarks which collect about a country house as nowhere else. Every June at least one young couple take a cottage for the period of a honeymoon because the place has become associated with beauty and romance. The Bowen Country Club really illustrates perhaps better than anything else

Hull-House has been able to achieve, the results of the play instinct coming to flower in a sheltered place where beauty and decorum are cherished.

The children who frequent the club, through the intriguing leadership of the superintendent, Thora Lund, have set up standards of conduct which they deem fitting to the place and public opinion tolerates no other. This standard was revealed when I once told a story to a group of Bowen Country Club children. It was met by so unanimous a cry—"She was selfish. She would have known better if she had ever been at the club!" "We would never stand for that at the club!" that I venture to repeat the story which a Hindu had told at the Chicago World's Fair.

It concerns a woman sent to the very bottom of the pit who petitioned the throne in Heaven again and again, that she might be released from her fearful punishment. The story goes that at last a message came down stating that if she could think of one unselfish act and would send up the record of it, that her petition would be taken under consideration.

The woman thought and thought a very long time before she could remember one unselfish act, but she finally recalled that once when she was sitting in her doorway preparing some carrots for dinner, a beggar had come by asking for food and that she had given him a rotten carrot.

It was with some misgiving that she sent up the record of this one act of unselfishness, but after a period for deliberation, she learned that she would be given a chance. A carrot, tied to a string, gradually came lower and lower until it reached the very bottom of the pit. She was told to take hold of it and it was possible that the good deed would pull her up. As she seized hold of the carrot, the string began to wind and she began to rise.

All went well until unfortunately she looked back and saw someone clinging to her feet, someone in turn clinging to his and so on all the way down until a large number of people were being pulled up with her. She was naturally very much alarmed because she knew that the carrot was rotten and she hastily cried out, "This is my carrot! Let go!" As soon as she had uttered these words, of course the carrot broke and they all went down together into the place where selfishness reigns supreme.

The kindly intercourse of good manners, so essential in collective living, finally becomes associated with the charm of the place itself, although it may exhibit the spirit of one of our Hull-House neighbors who loved to describe the beauty of the Bay of Naples. He always concluded with the same fervent remark: "And in Naples, the moon it shines every night!" All his other impressions had become submerged into a magic moon shining upon a glistening sea.

For me personally there is connected with the club, an association with two of my most enduring friendships; with Mary Rozet Smith, with whom I have studied, travelled and lived throughout all the years of Hull-House, and with Louise De Koven Bowen—the most active and ardent of the

Hull-House trustees. The latter has a habit of spending weekends during the spring and autumn months, in a cottage which she has built upon the grounds of the Bowen Country Club and which she constantly invites her friends to share; Miss Smith and myself occupy it not so much in the capacity of guests as of those who are at home— in that definition of a home as a place where they have to take you in.

It may be the withdrawal into the country after a week of haste and uproar, it may be the opportunity to read in leisurely fashion, to invite one's soul and to speak easily of the deeper issues of life and death, but I think that the peculiar charm of the place, the reason it seems to me germane to this chapter upon recreation in relation to the arts, is the sense of being basically at ease which can come only when the play instinct is reduced to relaxation and developed in an understanding atmosphere. Such basic experiences are hard to describe. I recall an early one which I received on my sixth birthday; the day so festive at breakfast was early marred by some childish misdeed and became filled with a heavy sense of guilt which enveloped me hour after hour until bedtime. When in my misery I at last approached my father to ask him if in spite of it all he still loved me, I can even now sense the reassurance which his voice brought, as he replied that of course he would always love me whatever I did, that my

conduct had nothing to do with his affection, although he definitely expressed the hope that we
would have no more such regrettable incidents.
That possession of an unalterable affection which
cannot be alienated, of a place in the universe
which cannot be shaken, is perhaps our first spiritual requirement and one of the most lasting as
it is certainly one of the most fundamental. Something of that has, I hope, been incorporated in the
relation of Hull-House to its neighborhood during the forty years of its existence, when much
of the population has changed but the Settlement has remained. It is certainly at the basis
of the relationships which I am trying to describe.

Both Miss Smith and Mrs. Bowen have been
committed to Hull-House for many years, during
our periods of bungling effort and in our identification with unpopular causes; they have erected
buildings in which experimental activities might
be housed; they have bailed men and women out
of jail who have been the unresisting victims of
public excitement; they have seen to it year after
year that those children surrounded by overwhelming temptations shall be rescued and the environment so far as possible modified that other children
may be protected from the same evils; they have
been ready with modest endowments that adventures such as an early music school and a country
club in contradistinction to a fresh air farm, might

be tried, and best of all, such experiments have always commanded their participation, resulting in that revelation of personality which comes only when the deed is added to the word.

III

Social life and art have always seemed to go best together at Hull-House. This is shown in what has been called the Big Studio, the large room where young people come year after year, partly making their own atmosphere and partly led by Enella Benedict, a teacher at the Art Institute, an early Hull-House resident, who brings books, pictures, reproductions, for them to share. Between them all, there seems to be created an atmosphere in which each can find his own way in art. Even here the medium is varied, for they make batiks in the studio and also use the adjoining room which contains a complete etching outfit.

From the beginnings in this studio a group of professional artists has been developed, four of whom are residents at Hull-House, occupying studios built upon the roofs of our two taller buildings. Two of these artists, who married each other, are now spending two years abroad with the keenest pleasure and profit; another who received a European scholarship at the Art Institute in Chicago, was able, because of his habits of frugal living, to take another man from the studio with him and they even stretched the scholarship into a second year of study which they spent in Spain. This fact caused a much more stirring interest in the studio than the news that one of the older men had received ten thousand dollars for a portrait in New York, and was fast growing famous. An illustration showing that the students felt more at home in the studio than anywhere else was afforded when one of their number returned from the war suffering from shell shock and insisted upon living there day and night for many weeks until he slowly recovered. He slept on a cot which his studio friends installed for him. They brought him food from the coffee house below and heated it upon the gas ring used for batiks. He painted hard and furiously by day and at last slept peacefully at night, gradually readjusting himself to the world outside. It is rather interesting that out of ten of these artists who may be said to have "arrived," at least half of them are Jewish. This may be partly because the Jewish youth seems more persistent in the pursuit of his object and partly because the family are willing to free the time of a gifted young man, as Jewish families, however meager their resources, have for ages supported the Talmud scholar.

The people who seize upon the plastic arts with the most enthusiasm are the Mexicans. A few weeks spent in Mexico one gorgeous spring convinced me that the Mexicans took their art seriously. We saw the enthusiasm on the part of Saens, assistant secretary of Education, of Vasconcelos who was previously secretary, of the school of gifted artists who decorated the vast halls of the educational buildings with scenes from the history of Mexico. The artists always bear in mind the progressive educational theory as they conceive it. They showed us a wall in a boys' school upon which the paintings had been deliberately defaced because the French artists who did them "had violated the canons of the new education" and had "imitated the frivolities of a dead art."

One of the resident artists at Hull-House spends several months of every year in Mexico, and comes back with fresh material and fresh enthusiasm for the possibilities of all their abundant talent. A few of the Mexicans in the neighborhood of Hull-House come from the Indian tribes in which the making of pottery has been traditional. Several of these men are able to support themselves by what they produce in our shops and in a little factory set up in the basement of one of our buildings called the Hull-House Kilns which we hope may fill a definite need in the scheme of the art school. It is not only that the children are under the economic stress and pressure of life more and more as they grow older and that their families ask for promise of some practical returns upon their work, but that the faculty of the art school itself is constantly driven to make plans out of respect for the talent which the school uncovers. They want to give young talent a chance to try itself out, young powers an opportunity to make good while they are young.

Critics of the Cizek School in Vienna and of other attempts to connect the play instinct with forms of art, are always certain to point out that at the period of adolescence when the child becomes self-conscious and actually looks at the world about him his work suffers a collapse, sometimes he refuses to go on with it and often continues only half-heartedly. The reply to such an indictment must be that the educational methods are at fault, that a gradual adaptation should be made to the inner changes which come so gradually to the child. The environment which the child encounters in real life may also have to be modified, but what better clue could be followed in making needed changes in our industries. Certainly the Hull-House Kilns which were started three years ago under the able direction of Mrs. French, the head of the department of Ceramics in the Art Institute, who is also a resident at Hull-House, have been very satisfactory. One of our most gifted young men finds permanent occupation there as foreman. He had earned much more money as a prize fighter with a reputation growing beyond the Italian colony into national fame. He yielded at last to the lure of creative activity, perhaps the most intriguing occupation vouchsafed to mankind.

IV

It is to be hoped that such experiments as are carried on in the art school at Hull-House and in many other places in America, including the advanced public schools, will at last influence the entire system of public education. To give every child in our schools the ability to use his hands with ease and pleasure, not upon the narrow basis of fitting him for factory life as educated clerks have been formerly prepared for the merchants, but in order to retain that power of unfolding human life which is implicit in the play instinct. If it had a natural expression it would normally develop into the art impulse with that power of variation which industry so sadly needs to redeem it from its extreme mechanization. In the minority report on the English Poor Law, all the English speaking world was told that it was a mistake to put young people under eighteen at work which did not have educational content; that England was preparing for herself a new crop of dependents and unemployables. We might add that the immature human creature should not be put into a certain type of monotonous work because society is losing something too valuable by thus prematurely extinguishing that variety and promise and bloom of life which are the unique possession of youth and the basis of the arts.

The United States perhaps more than any other

country in the world can demonstrate what applied science has accomplished for industry through invention of machinery and the utilization of all sorts of unpromising raw material. It would be unfortunate if we should become content with this achievement and oblivious to the fact that the next industrial advance lies in the discovery and education of the workman himself to the end that his mind, his power of variation and his instinct for art may ultimately be reflected in the industrial product. The purchasing public including both consumers and producers—although it is impossible to regard them as two classes if we accept the dictum that the nation is most prosperous in which its producers are at the same time its best consumers—may in time refuse to be surrounded by manufactured objects which do not represent some gleam of intelligence on the part of the men who made them. Hundreds of people have already taken that very short step so far as all decoration and ornament are concerned. Such a change in industry will be but a recognition of the play instinct, of the charm and spontaneity of life which might be reflected in the most prosaic of products. But first industry must be seized upon by the educators who now either avoid it altogether or beg the question by teaching a tool industry, advocated by Ruskin and Morris in their first revolt against the iniquities of the present system.

The result of monotonous factory work is quickly

trial world than many of them had been at fourteen, but were actually less educated and in every
way less fitted to face life. I do not believe that
this state of affairs is more true of England than of
the United States. I have known Italian children
who leave school able to read quite readily in the
third and fourth readers, and who five or six years
afterwards could not read a sentence from a newspaper. After leaving school they had worked in
a factory with other Italians and at home had used
the same tongue, until their hard-earned education
had simply fallen away from them. It was found
that the only things they really remembered were
those which the daily task required them to use—
the subjects which were put into use were not only
remembered but were quite often extended. We
have also discovered that as boys become familiar
with electricity and machinery, understanding
something of the application of modern science to
industry, they are more receptive and eager to
develop their general knowledge, rising occasionally to intellectual interests.

There are many indications that public education is moving in this direction. Public schools
equipped for electrical engineering, aviation, automobile construction and other of the mechanical
arts are filled day after day by young workers who
are in the continuation schools, with attendance
arranged out of their employers' time. The present development is the result of much effort on the

part of many people to secure freedom from too early labor and also the prolongation of education for self-supporting youth. This general integration of child labor regulation and educational requirement has been carried on for years from Hull-House but never more effectively than at the present moment by Mrs. Alfred D. Kohn who is chairman of the Child Labor Committee of the Illinois League of Women Voters.

V

But if the play instinct has been ignored in industry it has also failed to assert itself in large areas of social life where it is sadly needed. After all, a city is made up of an infinitely varying multitude, working their way, through much pain and confusion, toward better social relations and just because men are crowded into hotels, lodging houses and tenements, and constantly jostle each other upon the street, they are often deluded into thinking they have it. In many parts of the city the homes are overfull and small, and the boys are not expected to invite their comrades to them. They therefore initiate a free life of their own in the streets, in the alleys, and upon vacant lots where they inevitably drift into definite groups of congenial spirits. Much of this group life of boys is innocuous and if they have enough outlet for play they keep busy and happy. They may get through an entire summer without difficulty if

ter of warmth and loyalty. Certainly nothing is more forlorn than the boy who has no gang at whose fire of friendship he may warm himself. I recall a boy who used to hang about Hull-House who had long been an outlaw and a solitary because he had once stolen from his own gang, the unforgivable offense which kept him out of all neighborhood groups. In the Art School, however, where he exhibited unusual talent, he obtained a position accorded by the judgment of his peers which gradually restored him to the social order. He acknowledged it himself one day when contemplating his own work he was heard to remark in the language of the movie "from crook to artist."

But this independent gang life which so many city boys lead quite often loses all its instinct for play and they come to conduct a purely predatory existence, each gang more or less against the existing order and always ready to exploit it. A survey of the gangs of Chicago, made by a student in the Department of Sociology of the University of Chicago, divided the city into concentric zones, giving each the predominant type of group life among the boys living there. The portrayal of the loyalty of the gang for its own members was astonishing —a gang loyalty so great that it inhibits the loyalties and affections to the family itself, which we long supposed was the basis of our social order. When as a committee on behalf of the Quakers we went into Germany immediately after the war, we

were told by the probation officers of the Juvenile
Court of Berlin that the long continued starvation
had so broken down family loyalty that the children continually stole from their parents, clothing,
rugs, books, kitchen utensils, whatever was re-
movable. To those of us who know how strong
the sense of family possession is with most children, who talk of "our" house and "our" things,
this seemed one of the shocking manifestations of
war, and yet something similar is going on in all
our great cities. Members of the gang who are
expected to take their turn procuring a "feed"
often have no way of obtaining money except by
stealing from their parents, and many of them
ruthlessly do it. The hideous story comes from
New York of a boy who was killed by the members of his own gang because he turned over to
the landlord thirty-two dollars his mother had sent
to pay for the rent when, according to all gang
ethics, he should have brought it to them. They
meant to teach him a "good lesson" but the torture
went too far and the child died as a consequence.

It is easy to see how such limited and intensified
loyalty develops groups of racketeers and of corrupt politicians; if a man is loyal to his "own fellows" the standards of the world outside do not
touch him. In fact as he successfully defies the
outside world and brings in the loot he rises higher
in gang estimation. I was much startled some
years ago when Hull-House was interested in a

campaign against a corrupt local politician, to be told by a wise man in our ward that such a politician could never be defeated save by a candidate who had had a long experience in a gang. I have since learned to understand what he meant. The leader of a gang of boys gains his prestige largely through his power of obtaining favors for his followers. He discovers the alley in which they may play a game of craps undisturbed because the policeman is willing not to see them; he later finds the gambling and drinking places which are protected by obscure yet powerful influences. It is but a step further when his followers are voters and he an officeholder, to extend the same kind of protection to all the faithful from the operations of any law which may prove to be inconvenient to them. He merely continues on a larger scale to utilize those old human motives—personal affection, desire for favors, fear of ridicule, and loyalty to comrades.

Again the desire for play, for sports fitted to the ages of such boys I believe will be the only agency powerful enough to break into this intensified and unwholesome life. In fact I have seen it thus broken when gangs of boys were finally induced to patronize the public playgrounds of Chicago. When such a gang enters the recreation field the gang leader finds that the special power of manipulation which he has developed, is of no use there. The boy who is admired is not the one who can secure secret favors but the one who can best meet those standards maintained by the athletic director with competition open to all for swimming, running and turning. The boys come to despise and to cover with opprobrium any comrade who wishes to receive special consideration either for himself or his followers. A rude sort of justice which prevails may become the basis for a new citizenship which will in the end overthrow both the gang leader and the corrupt politician.

In the old city-states, such as Athens or Florence, the citizens were held in a common bond and could draw from a fund of similar experiences. The area of government corresponded to the area of acquaintance, or at least to one of memory and filial piety. But in the modern city, and especially the cities in America, solidarity cannot depend upon any of these sanctions, for the state is composed of people brought together from all the nations of the earth. The patriotism of the modern state must be based not upon a consciousness of homogeneity but upon a respect for variation, not upon inherited memory but upon trained imagination. We are told that the imaginative powers are realized most easily in an atmosphere of joy and release, that which we have come to call recreation. This must be held in mind if the city would preserve for its inhabitants the greatest gift in its possession—that which alone justifies the existence of the city—the opportunity for varied and human-

there had a greater sense of participation than the Marionette Club, of which he had been a member for many years. One young woman who began her training at Hull-House as a little child is now a member of the faculty in the Department of Dramatics at Yale University. These achievements as professionals have been in a sense secondary to the fact that the young people as a whole have been able to refine the play instinct into dramatic expression, to realize the pleasure which a devotion to an art entails. I should like to describe these clubs by quoting from an address given by their gifted director, Edith de Nancrede, at the Yale Drama Conference, held in 1927, to those representing at least a few of the three thousand little theaters scattered all over the United States:

One of the interesting facts that Hull-House has brought out in its dramatic work is the almost unique power a dramatic club has of holding a group of people together from childhood, through adolescence and into maturity. The need of some means of making life more interesting and beautiful, the need of something to stimulate the mind and imagination, is peculiarly felt in neighborhoods such as that of Hull-House.

Through such plays as "Mid-Summer Night's Dream," the "Sunken Bell," "Prunella," with their opportunity for beautiful and imaginative settings and lovely incidental music, a real love and appreciation of beauty has been developed. Fortunately there are several artists and musicians among the Hull-House residents and, in the groups themselves, there are young artists and musicians developed by our Music School and our Art School. The dramatic clubs care so much for the beauty of their performances that they spend a tremendous amount of time and energy, and all the money that they take in at their productions, upon costumes, scenery and lighting. As all of the members, including the director, are engaged all day in earning a living, the painting of scenery and experimenting in lighting, as well as all rehearsals, are done at night. And often, just before a play, the work on the stage goes on all night. The result of such devotion is that the Hull-House productions are often quite beautiful to look at, and the music, performed by a quartette trained in the Music School, is lovely to listen to. . . . .

After observing for some twenty-five years its remarkable results in the form of charming and interesting young people, I am fully convinced that there is no force so powerful as that of the drama in awakening and stimulating an interest in intellectual and beautiful things. And to me it has an even greater quality —the power of freeing people from inhibitions and repressions. It seems to me the drama is like Josephine Preston Peabody's "Piper"—always letting things out of cages—and sometimes, as I watch some young, self-conscious creature expanding and growing under the influence of the inspiring or poetic thought he is expressing, the drama seems to me like one of those Eastern magicians, who puts a seed into the earth and immediately before one's eyes, it sends forth roots, branches, leaves, buds, and opens wide a flower. I have seen such miracles, such incredible growth on the Hull-House stage.

The National Federation of Settlements which has been so great a factor in unifying settlement activities throughout the country, has sustained committees on dramatics, on music—the latter has been able to report an astonishing growth in music schools in Philadelphia, New York and in other cities—and one on poetry. The last both encourages children to care for poetry and to write it if they choose. One of the best methods of obtaining the first object is to have the children recite in chorus somewhat in the spirit of the speaking choruses, which John Masefield has so skillfully encouraged in England that hundreds of people, the timbre of whose voices has been carefully selected, can recite together with great beauty. We find the children at Hull-House will fit their rhythm to music or easily chant to a distinct meter. We have had one or two rather heartbreaking experiences with regard to composition. The following verse was written by a little girl whose uncle had been executed for murder. There was no possible way of knowing that the child would select such a theme of which these are the last lines:

> He was doomed to die that night
> Oh, it was a dreadful sight
> They brought him coffee to make it right
> But a shock came and he was dead.

VII

Perhaps I can best illustrate the aims of our music school by quoting from the journal published qaurterly by the National Federation of

Settlements. The review was written by the editor, Albert Kennedy.

The Merman's Bride is a cantata by Eleanor Smith, one of the most finely creative minds in the Hull-House group, a composer of note, and founder and director of the Hull-House Music School. It is naturally a matter of considerable significance to all who are interested in Settlements when a work of art of notable quality comes to birth in a Neighborhood House. An agency such as the Settlement, whose basic purpose is to raise the quality of civilization cannot but thrill when its angel grants it the supreme joy of participating in a creative process. . . . The score of *The Merman's Bride* calls for two pianos, a string quartette, four solo voices, a chorus, actors and dancers to mime the characters of the story. The junior division of the Hull-House Dramatic Department takes the responsibility of the visual presentation upon the stage. . . .

The pupils of the Music School are peculiarly fortunate in being permitted to participate in bringing so distinguished a composition to performance. There is an enlargement that comes with being involved in a creative process. Possibly the cantata was conceived through some vital interplay between the children of the school and their director. One feels both in the story and in the choruses something of the actual life of these girls who sing and play. Quite obviously its melodies had already become part of their mental and emotional heritage, and as the years go by they will recall the birth of the work as one of the choicest experiences of their lives. Of all the gifts that the creator, the artist and the teacher can give to youth, surely none is so precious as this, that the pupil is

the twenty-fifth anniversary of the opening of Hull-House in September, 1914, only a few weeks after the beginning of the World War, it seemed impossible to arrange for an occasion of rejoicing at such a moment. We decided, however, to record the ending of our first quarter of a century by publishing five Hull-House songs composed by the head of the Music School. The four songs written in response to public efforts were on the protection of sweatshop workers, the abolition of child labor, the relief of the anthracite coal miners during a great strike, and the movement for granting votes to women. The fifth song set to a poem of Matthew Arnold's was really a prayer to be saved from the eternal question as to whether in any real sense the world is governed in the interest of righteousness. It voices the doubt which so inevitably dogs the footsteps of all those who venture into the jungle of social wretchedness. Because old-fashioned songs, with the exception of those of religion and patriotism, chiefly expressed the essentially individualistic emotions of love, hope or melancholy, it is perhaps all the more imperative that socialized emotions should also find musical expression, if the manifold movements of our contemporaries are to have the inspiration and solace they so obviously need. We believed that all the songs in this collection fulfilled the highest mission in music, first in giving expression to the type of emotional experience which quickly tends to get

beyond words, and second in affording an escape
from the unnecessary disorder of actual life, into
the wider region of the spirit which, under the
laws of a great art, may be filled with an austere
beauty and peace.

VIII

The release function of art, the offering of an
escape from the monotony of daily living is doubtless provided most widely by the movie and its new
child the talkie. Whether the audience in a movie
house is composed of adults or children, there is
no doubt that they all come with a simple desire
to be amused or a willingness to be instructed if
done entertainingly. The fact that a tired man has
to be jerked away from his preoccupation rather
violently may account for the popularity of the
detective and murder plays. They seem as innocent as any other form of puzzle although they
doubtless tend to a view of crime which is at once
romantic and sordid, losing sight of the human
and social reactions and abstracting all moral
judgments. Interest centers on the cleverness of
the two parties to the game, the criminal and the
detective and he wins who "gets away with it."
The exception to the desire for pure entertainment
is afforded by the girls who frankly announce that
some films are valuable in showing them how to
secure a husband and that other films are no good
for that purpose. It is also said that a certain sort

of young man tests a girl's resistance by what she will stand for in a movie, and that he boasts that it is possible, by a continuous selection of movies, to undermine a girl's standards, a new type of seduction as it were, as if the moving picture films still exhibited traces of their furtive origin in the peep shows.

But allowing for these disabilities and many others which could readily be found there is no doubt that the function of release in neighborhoods such as ours, is marvelously performed by the movies. It is no small achievement that millions of men, women and children with no hope for an opportunity for travel, are still easily familiar with ships on wide seas, with a moon shining on snow-capped mountains, with the rice fields of China, and the temples in India and Egypt. To have made thousands of immigrants familiar with the life of the wild west is to give them the background for at least one aspect in our national development. One may safely assume that certain standard pictures will arise in the minds of the simplest audience when given subjects are discussed.

From my own experience I should say that one of the most beneficent features of the movie is the recreation and release it offers to old people. I recall an old Scotchwoman whose declining years were quite made over by the movies. She lived in an apartment house on Halsted Street, whose lower floor of two stores had been turned into a moving

picture house. By using the back stairs she did not
need to go out of doors and the kind proprietor
saved her a seat night after night so near to her
point of entrance that she could reach it unob-
served and, therefore, she "never had to dress for
the show." As she sat there in the dark her poverty, her deafness and all her other disabilities
slipped from her and she was transported to one
absorbing scene after another. At first she saved
out Wednesday evenings for prayer meeting, but
as she had the genuine excuse of the difficulty of
walking three blocks with a lame knee, she gradually gave that up, and for a modest lump sum was
entitled to the first performance during six nights
a week, for her Presbyterianism held out against
Sunday night until the very end. Her old eyes
would shine with the light of youth as she told us
of yet another wonderful experience in this world
of ours which she had never had a chance to
explore until she was about to leave it.

It is impossible to attend international meetings
of any sort without encountering discussion upon
motion pictures, their influence upon international
opinion, and upon the estimate accorded by one
nation to another. In a congress of Pan-Pacific
women, I heard an Australian delegate tell of a
governmental investigation into the cinema situation, especially as to how far the film portrayal of
Western civilization affected the attitude of the
village population toward the mother country; in

India, a similar investigation had been made of the films exhibited there, seventy per cent of which were manufactured in America. The Pan-Pacific women passed a resolution which was sent to various producers, begging them to send representations of the better type of Western life and not so often of the baser. Certainly we all recall seeing cinemas in foreign countries which had little to do with the higher values of life. "Chicago, oh, yes; that is where they pursue the thief over the tops of the roofs," was said to me in Tokio. At the moment, the Japanese newspapers were full of what they termed a new stage in the "westernization" of Japan. The criminal element in Japan was, according to their news reports, copying the West in its methodology and the police were greatly worried over the change in tactics of the lawless element with which they had to deal. They credited these marked changes in violence to the criminal procedure of Chicago and other Western metropolitan centers, as presented by the "cultural medium" of the movies.

A sponsoring committee is being organized, with headquarters in New York, for "A Proposed Study of the Influence of Motion Pictures on International Relations, especially as regards the Attitudes set up in Foreign Lands towards Americans and America." It is impossible to anticipate the report, but that a committee of responsible people should be committed to such an arduous undertaking is in itself a testimony of the gravity of the situation.

This sordid condition may have come about because so-called recreation has been allowed to get too far away from art expression which while universal in its interests still imposes long-established restraints upon a portrayal of the individual experience, connecting it in some subtle fashion with those permanent experiences forming the basis of our human heritage.

I recall that H. G. Wells once contended that mankind is developing a genuine pleasure in co-operation and is evincing a new craving for that sort of associative effort which transcends personal motives. He believes that we can in time count upon this new factor in human affairs as we have already learned to depend upon intellectual curiosity which also only gradually became disinterested. Doubtless our scientific advance depends more upon disinterested intellectual curiosity than upon any other human trait but we may be faced at this moment with an opportunity to so revitalize our own experiences that we may score as never before in the very Art of Living itself. We may drink from a fountain into which are flowing fresh waters from remote mountain ranges which only the artists could have discovered and made part of our familiar world.

CHAPTER XII

EDUCATION BY THE CURRENT EVENT

THE settlements early founded their educational theories upon a conviction that in every social grade and class in the whole circle of genuine occupations there are mature men and women of moral purpose and specialized knowledge, who because they have become efficient unto life, may contribute an enrichment to the pattern of human culture. We knew that much of this possible enrichment was lost because he who would incorporate these experiences into the common heritage must constantly depend upon fresh knowledge and must further be equipped with a wide and familiar acquaintance with the human spirit and its productions. The difficulties involved would be almost insurmountable but that life has a curious trick of suddenly regarding as a living moral issue, vital and unappeasable, some old outworn theme which has been kicked about for years as mere controversial material. The newly moralized issue, almost as if by accident, suddenly takes fire and sets whole communities in a blaze, lighting up human relationships and public duty with new meaning. The event suddenly transforms abstract social idealism into violent political demands, entangling itself with the widest human aspiration.

When that blaze actually starts, when the theme is heated, molten as it were with human passion and desire, the settlement can best use it in its unending effort to make culture and the issue of things go together. From time to time during the last twenty years, when such a blaze did start it seemed for the moment that the peculiar aspect of the world which marks each age for what it is— the summary of its experiences, knowledge and affections, in which are found the very roots of its social existence was fused into a glowing whole. At such a moment, it seemed possible to educate the entire community by a wonderful unification of effort and if the community had been able to command open discussion and a full expression of honest opinion the educational opportunity would have been incomparable.

II

'As an example of sudden interest, resulting in widespread education upon a given theme, the trial at Dayton, Tennessee, upon the general subject of the theory of evolution, forms a striking example.

I had been in England the summer of the trial and had been so often challenged as to our situation in contrast to theirs, because Huxley and Dean Wace presided over by Bishop Wilberforce had publicly discussed the so-called conflict between science and religion in an atmosphere of scholarly tolerance. I had tried to point out that the United States could doubtless at any moment stage a debate between a polished churchman and a kindly scientist, but that such a debate would leave the situation very much where it was before; that what made the Tennessee incident so significant was the fact that legislative action had been taken against the teaching of the theory of evolution in tax-supported schools, by people who had a chance to express their actual desires through their government representatives. I was quite sure that Englishmen could be found in remote quarters of the British Isles who believed exactly what these Tennessee mountaineers believed in regard to the acts of creation; thousands of them had received their education, as had these Americans, through those who had expounded the

"Book" as a sole and abiding authority. Such men in England were as totally untouched by scholarly debates as were the Tennessee mountaineers; there was this difference, however, that the latter found self-expression through the processes of local government and eagerly determined what their children should be taught upon the subject that they regarded as the most important in the world.

During the trial the situation was so sharply defined that it brought before the entire country a public discussion of fundamentalism versus evolution. That such a situation arose was in one sense a demonstration of our democratic purpose, which is, after all, an attempt at self-expression for each man. Democracy believes that the man at the bottom may realize his aim only through an unfolding of his own being, and that he must have an efficacious share in the regulation of his own life. While there was no doubt that the overwhelming public opinion concerning the Tennessee trial was on the side of liberality both in politics and religion, the group of so-called narrow-minded men had made their own contribution to our national education. In the first place, they had asserted the actuality of religion. It is always difficult to convince youth that reality reaches upward as well as outward, and that the higher planes of life contain anything but chilly sentiments. The educator dealing with religious topics often finds that young people receive his statements with polite attention, but when it comes to action, they who are fretting with impatience to throw themselves into the stream of life and to become a part of its fast-flowing current, carefully imitate the really desirable world inhabited by successful men of affairs. But suddenly there came from a group of remote mountaineers a demonstration of a vivid and sustained interest in matters of religion, resulting in a sharp clash of doctrine between themselves and thousands of our fellow citizens, who all hung upon the issues of the trial with avid interest.

It was at times almost comic to hear the "hard-boiled" city youth in his bewilderment talk about the situation. In the first place, modern economics had taught him—or he thought that it had—that a man was abjectly dependent upon the material world about him and must succumb to the iron clamp which industry imposes upon life; moreover, the youth himself gravely asserted that man's very freedom, morality and progress is determined by the material conditions which surround him and he had bodily taken over this theory into ethics and philosophy. He quoted those students of the social order who in what they considered the scientific spirit had collected and arranged data, to demonstrate the sole reaction of economic forces upon human life. These young people had for the most part lightly disregarded all teleological considerations, as they had long before renounced the theological explanations of a final cause. And yet many of them were secretly glad of this opportunity for discussion with old Jewish fathers who had never ceased to attest to the life of the spirit and who on their side caught their first glimpse in those sons hotly defending the theory of evolution, of the same zeal which they and their fathers had expended upon religion. These same young men so devoted to economic determinism as a theory of life had been already somewhat disconcerted by a recent movement in psychiatry with the emphasis upon the emotional and subconscious life versus the exclusive response to environmental stimuli. But if they were startled they were also much interested in this ardent inner life which was apparently to be found among so many different types of people who were everywhere responding to the blaze of interest started in Tennessee.

The repercussions of the trial were the more interesting because the incident brought into the circle of their discussion a large number of people who had hitherto been quite outside their zone of interest. These remote farmers were isolated, save on the occasional Sundays when a circuit rider came to preach, by their discouraging occupation of extracting a living from a rock-bound soil. Nothing could have been further from the experiences and mental processes of the intelligentsia of a cosmopolitan city than these mountaineers, nothing more diverse than the two methods of approach to the time-old question of the origin of

nearly approach international usage. The fact that in many European nations the socialists were among the major political parties, that a "Labor" Party had come to office in England was in itself an education in the use of words as they are current throughout civilization. Perhaps more important still the man of affairs began to contrast such attempts at political control of industrial situations with the associative business control which has been worked out in the United States.

There had never developed in our American cities, on the surface at any rate, either an adequate economic motive for substantial change deliberately undertaken as a conscious policy nor the personal elements for a new party to advocate such changes, not at least with sufficient influence to materially modify the situation. This is true in spite of the affection poured out upon Eugene Debs, and in spite of the great respect commanded by the abilities and character of Norman Thomas. So nearly as I was able to formulate it from the Chicago situation, the United States was making an experiment of its own, largely unconsciously and to a great extent through the empirical education of its business men. It is still trying to develope on the existing political and economic situation in general, an industrial system which will produce through scientific discovery and skillful organization, a maximum of general welfare in which the workers shall share. The employers hope to eliminate all avoidable waste of labor, of material and of processes and to develop to the utmost points the efficiency of personnel and machines. It has further tried to make the workers "contented" by giving them a share in profits and a stake in industry by holding stock, on one hand, and on the other by giving them a voice in the management and a sense of being a coöperating part of the whole organization; creating such conditions as would awaken the workingmen's interest and make them more participative in the job; one could also mention the extensive health schemes with their periodic examinations. The earliest extension of the regular summer vacation to "the man at the bench"—to the industrial worker in addition to the office force and the salesman—was made in Chicago by the International Harvester Company. Dr. James A. Britton, a long-time resident at Hull-House, was then in charge of the medical service in their Chicago plants and he is at present the medical director of all their plants throughout the United States. In his efforts to reduce tuberculosis and other diseases superinduced by fatigue, he was convinced of the necesisty for regular periods of vacation and the response of the company to this conviction set up a milestone in the long effort for bettering health conditions for industrial workers.

His wife, Gertrude Howe Britton, who was the superintendent of the largest dispensary of the city and is at present executive of the Society for the Prevention of Heart Disease, has constantly pressed upon employers a sense of responsibility for the continuing health of their employees, even when such employers had no medical service of their own. What she has been able to do in the way of placing both men and women whose hearts require special care is very impressive. In time it may be demonstrated that the workingmen's fear of health inspection because it would afford still another opportunity to eliminate the handicapped is unfounded. It should in reality conserve places for such men, who without this scientific supervision, would be thrown out of industry.

This American effort to combine industrial and commercial activities that shall operate by consent, is an alternative to the strong-arm control by employers or the constant struggle between organized capital and organized labor with the result in some trades of trade-union tyranny, and in others of employers' tyranny, in either case accompanied by conflict and instability. This development of a system resting on individualism, competition and private profits, has its weaknesses and ugly sides, visible even to those who accept it in principle, but it appears likely to be the substance of the next chapter in our economic history.

There is nothing in this apparently which is inconsistent with a concomitant development in the socialization of large economic areas; certain cities will continue to standardize and unify existing public utilities through the municipalization of electric systems and the Federal government will doubtless undertake other large inter-state activities like Boulder Dam. It seems reasonable to look forward to a system in which a corps of public agents carrying on business for the benefit of the community, will be surrounded or interpenetrated by privately run economic activities. If the latter can be controlled when specifically dangerous or anti-social, the experiment will be valuable. This condition of things certainly at present tends to provide (a) for various psychological types of human beings and for the very wide varieties of ways in which different persons function best; and (b) for a possibility of progress and change, with comparison and criticism to serve as a solvent for the tendencies to inertia said to be inherent in bureaucratic organization.

It would seem obvious that the most important condition for the peaceful and fruitful development of the world would be at the lowest, a theory of live and let live between countries organized on different economic systems. If the Soviet Republics are to foment revolution and unrest in countries where the basis of communism does not exist, and if countries organized by private business are determined to keep Russia outside the comity of nations, it is clear that the two economic systems will never learn much from one another.

very curious that the conversatives are always
afraid of change and persistently fail to realize
that the greatest dangers in the existing state of
affairs are those which arise from inadaptability.
Many difficulties come from the simple failure of
our ideas and conventions, not to mention our prejudices, to keep up with the pace of material
change. Our environment moves much faster than
we do. If we would keep the world contemporaneous, we must hasten to mold the plastic material of life into our own current image. It is hard
to recruit people to render such service from the
Right, they come more easily from the Left, and
yet it might be possible to persuade the type of
man whose abilities are now involved in creating
a great business that there are still larger undertakings which might profitably engage his
energies. Perhaps something of this is already
coming to pass through the participation of American business men in the Reparations Commission
and in the international banking situation. It is
possible that owing to the rapid changes in business administration more than anywhere else, the
flow of personal experience comes to pause at
nodal points where a man first grows vividly
aware of the whole situation as calling for new adjustments. The course of circumstances has outstripped his capacity for those offhand and instinctive responses which up to that moment had
kept him unshattered in a world of change.

The tremendous flux of business in relation to one set of inventions was dramatically portrayed at a birthday party to Thomas Edison given in the autumn of 1929 by Henry Ford. That which seemed most significant to me as a humble guest was the enormous variety of transformations which the inventions, directly or indirectly, had brought about. This was dramatized by the presence of officials of companies and of mergers of companies, in transportation, in telephone and television communication, in moving pictures and radios. It was all made the more graphic because Mr. Ford had carefully reproduced the baggage car in which Edison's first boyish experiments were made and from which he and his apparatus had been ejected by an irate conductor. Mr. Ford had also carefully assembled the actual long wooden shop with its entire contents in which Edison had carried forward and consummated the invention of electric light. When the venerable guest carefully repeated the final tests which he had made just fifty years earlier and lifted up the freshly created light in the presence of the President of the United States and other distinguished men, all trained in technological processes, it was as if a veritable play had been staged with the actual miracle reproduced.

I have been accustomed to meet former Hull-House residents in economic congresses and international gatherings but I also found them at Mr.

Ford's party. Their presence reminded me of a conversation I had long ago held with the head of an electrical factory near Hull-House. The fine old man sitting before the hickory log fire in his office, which was always burning there if the weather offered any possible excuse for it, said to me: "Several of our most promising young men are living at Hull-House and it is a good place for them. Let them see all they can of all kinds of people and of their requirements. It would be the best possible preparation in this business of electricity which is pushing out so rapidly into so many new fields in response to the incredible variety of human needs." How much had the varied business concerns represented at Mr. Ford's party depended not only upon a comprenhensive type of organization and upon the prompt utilization of new inventions but also upon an understanding of the growth and change implicit in the very stuff with which they were dealing and in its power to evoke as well as to supply a rising standard of living. This business adaptability represented by so many men at the Edison birthday party had of course extended into international fields, the most obvious was the manufacturing of European films and the definition of wave-lengths designed for international radio use. It was interesting to see the expressions on the faces of the banqueters when the radio message Einstein was sending from Berlin, halted and failed. The faces of the radio men reproduced exactly the expression of a mother with her face turned toward the stage upon which her child falteringly recites a poem—both disappointment and chagrin are there but unable to dim the overbearing maternal affection.

The Edison birthday party itself was broadcast by every possible device and afforded an illustration of education by the current event indefinitely multiplied in its carrying power by cinemas and radios. Possibly the enormous extension of the use of both of them in the United States, is part of our national reaction to the educational process arising from things as they are.

A very striking example of business economics spreading out internationally was afforded by the host at the Edison party. It was perhaps another example of Ford adaptability that he was then arranging for a report upon the purchasing power of the wages paid by his plant in Ireland that he might compare them with the wages in Detroit.

At that very moment the President of the General Electric Company who I am happy to claim had been for several years a resident at Hull-House, was preparing to announce an unemployment plan designed to make funds available for such of the company's 75,000 employees as may be forced into idleness in time of business depression. This was coupled with an ingenious plan for the stabilization of business to the end that unemployment should be reduced to a minimum. Because the company is international in its organization the plan has been declared by an expert to be "of world-wide significance and to embody a piece of industrial statesmanship of the first order." I recalled the General Electric plants we had visited in China and Japan and saw the workers of those countries, so long regarded as mere labor power, lifted into the regions where a standard of living became a matter of world-wide concern.

IV

Another instance of education through the discussion of current social developments, took place in regard to the problem of race relations when the industrial needs of war-time and the immigration restriction following the war, resulted in a great increase of Negroes in the urban populations throughout the country. This was brought to a head in Chicago as in many other places by the question of housing, when real estate values became confused as always with the subject of segregation. Whatever may be the practical solution it is still true that a complete segregation of the Negro in definite parts of the city, tends in itself to put him outside the immediate action of that imperceptible but powerful social control which influences the rest of the population. Those inherited resources of civilization which are embodied in custom and kindly intercourse, make more for social restraint than does legal enactment itself.

One could easily illustrate this lack of inherited control by comparing the experience of a group of colored girls with those of a group representing the daughters of Italian immigrants or of any other South European peoples. The Italian girls very much enjoy the novelty of factory work, the opportunity to earn money and to dress as Americans do, but only very gradually do they obtain freedom in the direction of their own social affairs. Italian fathers consider it a point of honor that their daughters shall not be alone upon the street after dark, and only slowly modify their social traditions. The fathers of colored girls, on the other hand, are quite without those traditions, and fail to give their daughters the resulting protection. If colored girls yield more easily to the temptations of a city than the Italian girls do, who shall say how far the lack of social restraint is responsible for it? The Italian parents represent the social traditions which have been worked out during centuries and although such customs often become a deterrent to progress through the very bigotry of their adherents, nevertheless it is largely through a modification of these customs and manners that alien groups are assimilated into American life. The civilizations in Africa are even older than those in Italy and naturally tribal life everywhere has its own traditions and taboos which control the relations between the sexes and between parents and children. But of course these were broken up during the period of chattel slavery for very seldom were family ties permitted to stand in the way of profitable slave sales. It was inevitable that the traditions were lost and that customs had to be built up anew. It gives an American community less justification for withholding from a colony of colored people those restraints and customs which can only be communicated through social understanding. Another result of race antagonism is the readiness to irritation which inevitably results when one race is forced to demand as a right from the other those things which should be accorded as a courtesy. Every chance meeting between representatives of the two races is easily characterized either by insolence or arrogance. To the friction of city life and the complications of modern intercourse is added this primitive race animosity.

Happily in the midst of this current event discussion, there came to Chicago a distinguished Negro singer, various plays concerning colored people which portrayed something of that inner life upon which the kinship of races is founded and the Race Relations Committee of the Chicago Woman's Club arranged for a week of exhibits at the Art Institute and for recitals and lectures by well-known artists, poets and scholars. We have no exact knowledge of what has been and is being lost by the denial of free expression on the part of the Negro, it is difficult even to estimate it. One can easily suggest the sense of humor, unique and spontaneous, so different from the wit of the Yankee or the inimitable story telling prized in the South; the natural use of rhythm and onomatopœia which is now so often travestied in the grotesqueness of long words: the use of varied colors which makes it natural perhaps that the only scientific study made in America of the use of common clay as coloring material in the building of simple houses should have been done by a Negro so that we may hope some day to rival the pinks, yellows and blues of those European houses which afford the traveler such perpetual joy.

There is one exception to this lack of recognition, in the admiration of those melodies which we have learned to call the only American folksongs and which have become the basis of the Negroes' contribution to American music. Perhaps because an oppressed people have always been sustained by their dreams the spirituals became the support of their failing spirits. It may be that the wish-fulfillment was too slowly transferred to actual life but certainly an ever-increasing respect is coming from the Negroes' own achievements in the arts. Through their plays they have found the stimulus for conduct in the very field where it was possible to make the initial step toward social efficiency. It may be significant that the curtain falls on an advanced play like "Porgy" while the Negroes of Catfish Row are singing, "I'm on my way."

But even though fine demonstrations have been made by smaller groups of cultivated Negroes, we cannot truthfully say, however much we should like to do so, that recognition lies with the colored man himself and that the worthy will be worthily received. To make even the existing degree of recognition more general requires first of all a modicum of leisure and freedom from grinding poverty. An investigation made in 1929 by the Woman's Bureau of the Department of Labor gives an analysis of *Colored Women in Industry* from studies made in fifteen states. Their earnings were found to be far below the earnings of most white women, although they too must somehow meet the expenses of food, shelter and clothing. A great American industrialist had said, almost at the moment of the publication of the report, "American industry must for the future be based not on a living wage alone, nor on a saving wage, but on a cultural wage." No one needs the benefit of this dictum more than the ambitious Negro.

Because we are no longer stirred as the Abolitionists were, to remove fetters, to prevent cruelty, to lead the humblest to the banquet of civilization, we have allowed ourselves to become indifferent to

the gravest situation in our American life. The
abolitionists grappled with an evil intrenched
since the beginning of recorded history and it
seems at moments that we are not even preserving
what was so hardly won. To continually suspect,
suppress or fear any large group in a community
must finally result in a loss of enthusiasm for that
type of government which gives free play to the
self-development of a majority of its citizens. It
means an enormous loss of capacity to the nation
when great ranges of human life are hedged about
with antagonism. We forget that whatever is
spontaneous in a people, in an individual, a class
or a nation, is always a source of life.

In the world-wide effort to relieve the colored
races from the odium and discrimination which
white races have placed upon them, no man living
on the planet today has done more than has Ma-
hatma Gandhi, first in South Africa in the struggle
for civil rights against the Transvaal Government,
which absorbed his energy for almost twenty years,
and later in the undertaking, the most difficult of
all, directed against customs intrenched in the religious traditions of India, to free the fifty million
untouchables or pariahs, who are subject to many
harsh rules of segregation. While the differences
of race between the Brahmans and Pariahs is not
the sole basis of the insupportable division between them, the situation is essentially the same as
that which faces any effort to break down barriers

of race or caste. Gandhi's most striking success in his protest against untouchability was the opening of the roads, which because they passed near the temples were forbidden to the Pariahs. His followers faced a cordon of police for twelve hours every day during a year and four months before the orthodox Brahmans yielded. Such devotion opened to the untouchables not only that one forbidden road but all the roads that had been forbidden to them in southern India and gave the doctrine of untouchability its severest blow. Such a long and courageous effort may indicate that only sustained moral energy will be able to break through long-established restrictions. Perhaps it is only protests such as these which could offset those protests made in Paris restaurants and elsewhere by Americans whose influence it is said is gradually breaking down the traditional Latin attitude toward race equality. It looks at moments as if we should be late in the movement to abolish race discrimination as we were very late in the abolition of slavery. We were more than thirty years behind England who abolished her colonial slavery in 1832.

We were all very grateful when the Inquiry undertook the study of race relations not by employing a group of experts but by helping people to study effectively their own experiences and desires, although all they may have known about their desire for study was an uneasy feeling on their part that friction was gradually developing between white and colored sections of the community and that something ought to be done about it. The cause of the reported friction may be primarily due to industrial competition or to a housing shortage, or again to the machinations of a small minority of trouble-makers. In any case, what is needed is a technique for helping people to find the sore spot and to secure a quick and effective diagnosis."

The Inquiry through its commission on Race Relations has endeavored to find the causes of inter-racial friction in economic competition by interesting groups in different centers to bring to light those factors that make for racial antagonism —whether these are found in the policies of the industries themselves, in the attitudes of their workers or in the traditional racial experiences of the whole community. The committee has discovered that problems of race relations may arise in situations where a group of people regard themselves, or are regarded by others, as racially homogeneous, even where such an assumption does not correspond to scientific reality. Merely to inform people that such and such a group conflict is based upon an ethnological misunderstanding, will not do away either with the conflict or its emotional associations in the minds of those implicated. The entire race situation demonstrates once more that mere information is not enough and that the various research bodies need to be constantly supplemented.

V

This was something we learned in the early days of Hull-House. We used to say that the settlement had a distinct place in the educational field and we were even bold enough to compare ourselves with universities and colleges. It was the business of the universities, we said, to carry on research, they were committed to an unwearying effort to reduce the black region of ignorance by bringing to light that which would increase the sum total of human knowledge. It was the business of the colleges, broadly speaking, to hand down the knowledge that had thus been accumulated and if they kindled an ardor for truth, each succeeding generation would add to the building of civilization. It was the business of the settlements to do something unlike either of these things. It was the function of the settlements to bring into the circle of knowledge and fuller life, men and women who might otherwise be left outside. Some of these men and women were outside simply because of their ignorance, some of them because they led lives of hard work that narrowed their interests, and others because they were unaware of the possibilities of life and needed a friendly touch to awaken them. The colleges and universities had made a little inner circle of illuminated space beyond which there stretched a region of darkness, and it was the duty of the settlements to draw into the light those who were out of it. It seemed to us that our mission was just as important as that of either the university or the college.

It is easy for young settlements, as it is for all youth, to be boastful. It is easy to say what you are going to do before you have had a chance to try. Our achievement was halting but I still think there was something fine in that youthful statement, and that our contention was well-founded that the man who breaks new soil and makes it ready for the seed, may be quite as useful as the sower himself or even the triumphant harvester. We came rather slowly to the conviction that this could best be done through the use of the current event.

VI

During its first two decades, Hull-House with other American settlements, issued various studies and fact-finding analyses of the city areas with which they were most familiar. The settlements had antedated by three years the first sociological departments in the universities and by ten years the establishment of the first Foundations so that in a sense we were the actual pioneers in field research. We based the value of our efforts not upon any special training, but upon the old belief that he who lives near the life of the poor, he who knows the devastating effects of disease and vice, has at least an unrivaled opportunity to make a genuine contribution to their understanding.

We used to say that it would be easy to throw away that opportunity, either because we shirked intellectual effort, because we lacked courage or because we failed to see our obligations.

These early efforts of the settlements in research, gradually made for a cordial coöperation between the social workers and the university men. The School of Civics and Philanthropy founded by Graham Taylor of the Chicago Commons, with which Julia Lathrop of Hull-House was early associated, after a useful career of twenty years, was taken over by the University of Chicago, and has developed into a graduate school of "Social Service Administration," of which the dean, Edith Abbott, and Sophanisba Breckinridge, long-time residents of Hull-House, are the executives; two other former residents of Hull-House are identified with the studies in social and family welfare carried on at the Northwestern University where Professor Arthur Todd is head of the department in which William F. Bryon is also teaching.

The early companionship between the settlements and the universities has been described by Charles Beard "as exerting beyond all question a direct and immediate influence on American thinking about industrial questions, and on the course of social practice." It was partly due to the custom of the early settlements—in Chicago at least this was true of the Chicago Commons and Hull-House—of giving the radicals in the city an opportunity to debate upon a free floor, believing that no one can be really useful in the long and delicate task of social amelioration unless he knows the changes being urged by various bodies of people for a world which they honestly believe to be upon the brink of destruction. The newspapers tended to judge these men as disturbers of the peace and for a long time they unintelligently insisted that because the settlements promoted free discussion, they therefore endorsed what everybody said. They little realized that had we endorsed all these conflicting beliefs we should have been burst asunder as was the chameleon placed upon a piece of plaid.

In one sense it was easier to be patient with the radicals during the first two decades than to prove the thesis which emerged in the third decade of our existence as a sort of settlement creed that the processes of social amelioration are of necessity the results of gradual modification. We learned to act upon a belief that the hoary abominations of society can only be done away with through the "steady effort to accumulate facts and exalt the human will." But because such an undertaking requires the coöperation of many people and because with the best will in the world it is impossible to get the interest of the entire community centered upon any given theme, we gradually discovered that the use of the current event is valuable beyond all other methods of education. In time we came to define a settlement as an institution attempting to learn from life itself in which undertaking we did not hesitate to admit that we encountered many difficulties and failures. But this effort to interpret the contemporaneous situation and to make it usable demanded an ever-widening public who should have a sympathetic understanding of those social problems which are of such moment to all of us. To allow a large number of persons to remain outside the circle of those interests because they have not been given a sense of participation would at last not only cripple our national life but limit our human possibilities.

We had discovered the use of a genuine interest in life itself by accident, in the early days of Hull-House, in such a simple matter as teaching English to our foreign-born neighbors. We were surrounded by a great many Italians in those days when unified Italy was still comparatively new and many of our neighbors had taken part in that great movement for nationalism. In our first Hull-House reading club for foreign-born students we tried to read an English translation of Mazzini's on *The Duties of Man*. It was very good reading but not always easy reading, although a shared interest that is genuine is the best possible basis for

stimulating factor in their development and ours. There is a theory of culture which contends that when people journeyed on foot or on camels or by other means into a strange part of the world, their contact with the established civilization there produced a curious excitement that often resulted in the creation of a new culture that never had existed before. I believe that we may get, and should get, something of that revivifying and upspringing of culture from our contact with the groups who come to us from foreign countries, and that we can get it in no other way. It implies of course a mutual interest in the life which is being lived in various parts of the globe. The settlement makes a constant effort through books, through the drama and through exhibits, to connect passing experiences with those expressions of permanent values which lie at the basis of world culture. If this is well done, it should heighten the sense of companionship in the neighborhood itself. The Italians have a saying that probably originated with St. Francis that the poor little brethren gathered with us under the Madonna's cloak, keep us warm quite as much as the great blue mantle itself.

Settlements are trying through all these years, to build up a technique, although with only a few scientific generalizations to go upon in order to use the group itself for educational ends. Perhaps the best efforts in this direction have been carried out through the National Federation of Settlements.

A national association is driven to find a new technique if its annual meetings are to be in any real sense a conference. Certain enthusiasts for creative discussion, such as the national Y. W. C. A., in their widespread organization of committees, boards, and clubs, have accepted the growing change of basis in modern life from individual to organized activities, and seek ways by which people in group relations shall find the mutual stimulus and enhancement of shared purposes and pooled resources. In such undertakings the settlements inevitably encounter more difficulties than the more homogeneous organizations do, for from the nature of the case settlement activities must respond to the diversity of their clientele.

The settlements have often been accused of scattering their forces; as institutions they are both philanthropic and educational; in their approach to social problems they call now upon the sociologist, now upon the psychiatrist; they seek the services of artists, economists, gymnasts, case-workers, dramatists, trained nurses; one day they beg the anthropologist for a clue to a new immigration, and the next they boast that one of their pupils is playing in the symphony orchestra. In response to the irrefutable charge of weakness in multiform activity, we are accustomed to reply that even so we are not as varied and complex as life itself. I recall my sense of relief the first time I heard a sociologist use the phrase, "vortex causation"; the universities were at last defining the situation and it was possible that they would later enter this inter-related field of personal difficulties, bewildering legal requirements, ill health and conflicting cultures which the settlements find so baffling.

The very recent attempts of several graduate schools to find a methodology applicable to more than one field of science promises to throw light on those problems of frustrated human beings with which a settlement becomes so painfully familiar. In spite of the fact that a large proportion of the children of immigrants avail themselves of the educational opportunities which America offers—in a Hull-House club of twenty-four Russian Jewish boys, all of whose parents were immigrants, eleven have graduated from universities or from professional schools—nevertheless, a neighborhood such as ours contains many men and women who have been left behind. The social relationships in a modern city are hastily made and often superficial. Common sense, the household tradition, the inherited custom, the desultory reading by which so much of life is directed, the stream of advice constantly poured over the radio, break down the restraints long sustained in smaller communities by public opinion, and in the end certain areas of city life seem to be in a state of dire confusion.

I do not believe that throughout America there are any groups more grateful than ours for the

Social Science Research Council and its investigations of the scientific aspect of human migrations, broadening into general population studies and for the notable series of reports on international and domestic topics, produced by the Institute of Economics in Washington. All these demonstrate that education should be continued throughout life and should play a leading rôle in the interpretation of contemporaneous developments. Possibly education in a democracy must in the end depend upon action, for raw theory cannot immediately be applied to life without grave results. In addition to the League of Nations Commission upon Intellectual Coöperation with its headquarters in Washington where one of the former Hull-House residents is acting as secretary, all these national research bodies are inevitably carried into the international aspects of their subjects. They demonstrate that each current event in this interrelated world may be the result of a repercussion from any part of the globe, or due to the same impulse manifesting itself in widely separated areas.

Dr. Dewey has told us that the general intelligence is dormant with its communications broken and faint until it possesses the public as its medium. It seems at moments as if we were about to extend indefinitely what we call our public, and that unless it were stretched to world dimensions, the most significant messages of our times might easily escape us.